DOING
INTERNET
RESEARCH

Other books authored or edited by Steve Jones:

CyberSociety 2.0: Revisiting CMC and Community

Virtual Culture: Identity and Communication in Cybersociety

CyberSociety: Computer-Mediated Communication and Community

Rock Formation: Popular Music, Technology and Mass Communication

DOING
INTERNET
RESEARCH

Critical Issues and Methods
for Examining the Net

STEVE JONES
Editor

SAGE Publications
International Educational and Professional Publisher
Thousand Oaks London New Delhi

For information:

SAGE Publications, Inc.
2455 Teller Road
Thousand Oaks, California 91320
E-mail: order@sagepub.com

SAGE Publications Ltd.
6 Bonhill Street
London EC2A 4PU
United Kingdom

SAGE Publications India Pvt. Ltd.
M-32 Market
Greater Kailash I
New Delhi 110 048 India

Printed in the United States of America

Library of Congress Cataloging-in-Publication Data

Main entry under title:

Doing Internet research: Critical issues and methods for examining
    the Net / edited by Steven G. Jones.
            p. cm.
        Includes bibliographical references and index.
        ISBN 0-7619-1594-X (cloth : acid-free paper)
        ISBN 0-7619-1595-8 (pbk. : acid-free paper)
            1. Internet (Computer network)—Social aspects—Research—Methodology.
        2. Internet (Computer network)—Social aspects—United States—Research—Methodology.
        3. Telematics—Social aspects—Research—Methodology. 4. Telematics—Social aspects—
        United States—Research—Methodology. 5. Cyberspace—Social aspects—Research—
        Methodology. 6. Cyberspace—Social aspects—United States—Research—Methodology.
        I. Jones, Steve, 1961–
        ZA4201.D65   1998
        303.48′33—ddc21   98-19758

This book is printed on acid-free paper.

        01   02   03   04   05   7   6   5

Acquiring Editor: Margaret Seawell
Editorial Assistant: Renée Piernot
Production Editor: Sherrise M. Roehr
Editorial Assistant: Denise Santoyo
Copy Editor: Linda Gray
Typesetter/Designer: Christina M. Hill
Cover Designer: Candice Harmon

For Ted, Don, Linda, and Beth

**Someone's always missing
From the picture
Of the perfect scene we're all headed for
Someday**

—Lynn Canfield/Area, "Puzzle Boy," 1990

Contents

Preface

No one ever said that change
Had to make the kind of sense we swear
Is only right
—Lynn Canfield/Area, "Larger Than Life," 1990

Don MacDonald and John Pauly, professors of communication at the University of Tulsa, developed and regularly taught a course titled "Inquiry in Communication" offered in that department. At the very start of the term, they challenged undergraduates to unfailingly ask So what? and Who cares? questions when the students read research or began to plan research projects of their own. Those questions are critically important to research, not merely because they should drive scholars to justify their work or simply because they may give us insight into the motivation(s) of scholarship, but rather, they engage scholar and reader in a conversation about values.

But such questions continue to be easily dismissed when it comes to Internet research: The Internet's very ubiquitousness (if due only to its coverage in the media) has ingrained in us its importance. Of course, many people *do* care about the Internet and what goes on within and through it, and as well we should care. As a medium of communication new to us (newer than television, the former undisputed champion of research of assumed importance), a medium that intersects with everyday life in ways both strange and omnipresent, popular interest in the Internet is enormous—not just in industrial countries, but worldwide.

We are still coming to grips with the changes that we feel are brought about by networked communication of the type so prominently made visible by the Internet. In some cases, it is even possible that we feel change where there is not any, from anticipation bred by being accustomed as we are to its occurrence. Change is what motivated this book's creation, as did the frequency with which I find myself wondering if change makes sense in regard to the methods we have been using to study the Internet's convergence with modern life. It is the result of discussions with many scholars from a wide variety of disciplines who believe, as do I, that simply applying existing theories and methods to the study of Internet-related phenomena is not a satisfactory way to build our knowledge of the Internet as a social medium. Consequently, this is not a book that will (at least in any direct way) help people to use the Internet as a research tool. Rather, its goal is to assist in the search for, and critique of, methods with which we can study the Internet and the social, political, economic, artistic, and communicative phenomena occurring within, through, and in some cases, apart from but nevertheless related to, the Internet. As Rice and Williams (1984) caution,

> We need not jettison useful communication theories when we wish to understand the new media . . . we should take advantage . . . of the new media to further specify and modify those theories. . . . The new media need to be included in traditional communication research, but we need to look at those traditional theories untraditionally. (pp. 55, 80)

Rice and Williams's call for interdisciplinarity in new media research is one heeded by contributors to this volume and one that I hope will continue to suffuse Internet research.

Disciplinarity is useful for a variety of reasons, however, including that it provides a starting point and structure for systematic scholarship. Because another goal of the book is to help people get started . . . well, doing Internet research . . . structure and disciplinarity will be evident. Yet disciplinarity should never lead us to abandon inquiry. The instant it structures to the extent that it disengages curiosity, disciplinarity will ruin scholarship. We must keep asking, What are the methods that scholars are already using to study the Internet? What are ones that we could use but have not yet? What are the advantages and disadvantages to these methods and others? There is not yet a field known as "Internet studies," although there may well be one before long. Although it is not a goal of this volume to create such a field, it has as one of its goals to get us to begin thinking about how we might go about systematically studying this medium. On the other hand, the last thing I would like to have happen is for the study of the Internet and related social phenomena to get systematized to the point of bureaucratic rigidity. There are no "traditional" methods for studying the World Wide Web or e-mail or Usenet or, for that matter, anything Internet related.

As I have examined my own feelings during the making of this book, I have found myself less in favor of the formation of a field of study, in large part because we would do well to avoid what Stephen Jay Gould (1993) succinctly pointed out in an essay on field research:

> All field naturalists know and respect the phenomenon of "search image"—the best proof that observation is an interaction of mind and nature, not a fully objective and reproducible mapping of outside upon inside, done in the same way by all careful and competent people. In short, you see what you are trained to view—and observation of different sorts of objects often requires a conscious shift of focus, not a total and indiscriminate expansion in the hopes of seeing everything. The world is too crowded with wonders for simultaneous perception of all; we learn our fruitful selectivities. (p. 213)

The Internet is a "different sort of object" (if it is, indeed, an object at all), and studying it does require a "conscious shift of focus." However, I will hope that we can continuously shift both focus and method in the pursuit of understanding and hope that we do not fix our gaze one way or another, lest we fail to grasp the Internet's essential changeability.

There are, of course, methods that have been traditionally, and successfully, used to study other media that are now being used to study the Internet, also with success. Ron Rice (1989) writes that "research on the uses and implications of CMCS (Computer-Mediated Communication Systems) reflects a variety of disciplinary paradigms, technological distinctions, and evaluation approaches" (p. 469). When it comes to Internet research, most of these are drawn from communication research, media studies, anthropology, sociology, literary criticism, cultural studies, psychology, and political economy. Some are quantitative, some qualitative. Some are rooted in the social sciences, others in the humanities, and others still cross over such boundaries. Which are useful? Which are not? Which do we believe will contribute most to our knowledge of the Internet? Those are the kinds of questions with which contributors to this volume have grappled. I must say that I hope these questions have been engaged but not quite answered, for if answers are that readily at hand, I may have been fooling myself that the study of the Internet is exciting and intriguing.

One might ask a priori, Why should we do Internet research? That question suffuses the work of contributors to this volume. Suffice to say for now that, whether or not one believes the hyperbolic claims about the Internet being the biggest thing since the invention of the wheel, the Internet is a medium with great consequences for social and economic life. To some extent, it simply does not matter whether one is on-line or not—one's life will be, in some way, for better or worse, touched by the Internet. As Rice (1989) notes, "Providing instruction, the delivery of health services, the retrieval of database information . . . the computerization of political campaigns" are among the activities "experiencing . . . convergence" with computer technology (p. 469), a convergence accelerated by the Internet. In a few years in the early 1990s, with a certain rapidity and inexorability, the Internet became a medium as widespread in the public mind, if not the physical world, as television and radio before it. Like technologies preceding it, the Internet has commanded the public imagination. What that says about us is even more important than what it says about the Internet. And what command it has: It is not often that a technology can so engage diverse interests in the public sphere. Consequently, the Internet matters—although precisely in what ways it is difficult to discern. It is my hope that you will find this book useful as a guide to the means by which we can better that discernment.

I hope, too, that as we find out more about what the Internet means to us, we will also find out what social life means to us. The Internet does not exist in isolation. To study it as if it was somehow apart from the "off-line" world that brought it into being would be a gross mistake. Internet users are as much a part of physical space as they are of cyberspace (more so, really, insofar as users' choices regarding place, identity, etc. are far more limited in physical space). As a result the notion that our research should be "grounded" takes on even greater significance when it comes to Internet research. That makes Internet research particularly interesting—and demanding. Not only is it important to be aware of and attuned to the diversity of on-line experience, it is important to recognize that on-line experience is at all times tethered in some fashion to off-line experience.

The bulk of research into the Internet has been essentially administrative, driven largely by the concerns of commercial interests seeking to get a grip on the demographics of on-line audiences in much the same way as that research is done on other media. Measures of web page "hits," domain name growth, and so on give us in broad strokes some sense of the Internet's shape. But I am not convinced such measures tell us much about Internet use. For example, measuring the number of domain names registered tells us nothing about the uses to which those domain names are put. Commercial Internet users hoard domain names and often do not use them. It is a form of trademarking—McDonald's not only reserves mcdonalds.com, but also hamburger.com, ronald.com, and so on. And often, if they do use all of these names, they all lead to the same web page. Educational domains are probably responsible for more web *content* than commercial ones: At my university, for instance, the top-level domain uic.edu contains tens of thousands of pages strewn across hundreds of servers (*.uic.edu). And each student, each staff and faculty member can, if he or she wishes, have web pages on uic.edu, denoted by syntax such as uic.edu/username. That may, however, not tell us about measures of Internet traffic either. But can we now even achieve a reliable measurement of Internet traffic, given the proliferation of agens and bots, software-based browsing mechanisms like the ones used by AltaVista, for instance, to search and catalog web sites? Those generate untold traffic—not human traffic, however. How shall we *account* for it and not simply measure it?

The point I wish to make is not that Internet research is difficult. That is obvious. Internet research, as I will discuss later in this book, must avoid being prescriptive. But it is extremely difficult for it even to be descriptive, given the ever-changing networks involved, the mutating software and hardware, and the elastic definitions. Writing in 1988, Williams, Rice, and Rogers stated, "Although we consider possible research methods for new media as mainly extensions of existing methods, we propose that the new media researcher should consider alternative methods, or even multiple methods, and to attempt a triangulation of methods" (p. 15). One hope that we should have is that the Internet itself can serve as a medium of communication of the research we conduct, that the triangulation Williams et al. seek can occur, at least in some small part, by the publication, hyperlinking, and communication of research findings on-line.

This collection may itself require some hyperlinking of a sort: It is far from exhaustive; it is not even complete. Many disciplines are not considered in these pages; many methods are overlooked, and in some cases, even the term *method* might be inappropriate. The goal of editing this volume never was to make it a complete one. In fact, I scarcely believe such completeness to be possible, just as I believe method itself should not solely drive inquiry. There is no one way, or even a set of ways, to go about studying the Internet, just as there is no one way or set of ways to study social relations and processes. Another goal of this volume is to consider methodological issues that arise when one tries to study and understand the social processes occurring within the Internet and, in a sense, apart from it, insofar as the Internet penetrates social life beyond its networks. The contributors to this volume do consider a broad range of methods and have their intellectual roots in various disciplines.

They have, in fact, done such a good job I scarcely know what to add. The contributors were asked, in essence, What can a particular method, area of interest, mode of inquiry, or way of asking questions contribute to Internet research? Their responses move us several steps along toward discovering ways with which to engage this emergent social word. Their responses also raise additional questions and bring to light further issues, in some ways moving us several steps to one side or the other (and appropriately, in some cases, back a step or two). As Ringer (1997) notes,

> The "intellectual field" [is] a constellation of positions that are meaningful only in relation to one another, a constellation further characterized by differences of power and authority, by the opposition between orthodoxy and heterodoxy, and by the role of the cultural preconscious, of tacit "doxa" that are transmitted by inherited practices, institutions, and social relations. (p. 5)

If this book manages to express some of those positions, then I believe it successful. It is my hope that this book will be but a beginning, that the steps we take here are part of a long walk that we are taking, talking all the while about cyberspace—and life, generally.

References

Gould, S. J. (1993). *Eight little piggies.* London: Jonathon Cape.

Rice, R. E. (1989). Issues and concepts in research on computer-mediated communication systems. *Communication Yearbook, 12,* 436-476.

Rice, R. E., & Williams, F. (1984). Theories old and new: The study of new media. In R. E. Rice (Ed.), *The new media* (pp. 55-80). Beverly Hills, CA: Sage.

Ringer, F. (1997). *Max Weber's methodology.* Cambridge, MA: Harvard University Press.

Williams, F., Rice, R. E., & Rogers, E. M. (1988). *Research methods and the new media.* New York: Free Press.

Acknowledgments

The well-known maxim goes, "Neither a borrower nor a lender be," and yet I have found it quite necessary to be indebted to the contributors to this volume, who gave of themselves so fully. I have learned much from their work, and it has given me great pleasure to work with them. I am privileged to be able to call them colleagues and friends.

I have, in fact, debts too numerous to list, much less discharge, that have accumulated during the making of this book. Among them are ones owed my editor at Sage, Margaret Seawell; Frank Christel, general manager of KWGS-FM at the University of Tulsa; the ADN/Academic Computer Center staff at the University of Illinois at Chicago; Jim Danowski and Emily Walker, colleagues in the Department of Communication at the University of Illinois at Chicago; Eric Gislason, Sidney B. Simpson, Jr., Larry Poston, and Steve Weaver in UIC's College of Liberal Arts and Sciences; Gary Szabo, Director of Information Systems, University of Washington—Bothell; and the Malnati family. Interest accrues on debts to my colleague in the Faculty of Communication at the University of Tulsa, Joli Jensen, and yet I am allowed to draw on her never-ending wisdom and inspiration. My mother and father are wonderfully supportive and encouraging.

Last, and most, thanks to Jodi White: Now that the book's done, I get the remote back.

Introduction

Forests, Trees, and Internet Research

James T. Costigan

I am not sure that I know what the Internet is; I am not sure that anyone does. The popular embrace of the concept of the Internet, and the market's enthusiasm to be a part of it, has certainly muddied the waters. I understand the Internet from its physical properties, and I know a little about computers and switches. I know about the Internet from the application point of view, why it was designed. I also know about use, how it is used and how I use it. I know about it from the market and social perspectives—the next "cool" thing. None of those perspectives seems to suffice in grasping the Internet.

The use of the Internet does not always adhere to its applications or its physical properties. I can think about the Internet using any two of the above concepts: technology, application, and/or use, but I have trouble using more. Trying to hold all of these constructs together creates the need to constantly modify the understanding or explanation of one of them, often resulting in incorrect changes in the others. All of these ideas are certainly related. Trying to connect them in some linear fashion may seem possible, but it is not.

The more you describe the Internet the less of it you seem to have; it is greater than the sum of its parts. In the book *Zen and the Art of Motorcycle Maintenance,* Robert Pirsig (1974) describes the beauty of the high plains. One of his companions is so awestruck that she takes 360 degrees worth of pictures to capture it, to show her friends the wonder of this place. When the pictures are developed they show very little. The pictures are accurate enough visually, but they do a disservice to the reality of the experience. The Internet cannot be captured in an individual "picture." Any single picture adds a frame and boundaries that do not exist, but the Internet cannot be contained. These pictures also add focus and prominence to individual items that are not universally prominent. The pictures are stagnant, but the Internet is in a constant state of flux. Just as the high plains have an all-encompassing vastness that is easily experienced but difficult to capture or reproduce, the Internet is often experienced but difficult to translate and express.

Perhaps that is the reason there are things wrong about some of our Internet research. But there are also many things right about it. The continuing discourse allows academics and researchers to build multiple perspectives, and this diversity is appropriate to the reality of the Internet. The Internet is a "network of networks," each with their own design and unique structure, yet they all follow some basic rules that allow them to interconnect. Social structures of the Internet mimic this design.

Consequently, when doing Internet research, definitions are difficult to come by. Yet good research should start with a definition of what is being studied. This is especially true with broad topics such as the Internet. Perhaps in this case any definition will do. A topic such as the Internet is large enough that starting points can be anywhere. Research often starts in the middle without stating that middle. The perception is, "I think we all know what we are talking about." Usually, the reality is, "I think I know something and assume that this is shared by all readers." The diversity of the Internet defies simple explanations or shared opinions.

Social science research on the Internet generally divides into two main categories. The first has to do with the abilities to search and retrieve data from large data stores. This information flood is not historically new; libraries hold large amounts of information and have search and retrieval capabilities. The Internet and constructs like the World Wide Web are simply faster and perhaps more culturally popular. Greater speed is allowing for, or causing, an information boom. The business and academic market is seeking out volumes of data to produce competitive advantage and improved understanding. (Many individuals feel this same competition in their personal life.) The sheer volume of information has made the access of this information almost impossible. Companies specializing in data mining are capitalizing on the notion that if there is record of specifically everything, any question can be answered specifically. For the researcher, this is perhaps the heart of our misguided pursuits. The thought occurs that if we can track all this, gather all this, then we will know more about all this. In fact, we may know less.

The second research area is into the interactive communication capabilities of the Internet. E-mail, chat rooms, MOOs (multi-user domains object oriented), and MUDs (multi-user domains) are all forms of text-based communication with variations in time, distance, and audience. Web-based publication is a new form of mass communication, and the ability to hyperlink brings a new form of interaction and structure. Research on these topics is truly unique to the Internet. There is no existing parallel social construct, and in many ways, the Internet creates wholly new social constructs. The medium and its use are creating communities that not only would not but could not have formed without the use of the Internet. The development and use of chat rooms, for example, has driven a language and community that is closely knit yet extremely diverse and dispersed.

Divisions do exist between those who study chat groups, listservs, e-mail, rhetoric, culture, race, cross-culture, sexual identity, and any other topic. Because of the sheer volume of archival and real-time data available on any subject, there is the thought that each of these areas holds a place of special regard on the Internet, and that is indeed true. There is often the assertion that this research discovers unique properties of the Internet, when actually, they are properties of the community or group being studied, modified by this new form of technology. Collectively perhaps, this diversity creates an accurate picture of the Internet as a social system.

In many large and small ways, the relationship between the Internet and its communities and academic life is parallel. Both tend to seek some sort of homeostasis and diversity that neither can obtain. Areas of the Internet appear to flourish with diversity of opinion, yet a political correctness is prevalent. Statements divergent from the consensus opinion in any of these groups are usually challenged with a direct relationship to the divergence of the statement. The expectable limits of this diversity are stated formally and informally in all socialized "areas." Support is given and a language developed recursively supporting the culture and group. These groups often tout their relationships and intermingling with other groups, but there is rarely a deep relationship without one group's swallowing the other.

How We Write the History of the Internet

Many scholars are writing about the Internet; it is a popular and lucrative topic capturing the attention of much of the world. As we write, we are shaping the future of the Internet, shaping our ideas about it, and forming popular opinion. Much of what is written points to a personal perspective on the future of the Internet, based on how an individual thinks it will evolve. This is a history we are actively writing.

Our expressions of history and the Internet can be only personal and are valuable only when personalized. This limiting and frustrating result is driven by the personalized nature of the Internet's design. The Internet is sometimes referred to or envisioned as a "networked consciousness." This idea requires a "we" that does not exist. The Internet is more a networked schizophrenic, with multiple personalities that often have no idea that the others exist and a complex that there is something more unique happening where others are. But as long as one stays within one's communities, he or she is happy and safe. When one ventures out, one is often beaten soundly by varied and adamant opinion, which is interpreted and related as some different place or consciousness.

But who is the "we" in the title of this section? The society that reads articles on the implications of Internet research seems to be the same society that writes those articles. We are the "computer literate," the "on-line" defining our own societal impact. Does that matter? What are the implications of answers to questions such as, Who is writing the history of the Internet? Can the choir gain a correct social perspective on their church? Does the method of electronic publication and its often lower standards of critical review have an effect on the significance of this kind of writing? Does this technology drive academic research, or does research drive the technology?

A definitive history of the Internet of our times is decades from being written. The various perspectives being written now are the basis on which we build this history. The continuing diversity of opinion and comment allow the continuing diversity of development that has been the hallmark of the Internet.

The Personal Perspective

Everything that I have seen, heard, and experienced has brought me to this point, and I understand nothing but in relationship to me at this point. That sentence is why I keep a journal; it keeps me from walking in circles. Every time I reach some place that appears to be the same, I reach it as a new me and can often then take a new road. This requires a frequent review of the paths chosen and the reasoning behind the choices.

Covey, Merrill, and Merrill (1994) in their book *First Things First* wrote about days of development. Day 1 must be completed before Day 2, and each of these days are different for each person. You can't "do" Day 7 until you have "done" the previous six, in order. One can hear and experience everything contained in day 7 but won't understand it until all of the other days are experienced. For computer users, Day 1 finds us thinking that computers are "against" us. The boolean design of operating systems seems to have an adversarial relationship with users: Who will be the master and who the slave? Everyone at some point realizes that a computer will save and delete files only when told—and without regard to significance or personal investment. (Yes, I just hit save.) Dominance and submission involve systems of values, and we are only beginning to understand how values are embedded in our technologies. We are only scratching the surface of understanding the relationships between software and hardware and the different types of "embeddedness" those involve.

It is important that academics write about their "discovery" of the Internet and its application, because sometimes Day 1 is different in significant ways. The design of the Internet and its social constructs will embrace wholly new dimensions and ideas. Although the underlying structure may remain, the application of it may be completely new, perhaps by accident. Every user takes a slightly different approach to his or her use of the Internet, and each has a slightly different expectation. These variations can create whole new uses. Internet-unique forms of communication have been driven this way; various acronyms (LOL—laughing out loud), symbol systems such as emoticons ("smilies") ;^), and fantasy environments such as textual virtual reality were all created by users to make the Internet more robust. These advances often result from a poor understanding of the existing social or practical "rules" of the Internet.

Researchers paying careful attention to these phenomena can produce a very thick and interesting description of the acquisition of a new form of communication. Multiple examples of this acquisition can provide bedrock for the research on, and the history of, the Internet.

The Community of the Internet

Community as a construct is perhaps the most interesting aspect of the Internet and one that is too rarely discussed. Community on-line is fluid— perhaps because persona and identity are different, perhaps because structure and time are different, perhaps because the channels are different. Unlike off-line, on-line communities are often constructed and destroyed not because they have challenges with structure, as Carey (see Munson & Warren, 1997) suggests, but because the connection is not time sensitive. Messages are not necessarily sent in real time and can often remain on listservs or in digests for months or years. If you believe that the community exists as long as people are reading and participating with and through these messages, then the community may come and go as people discover the messages.

It takes little time or structure to create community on-line, and therefore, the effort to maintain structure and community is not as highly valued. The maintenance of on-line community is different, making the community different. There is no need to actively seek out and interact with on-line communities, to perform relational maintenance. When there is something to say, the community comes to you or you go to the community. Often, people post messages to a "community" asking if the community is still there. Who can answer that question? If the servers and addresses are functional, is the community there? Do you have to respond for the community to exist? Is the simple fact that you get a message confirmation of the community?

The academic and professional communities formed on the Internet are "together" on-line, and although we are physically closer at conventions and conferences, the sense of on-line community is lost by physical co-location. The medium has changed and so has the community. The medium has such an effect on the community as to define it. Community relationships formed on-line allow an access and intimacy not transferred to other situations. On-line messages can be sent at any time and to anyone and can be responded to when time is available. This level of access does not transfer to face-to-face situations where different social, personal, and community rules exist.

Owning the New Frontier

The Internet is available with the correct hardware and connection; one does not have to sign in or pay an initiation fee, insofar as the actual connections (as opposed to access) to the Internet, and its contents are without charge. The connection point is not significant in terms of entrance. The Internet is not in one place more than it is in another. Where a piece of information is when it is on the Internet is a little hard to describe. It is on some computer somewhere (maybe even on one's own), but it is available anywhere the Internet is.

This collapse of distance between the source and the receiver is unique to human experience and creates a setting in which negotiation for ownership and fair use is a constant debate. The Internet is in many ways the Wild West, the new frontier of our times, but its limits will not be reached. The Internet, as a place, is finite in size. At any one time, it has a definable size; there are a certain number of computers, a certain number of nodes, and so on. The Internet does not have an edge to push past, no wall or ocean to contain it. Its size and shape change constantly, and additions and subtractions do not inherently make something new or different. Local computer systems often create a "firewall," a hardware and software division that keeps the Internet out and the internal information in. For social scientists, a firewall should not be thought of as a wall but as a different existence. Things that are on the Internet exist there; things with passwords or limited availability are parts of a different network, which may share some of the same hardware.

This point of view makes ownership a complicated thing. If you put something on the Internet, it exists there. Limiting where it can be, given the above perspective, takes it off the Internet and puts it somewhere else. If you cannot control the access and use of something, can you own it in the traditional sense of the word? The Internet has gained popularity and acceptance by allowing free access to valuable information. For something to have value, in the Western sense of the word, there must be some way to collect that value, some form, although possibly indirect, of monetary compensation, of exchange of capital. For the next few years, the Internet and those on it will fight a battle of value: How shall we keep something universally accessible and of value? The situation is similar to the development of the American West from the West known to Native Americans. The new frontier of the Internet is in some senses being overrun by the advance of commerce. The divisions and rules of ownership that established territories, and then states, out of an untamed and largely unregulated land built the American West and destroyed forever the free and untamed lands. Perhaps the "advance" is inevitable, for all its good and bad. Luckily, the ability to archive and store data, and the very nature of time on the Internet, produces electronic ghost towns that can be revived. The flexibility of the Internet allows for rapid progress—and if need be, a rapid retreat. The variety of networks, in this network of networks, allows for a rich and diverse social experiment centered on how the Internet defines its value. It is the responsibility of those researching the Internet to view critically these various experiments and comment on their implications.

Conclusion

As I said at the beginning, I am not sure I know what the Internet is, and I don't know if that matters. Given the rapid pace of development and the way the world has rushed to adopt this new technology, any definition is fleeting. As for Internet research, researching the hard to understand, the hard to define, and the rapidly changing is perhaps one of the most invigorating of academic pursuits. The analogy of the Internet as a forest composed of thousands of separate and unique trees is appropriate, but we are still at the point where we have to gain a better understanding of the trees themselves, before the forest makes any sense.

References

Covey, S. R., Merrill, R. A., & Merrill, R. R. (1994). *First things first: To live, to love, to learn, to leave a legacy.* New York: Simon & Schuster.

Munson, E. S., & Warren, C. A. (1997). *James Carey: A critical reader.* Minneapolis: University of Minnesota Press.

Pirsig, R. M. (1974). *Zen and the art of motorcycle maintenance.* New York: Bantam.

1

Studying the Net
Intricacies and Issues

STEVE JONES

Even after all the research, and the most skillful storytelling,
reality remains obdurate.

—John Pauly (1991, p. 23)

We look for evidence of culture at those minute points of contact between new
things and old habits, and . . . we include in our sense of history the power of
things themselves to impress and shape and evoke a response within
consciousness.

—Alan Trachtenberg (1986, p. xiii)

There is always risk in probing into mysteries.

—David Plath (1980, 218)

FOR ALL THE NEWNESS AND HOOPLA associated with the Internet, much of
the narrative surrounding it is quite predictable. As I have noted in other
essays (Jones, 1995, 1997b), the hype about the Internet, whether accurate
or not, is tellingly like that which accompanied the introduction of earlier

media technologies. It is possible to go so far as to say that technology itself (and the uses to which it is put) is less predictable than the hopes and promises for it that we harbor.

The Internet is not only a technology but an engine of social change, one that has modified work habits, education, social relations generally, and, maybe most important, our hopes and dreams. It is in some ways the technological embodiment of a particularly American social project (Jones, 1995, 1997b), and importantly, it is a social project rooted in what James Carey (1997b) aptly describes as "the union of science and state" (p. 3). In this regard, our metaphors have led us astray: The Internet is not an information highway; it is in reality only peripherally about information. It is, instead, the first evidence we have of what we have believed that we are for quite some time—an information society. It is not that the Internet illustrates that the public has made a leap to becoming an information society. It is that for the first time we can point to something outside of society as we know it and say, "There—that is a society made up of information," in a somewhat literal sense. The Internet is a social space, a milieu, made up of, and made possible by, communication (the cornerstone of community and society). Of course, this is facile: Information is hardly the only thing necessary for society, and information is hardly communication (Ong, 1996). However, both the notion of an "information society" and modern conceptualizations of the Internet as a self-regulating "entity" (however one may envision its shape)—that arena in which our "digital being" lives—at least evade, if not altogether avoid, the centrality of values to the processes of communication that the Internet, as a form and medium of communication and meaning, sustains.

The Internet and the Market

Our historical work is only just begun when it comes to the Internet, and the sooner we get on with it, the better. Our histories *must* go beyond the origins of ARPANET (the Advanced Research Projects Agency Network precursor to the Internet), a starting point often misinterpreted as to mean that the Internet was created solely as a command-and-control mechanism to ready the United States for nuclear war. The work of Vannevar Bush, J. C. R. Licklider, Vint Cerf, and researchers at Xerox PARC—that ran along with, and parallel to, ARPANET—was itself from the start co-opted, and not only by academics. Our histories must go into greater depth, and recent and forthcoming research efforts such as Ronda and Michael Hauben's (1997) *Netizens* and a forthcoming book by Janet Abbate represent the first scholarly efforts that systematically delve into Internet history. It is important to note that Internetworking was co-opted by various cultures; as Steven Levy (1984) shows, by 1960s MIT hackers; as Katie Hafner (1991) shows, by computer hobbyists and academics; as Bruce Sterling (1992) shows by the 1980s, hackers and bulletin board system operators and users; as Gary Chapman, columnist and director of the 21st Century Project at the University of Texas—Austin has said, by professional organizations such as Computer Professionals for Social Responsibility and the Electronic Frontier Foundation; and even perhaps by the media itself, which gives us images of cyberspace pioneers such as John Perry Barlow, wily hackers such as Knight Lightning, and the Chaos Computer Club and the Legion of Doom—images of teachers and students somehow transforming educational processes and images of danger and delight.

These intertwined histories are particularly critical to understanding the origins of the Internet in the early 1960s culture of science, at least because our present conceptualizations of the Internet still operate within their framework. The frame has, however, shifted slightly, as capitalism has come to preoccupy science and the state. Instead of a culture of science, science (and likely even culture, too) has been disguised in the sphere of the popular press (and popular imagination) by the market, a guise that allows value to be . . . well, valueless, empty, in regard to the human dimensions of social relations and "value-able" in regard to commodity and capital. This is a guise that the media of mass communication have long adopted (Peterson, 1956), and one in which audiences and markets are summarily conflated. The Internet in this guise is both a medium of communication and a medium of choice. On it, within it, we are to choose from among communities of interest and to participate in what we are led to believe is essentially democratic (Jones, 1995, 1997b). But as Carey (1997b) notes, the conception of the self in such a system is ultimately characterized as "unfit for democracy," because "freedom consists solely in the capacity of people to choose their own ends and all social arrangements [are] mere means to be manipulated in satisfying individual desire" (p. 9).

Such a positivist conception frames much of the discourse about what the Internet is and should be. In turn, there is both the sense that Internet research can be eminently predictive and the sense that the Internet is the ultimate (or at least so far the best) means of delivering *personalized* mass media. The Internet-as-market metaphor derives its power from the notion that the market is not only theoretically based but quite practically functional, at the level of the individual, thanks to new technologies. But the development of various "push" technologies (e.g., the use of web-based "cookies"[1] and the like), the trading of personal information for personal service, is little more than a technical version of what has long sustained barter economies, and even government, for centuries. For example, when I launch my web browser, its default page is at excite.com; I have personalized it through use of keywords and other means. Consequently, the first web page I see is filled with news filtered for me, a near-equivalent of Nicholas Negroponte's (1995) "Daily Me" newspaper. In some ways, this is no different from exchanging gossip: I tell you something, you tell me something, and those "somethings" are usually things we think the other wants or needs to know. What is different in these scenarios involving technology is the speed and accuracy of information trading, the accumulation and accretion of information, and the uses (in terms of variety and scope) to which the information can be put.

The metaphor of the Internet as a market-driven social space lends itself particularly well to market research that has long desired predictive precision at the level of the individual consumer and has employed a variety of technologies with which to gather sufficient information in an attempt to ensure predictive power. For example, when I shop at a grocery store, to get discounts and to use a form of payment other than cash, I have to hand over a "preferred customer card" (a misnomer, really, because most all customers have one). To get such a card, I had to fill out a form providing all manner of personal information, usually demographic but also psychographic, information subsequently used to set up a file on me in a database. When I go through the checkout lane, I hand over my card to be scanned, and I am identified. My purchases are then scanned *and* recorded (it's relevant that this activity is performed as a service of A. C. Nielsen in most markets). When a receipt is printed, on the reverse are coupons directed *right at me* based on my purchasing history. They may be for products I already buy, or from competing brands—either way, Nielsen profits as it plays off one firm against another in a struggle over my loyalties, and presumably, the store profits from my return visits to use the coupons, and the brands in question profit from my continued purchasing.

But the important lesson is this: It is now possible to care less about the market and care more about the individual, or to put it another way, to *dis*aggregate the market that the media of mass communication had, of necessity, aggregated. One effect has been a tendency toward privileging loyalty and attention, as in the case of World Wide Web-based search engines that "are evolving into full-fledged online services where a company can be judged on its ability to earn user loyalty" (Vonder, 1998). Loyalty, construed and constructed from habit, has been the hallmark of the latest attempts to predict on-line behavior, the latest journey in "the quest for certainty (that) is the heritage of the objectivist epistemology" (Jensen, 1993, p. 71). The predictive tendencies of social science have led to the realization that it is much easier, in fact, to predict individual behavior when supplied with sufficient data than it is to determine the course of a mass audience irrespective of the amount of knowledge we have about it. It is important to remember, as Plath (1980) reminds us, that

> we are born individual: separate organisms each biologically unique. We grow jointly: each in the company of others mutually tending the wild genetic pulse, as we domesticate ourselves along pathways marked out for us by the vision of our group's heritage. (p. 215)

To have a holistic sense of our interactions (on-line or off-line) we must take good care to understand individuals and their relationships together—and to maintain a curiosity about Plath's notion of a "heritage," the lingering and persistent accumulation of our experiences that, somehow, goes beyond ourselves.

Information, Persistence, and the Net

Perhaps, in fact, one may consider personal information as a form of "heritage." My web-browsing habits, gleaned from cookies and the like, can be cross-referenced with credit card purchases I have made, the aforementioned grocery-shopping habits, and so on. There is thus another difference in kind from previous methods of information exchange, a difference related to the processing power gathered from the accumulated and seemingly dispersed and differentiated data. Networked communication is *not* only communication between people but between databases. But most important, the information, whatever it may be (grocery purchases, web sites visited, etc.) lingers; it is not forgotten, nor is it distorted over time, as gossip can become. It is not so much that it is necessarily accurate per se, but that, right or wrong, it is *persistent.*

This notion of persistence intrigues me. What about the Internet is persistent, and what about it is ephemeral? In regard to the notion of personalized

mass media, social theorists have begun to ask, What might be the consequences of such a personalized form of news consumption to our public,
common, conversations? To some extent, although we may have arguments
about what constitutes the public sphere, we have largely been in agreement
about the commonality that constitutes that conversation, that makes possible
a "public." Regardless of which theory one subscribes to concerning definitions of "the public," it has largely been taken for granted that the media of
mass communication are the forum within which public discourse occurs in
contemporary society (although it may not be so anymore). We have assumed, too, that in many ways, these media are ephemeral, regardless that
we can use recording technologies to make them replicable. The connections
between the ephemeral and our conception of ritual are worth exploring,
particularly when it comes to the Internet's forms of communication. The
notion of media "events" (Dayan & Katz, 1992) has been one way in which
we have denied the persistence, and emphasized the ritual nature, of mass-
mediated phenomena, continuing to rely on a Benjamin-esque (1968) sensi-
bility that an "aura" exists surrounding an event. In this age beyond mechanical reproduction, an era of digital reproduction, it is our memory that suffuses
an event with "aura" rather than our participation. Does persistence require
reproduction, ritual, memory, or some combination thereof?

But the Internet is not simply persistent due to its nature as a medium of
information. Were that to be the case, one must believe the Internet is only a
storage medium and not a medium of communication. Yet it is true that much
Internet research relies on a conceptualization of the Internet as a storage
medium, as one that "fixes" communication in a tangible (typically textual)
form, making it seem ripe for the picking by scholars. Newhagen and Rafaeli
(1997) noted the same in regard to

> the inviting empiricism inherent in Net behavior. Not only does it occur on a
> computer, communication on the Net leaves tracks to an extent unmatched by
> that in any other context—the content is easily observable, recorded, and
> copied. Participant demography and behaviors of consumption, choice, atten-
> tion, reaction, learning, and so forth, are widely captured and logged. Anyone
> who has an opportunity to watch logs of WWW servers, and who is even a little
> bit of a social scientist, cannot help but marvel at the research opportunities
> these logs open.

And yet the Internet is not nearly as "fixed" in these terms as one might
believe, given that it is a constantly changing medium. One may take

"snapshots" of it from time to time or of some portions of it. But in general, the Internet does not meet requirements for fixity that scholarship might require: Its very nature as a store-and-forward medium, one that is designed to act "intelligently" in regard to its network abilities, makes it an ever-changing medium.

What is persistent is not the information passed between us and among us, between us and "them" on the Internet, but an abstracted order of information that we leave behind as we move about cyberspace, information left behind in the form of cookies, filled-out web forms, e-mail, textual messages, and so on. As persistent is our own memory of our encounters in these media. These are the "memory" of the Internet, if you will, the connections between the connections. Rather than use it to predict future behavior, instead how might we get at it, "jog" it? What might it tell us about who, collectively, we are on-line, who we have been, what we have searched for, the past as it is remembered through associative links, hyperlinks, web pages, and visits come and gone? Might an understanding of the Internet as a connected space rather than a "cyberspace" allay some of the predictive tendencies at the forefront of Internet research thus far?

History, Prediction, or Both

In the case of Internet research, our vision of the future has a tendency to color our narratives of its history. Not only is the research we perform to discover its nature—its "flavor" of reality—predictable, but in a sense, the research itself is eminently predictive, based on notions of what we think the Internet will (or should) become, what it will (should) be, rather than on precise determination of what it has been. The predictability of the research stems in part from our use of tools, paradigms, theories, and so on currently available to us. And part of it stems from the difficulty to be precise about anything on-line. Neither of these are great cause for concern. The Internet changes, almost moment to moment. The tools we have, conceptually and otherwise, are the ones we should initially use. The overarching concern is that scholars, like programmers, businesspeople, and government officials, are part of the Internet "land grab," even if only symbolically. We rush to fill the vacuum of knowledge created by the extraordinary interest in the Internet. The metaphor of the Internet as an electronic frontier is one that still carries much power of suggestion. Scholars and educators are "out there" in covered wagons, sometimes circling them (as is the case with many traditional educational institutions' response to Internet-based "distance education" programs) and sometimes engaged in a frenzied land rush to colonize cyberspace with "virtual campuses." In some sense, we are doomed to repeat the future—the one we will create by establishing what is important to think about in regard to studying the Internet, the one we have already created countless times in our institutions, media, and relationships.

The Need for Reflection

The very publication of this book is implicated in the aforementioned "land grab." Can it, can we, as scholars, sufficiently eschew the prescriptive and predictive, embrace the critical and self-critical, and be sufficiently sensitive to language and meaning so that our work will be meaningful to those we study?

One imperative is for reflection. Scholars studying the Internet must be reflexive, for (at least) two reasons. First, because we have all, scholar and citizen alike, become savvy media consumers. The "I-know-that-you-know-that-I-know" game is played out every day in countless advertisements, marketing plans, newscasts, comedy programs, even in conversations between us (and perhaps within us), to the extent that one might suspect we can never again find naïveté. Whether this situation is labeled as the often-mentioned "postmodern condition," or the just-as-often-mentioned "information overload" is not as important as the conceptualization of audiences beyond "active" or "passive." Indeed, it may be necessary to reconceptualize the notion of "audience" altogether. Joli Jensen and John Pauly (1997), in a perceptive essay on the conceptualization of the audience in cultural studies, noted that "with each image [of the audience] come assumptions about who the research is in relation to the audience—who are 'we' in relation to 'them'?" (p. 155). They note that "doing cultural studies requires the work of heart and hands as well as head," but that "theoretical complexity marks one's status in the academy" (p. 168). I believe the Internet is a fertile site at which we can put to the test Jensen and Pauly's request that we take audience research "seriously as a democratic task," that we be "more modest about (our) theories and more respectful of vernacular accounts of experience" (p. 167). Indeed, one of the most fascinating elements to Internet research is that it so frequently and obviously intersects with the experience of the new. Indeed, as I have already mentioned, much Internet research is itself motivated by scholars "discovering" e-mail, Usenet, and so on. There is nothing inherently wrong with that: In fact, that is as it should be. However, we must be cautious about overlapping method and experience. If, as I believe, we have (at least for now) only the methodological tools available to us to which we are accustomed, it is critically important that we do not transfer the experiential demands they make (in regard to language, meaning, epistemology) to the realm of the Internet, lest we confine experience to that which *we* know but that others either may not know or, importantly, that which they experience as new, or experience in ways that we have not. The range of experience is somehow changed on-line, both qualitatively and quantitatively, and our explanatory abilities must change with it.

In regard to the media of mass communication, I have found it useful to ask, For whom are media made? For whom and to whom do media communicate? And what if the answer to those questions is, simply, "Us"? Audiences have become visibly fragmented, the media of mass communication seem less and less like they are, in fact, "mass" oriented. But it may be as well that our logics are fragmented, or to borrow from Jensen and Pauly, it is how we "imagine the audience" that is at stake. Rather than holding fast to an understanding of mass communication that has guided research for decades, an understanding that has, somehow, simultaneously encompassed and collapsed notions of consumption, production, and distribution, scholars must be savvy to the differences not only between those activities but within them as well. The complexity is, of course, staggering. In regard to the Internet, it is not only important to understand audiences—people—and what they do with media, it is important to understand what audiences think they do, what creators and producers think audiences do and what they think audiences *will* do, what venture capitalists think about audiences and producers, what software and hardware makers think and do, and so on.

In regard to the Internet as a medium of communication, this is a particularly critical line of questioning. It is still not clear, and it may be unclear for a long time to come, at which level of communication (mass, interpersonal, group, organizational, etc.) the Internet operates: whether it operates on multiple levels (it seems likely it does) and, if so, whether it can operate on multiple levels simultaneously (this, too, seems likely) and, if it can, with what consequences for our understanding of the people engaged in Internetworked communication? The situation is far from lamentable. We have come to understand, thanks in part to the visibility on the Internet of *process,* that we are all engaged in incredibly meaningful communicative processes, all the time. That it took our near-obsession with this technology to firmly point it out is ironic, for these are processes that have been going on throughout human history. The Internet, however, has made clear that even when it seems that we are a voice in the wilderness, there are other voices occupying the same space. Whether or not anyone hears the others is, however, one thing fundamentally at stake when we attempt to assess the Internet's intersection with social life and social being.

The Internet and the Academy

The second reason scholars of the Internet must be reflexive is that the Internet is both embedded in academic life and owes much of its existence and conceptualization to academia. According to Newhagen and Rafaeli (1997),

> Thinking about academia's role vis-à-vis the Net, we are reminded that what we call the Net today has roots in the Internet, Bitnet, and Arpanet, all partly academic institutions. Just at the point in history when critical voices speak of the decreasing relevance of research and universities, along come the Net and its attendant large-scale commercial, industrial, organizational, and social relevancies. In large measures, the Net can be considered an academic accomplishment. As you indicate, this alone behooves our involvement.

But the discourse concerning the Internet has shifted with tremendous rapidity from one with an academic and scientific basis to one based in commerce. We know that the Internet's growth since the development of the World Wide Web is attributable (at least in part if not in general) to its promise as an economic engine, at both the multinational corporate level as well as that of the individual. That it has become a commercial technology in multiple senses of that phrase (a technology itself for sale and used for selling) has become commonplace. But in regard to scholarship, the Internet still provides much: e-mail, networks, information with unparalleled speed, availability, and accessibility.

Academia is not without its connections to the world of commerce, of course, and the Internet is implicated in several such connections (not least being in connection to new forms of delivery for education, a matter of great import, but not directly related to those at hand). Academic fame and fortunes can be made: Scholars can be first to identify Internet-related phenomena; they might write that dissertation that Microsoft buys; or they might find themselves on the cover of *Wired* magazine, earning a $50,000 "Innovation Grant" from Merrill Lynch for "potentially profitable dissertations" (Secor, 1998), and so on. But are there dangers or hindrances to good, wise thought, brought about by this mixture? Quite likely our sense of discovery and wonder, senses that we rightly cultivate as scholars and senses that drove us to the academic life in the first place, are titillated by the sheer scale and penetration of the Internet. Perhaps the Internet can restore a bit of luster to the faded glory that came with being a PhD, a "scientist" in the post-Sputnik 1960s, the time when, not coincidentally, the Internet's conceptual and structural foundations were laid, and the time, again not coincidentally, when the "union between science and state" in the United States enfolded the social as well.

One perspective on technological development and the relationship of technology to society is based on the notion that technology is designed in anticipation of its effects, and it may well be that research is designed in anticipation of its effects, to borrow from Max Weber (1973). Such effects may, in addition, be ones beyond the outcomes of a research project's findings, ones that involve publication, funding, promotion, tenure, and the like. As Cathy Schwichtenberg (1993) noted in relation to Madonna studies, there may be an opportunity to assess the relationships between academia, the public, and the press, to "witness the fight over fragmented roles and fracturing power" (Jones, 1997c, p. 207) that erupts when an area of research suddenly becomes "hot." The research process is no less part of "the ongoing construction of individual and collective reality" (p. 215) than is the Internet—and discourse within it and external to it.

Framed that way, it is possible to consider the nature of research as a meaning-making process, as a version of reality by, and perhaps in some ways even for, scholars. The intersection of individual reality with that of collective reality produces some interesting results when both realities are shifting within, and between, disciplines. For instance, it is possible that we lose sight of the fact that few people are generally, in fact, pioneers when it comes to the Internet and Internet research. How many have "discovered" e-mail and written studies about it? How many analyses have been published or are underway that examine on-line discourse in MUDs (multi-user domains), MOOs (multi-user domains object oriented), and IRC (Internet relay chat)? I do not wish to disparage any such work, because it is important that we undertake it. I do wish to point out that no matter how interconnected we may become thanks to the Internet, we, as scholars, are as fragmented as the audiences that technologies of mass communication had once brought to-gether and now take apart. There is, and will be, of course, much more to be discovered about on-line communication, community, and social relations. But the penetration of the Internet across disciplines, as both an object of study *and* a channel of academic discourse, brings to light that no matter how we may value interdisciplinarity, academia is far from interdisciplinary in the way scholars communicate across disciplines.

How *Do* We Study the Internet?

As a friend and colleague, Jim Costigan, remarked, studying communication is a lot like getting a grip on Jell-O. The more you squeeze, the more it changes shape. The Internet is so fluid as to be rendered meaningless as a storage medium; it is never constant, never fixed, no matter that the textual traces left there seem to give it form. (That in and of itself may be the best argument for rallying us to the cause of ensuring that Internet studies not become institutionalized and structured as a discipline.)

In regard to the Internet as a social space, it is no easier to get a grip on the human dimensions of the Internet than it is to get a grip on human interaction, generally. It is easier, however, to be fooled into believing that we can have a firmer grip when the communicative aspects of interaction, particularly as they are rendered textual on-line, are fixed and available to us. To some degree, the sheer availability of chat sessions, MUD/MOO sessions, e-mail, and the like provide us with a seductive data set, and it takes little effort to be of the belief that such data represent . . . well, *something,* some semblance of reality, perhaps, or some "slice of life" on-line. Our own precepts about ideas relating communication and interaction, communica-tion and community, are as much engaged with determining whether such data "map" to reality or not.

So—how *do* we study the Internet, then? What, precisely, do we probe, analyze, scrutinize? The technology is not difficult to examine and is in its way rather seductive when it comes to research. One can get one's arms around the networking issues, the protocols, the components (routers, com-puters, cables, modems, etc.), the hardware and software. Plotting the net-work and determining the paths taken by messages, packets, and information is not so difficult and can be rather fascinating (How *does* this thing work? How, for instance, does my e-mail get broken up, each piece shipped, piecemeal, along different routes, reassembled, and delivered to me?). The "classic" model of communication (sender→message→receiver) is not only a tempting one with which to build analyses of the Internet, it can be a valuable first step.

Are the methods we have for studying other media (methods that scholars from many disciplines—such as communication, anthropology, sociology, psychology, history, and dozens of others—have contributed and used to assist us with understanding newspapers, speech, radio, television, telephony, and public life generally) ones that we can use to study the Internet and its position within modern life? Can the hypotheses, research questions, models, statistical procedures, close readings, and thick descriptions that we have used to study and describe media technologies, societies, media events, meanings, and intentions be (to borrow from the language of computing itself) "ported" over to study of the Internet and to what goes on within it and around it? Rice and Rogers (1984) noted that "the natural contexts of new media may limit how faithfully traditional research designs and methods may be applied . . . the nature of new media themselves may create limitations, as well as new opportunities" (p. 82).

An obvious step is to describe and interpret on-line communication. Thanks to the hardware and software, we have the artifactual textual traces of interaction created instantaneously, at the moment of utterance. For scholars with an interest in discourse analysis, literary criticism, rhetorical studies, textual analysis, and the like, the Internet is a research setting par excellence, practically irresistible in its availability. But the social issues surrounding the Internet are far more difficult to untangle than its texts. Most of the issues with which researchers, thus far, have been concerned, relate to the Internet's effects on society: Will it bring us closer together? Will it tear us apart, isolate us? Will it form the foundation on which electronic communities will flourish, or will it be the basis of the true "nuclear" family, allowing closeness via interaction at a distance? Will we divide into information "haves" and "have-nots" and with what consequences? (Have we not already been so divided: Is it simply clearer now that we are?) These are the obvious questions, and there are less obvious ones, such as those related to the epistemological consequences of the Internet. For instance, what does it mean for scholars and their scholarship when a particular technology with distinctive and peculiar modes of address, identity, behavior, and responsibility becomes a preeminent medium of information exchange? Or what of questions related to the insertion of the Internet into modern life, itself already replete with media of communication of all kinds, shapes, and sizes? What will be the interaction between scholars when they share the same "space" asynchronously, even invisibly? What will the subjective changes in our sense of the speed with which information can be moved bring to epistemology? As Breen (1997) put it,

> The resort to speed is a key feature of the contemporary communications mediascape. . . . Virtuality has served to heighten and individualize the speed at which information is gathered. What we cannot identify is where the information is grounded. . . . Scholarship may enjoy the benefits proposed by this sort of speed of access to digitized information. What that speed tells us little about are the organizing principles of the structures that bring the information to our screens and printers, research and publication efforts, not to mention the politics of our lives. In many respects, speed both empowers the user to gain access to pragmatic sources, while disempowering the critical apparatus of knowledge-history. It disarticulates one set of concerns—information retrieval and the re-creation of author information sets in the virtual world—from the field of knowledge.

Breen's concerns echo concepts that Schivelbusch (1986) set forth regarding changes in the perception brought about by the development of the railroad:

> The notion that the railroad annihilated space and time was not related to that expansion of space that resulted from the incorporation of new spaces into the transport network. What was experienced as being annihilated was the traditional space-time continuum which characterized the old transport technology. . . . What Bergson called the *durée* (duration, the time spent getting from one place to another on a road) is not an objective mathematical unit, but a subjective perception of space-time. If an essential element of a given sociocultural space-time continuum undergoes change, this will affect the entire structure; our perception of space-time will also lose its accustomed orientation. (p. 36)

In what ways might the research process, including, particularly, reflection and reflexivity, be affected by the kinds of changes Breen and Schivelbusch discuss? One issue may be the duration between elements in Dilthey's (1990) tripartite arrangement of the interpretive process, between immediate experience, expression, and interpretive understanding.

The traditional question to ask might be, What are the measures we can use to assess on-line phenomena? It is more useful, I believe, to adopt methods drawn from John Pauly's (1991) observations of qualitative research. In a superb monograph, Pauly notes three ways qualitative researchers have chosen to study mass communication: product, process, or commentary. To adapt such an approach to study of the Internet provides an opportunity for an interpretive turn lacking in much, if not most, of the literature to date.

For instance, to study the Internet as product might mean understanding on-line communication as, to paraphrase Pauly, symbolic forms by which experience is rendered and made "meaning-full." To study it as practice might direct us toward "cultural processes rather than products" and assist with an understanding of how, on-line, we "habitually organize and institutionalize the meaning-making process" (p. 4), as well as how, off-line, decisions are made about organizing the on-line. And to study the Internet as commentary might mean that we are sensitive to the ways it is "a useful thing to think with" (p. 5), as when we talk about the Internet as a realization of "the global village," or "networked consciousness," or even when we make claims about "Internet addiction," for these types of discourse "often articulate wider disputes over cultural style" (p. 5).

Commentary, as Pauly describes it, is something to which we should be particularly sensitive, as it frames and colors our own scholarly work. At every turn, we must encounter and face our assumptions. For instance, in regard to electronic communities (an area of study that has greatly interested me for many years), our arrogations about what is "good" about community (indeed, even that it seems to go unquestioned that community is of itself a good thing) color the positive and negative critiques of what the Internet will bring to social relations. One obvious critique is that electronic communities are, and will continue to be, elitist, no matter that it is widely believed that "community" implies some sort of "openness" and sense of belonging. Community is, in some ways, inherently elitist, at least insofar as it is predicated on the notion that some belong and others do not. At present, the elite are most likely to use computers and Internet services, and it may well be that the elite are finding community for *themselves.* Yet such communities go largely unresearched. Community is as exclusive as it is inclusive, as bad in some ways as it is good in others. Studies of community on-line will do well not to cast aside the study of some forms of community that seem less democratic, participative, "open," and so on, lest we ignore the range of experience on-line (and off-line) that enriches social relations.

In the realm of product and process, it is important to consider that community can have a wide range of meanings and that it can be institutionalized. Community, particularly on the Internet, is as marketable as any other commodity. Such marketing has been primarily the province of real estate and, to a degree, of city government (the naming of neighborhoods, developments, and subdivisions); had once been the province of social groups within those neighborhoods (and outside them); and is now simply the province of marketing generally.

One sees evidence of this even in broad terms. The Internet has become a segregated medium of entertainment, particularly since the announcement of plans to develop Internet 2/Next Generation Internet (I2 or NGI), to allow the once-ubiquitous (it is claimed) academic and research uses of the Internet to again proceed, unfettered by bandwidth constraints and overuse perpetuated by the incredible increase of commercial and entertainment web sites. Or perhaps to put it another way, the mix of the scientific and the prosaic, the elite and commoners, is again separating, and through technology one finds, among other things, status being mediated.

Perhaps the elite, too, can be thought of as diasporic communities (Mitra, 1997), even in terms once reserved for urban development (a form of "white flight" begins as the Internet is populated by the masses and the elite flee to I2, firewalls create "red-lined" neighborhoods, and so on). In the realm of real estate, elite communities were signified initially by suburbanization and the development of social and architectural structures such as gated buildings and communities. In the realm of what we might term "virtual estate," what we now find via the Internet are "Gates-ed" communities, ones cordoned off in other ways, by interest and by access. The acquisition, buying, selling, and trading of Internet domain names is the most visible representation of such activity. Less visible representations include the development of behavioral norms (MacKinnon, 1995, 1997; McLaughlin, Osborne, & Smith, 1995), establishment of limited-access "electronic communities," and importantly, maintenance of values prevalent on-line since the origins of hacking (Sterling, 1992). We may also consider academic communities diasporic, making annual pilgrimages to conferences and the like, and now able to meet virtually in cyberspace. Perhaps the nature of diaspora itself, or at least our usage of that term, has changed, alongside our changeable perceptions of space and distance. My point is not to broaden the scope of how we should conceptualize diaspora but to ask that we broaden the scope of our explorations and investigations into on-line communities and, most important, to ask that we do more than rejoice at the opportunities marginalized groups have to gather on-line, that we be sensitive to the broadest possible range of understandings of communities, incorporating understandings that those communities themselves have.

Going Native by Going ... On-Line?

As I discussed in *CyberSociety 2.0,* "Definitions of community have traditionally relied on unproblematized notions of place, a 'where' that social scientists can observe, visit, stay and go, engage in participant observation" (Jones, 1998). This brings up an important issue for Internet research: Although the artifactual elements of on-line social relationships seem readily available, in what ways is it possible for the researcher to travel to the "place" occupied by a community, to observe, participate, to use traditional ethnographic methods? As Lotfalian (1996) claims, studies of community have relied on terms

> that refer to group dynamics such as assimilation, acculturation, adaptation, and participation [and] to the opposite: expulsion, expatriation, and exile. [On-line] the terms used for indicating communities are different, such as posting, cross-posting, reading, lurking, and flaming, which don't imply being part of a whole. (p. 118)

Lotfalian's sensitivity to the language of on-line interaction is a very necessary first step if we are to get a "thick description" (Geertz, 1973) of on-line social groups. Geertz's assertion that "man is an animal suspended in webs of significance he himself has spun" (p. 5) has a particularly "Internet-friendly" ring to it, of course. It is important, however, to remember that Geertz ended his classic *The Interpretation of Cultures* by noting that "one can start anywhere in a culture's repertoire of forms and end up anywhere else. . . . One has only to learn how to gain access to them" (p. 453). Concerning Internet research, access is simultaneously an issue in regard to being able to log on and being able to participate, not only for scholars but for anyone else. It is also an object of study in its own right, insofar as issues of access are among ones paramount to Internet discourse, on-line and off-line. But access is also of concern to Internet research as it engages us in questions about our ability to make choices about what we will study and where we will study it. What are the boundaries of communities in cyber-space? Scholars have relied on being able to go places, to engage in partici-pant observation. In Geertz's terms, to "gain access" means not only to be able "to read over the shoulders of those to whom" (p. 452) a culture belongs, to not only participate and observe, but to understand and know. In cyber-space, is there a "there" *there?* What are the consequences of an "easy come, easy go" opportunity for sociological work? Can culture maintain itself even as people rapidly cycle in and out of its milieu?

Perhaps cyberspace is a place where communication must occur if for no other reason than because tradition is absent, as Carey (1997a) reminds us was characteristic of the American frontier. If so, we should examine not only the creation and maintenance of community but also its disruption and destruction. We should be aware of what Carey has described as the "anti-nomian counterpart" to the "creative aspect of culture":

> We ceaselessly create communities out of need, desire, and necessity but then continually try to escape from the authority of what we have created. We are forever building a city on the hill and then promptly planning to get out of town to avoid the authority and constraint of our creation. Both the creation and the escape, the organization and disorganization, involve intense episodes in sense-making, in the formation and reformation of human identity, in communication in its most fundamental sense. (p. 27)

Perhaps the formation of "personalized" mass media is, in its way, a mani-festation of a destructive tendency toward existing conceptions of commu-nity, one arising from a late 20th-century distrust of institutions (particularly governmental ones), and one given ground by the Internet, a medium itself "de-institutionalized."

If the Internet is a form of "personalized" mass media, perhaps researchers, too, should in some sense "personalize" their efforts, in two ways. First, to be sensitive to, and aware of, their own experiences on-line. Second, to focus not only on community but on individuals within social groups as well. If the Internet is the first truly "personal mass medium," as some have claimed (Negroponte, 1995), we must understand that it is not so for all. And we must understand the Internet in terms of processes engaging individuals and those that individuals engender as precursors to emergent, or as Daniel Dayan (1997) put it, fugitive, communities. Is it perhaps time that scholarship takes a page from marketing and disaggregates the market? Aside from gains and losses in terms of the traditional assessment of the quality of research (generalizability, replicability, sampling, validity, etc.), what might change about the explanatory and interpretive power of the research? If we do "disaggregate" so, we should also go to great lengths to ensure that we not erode "moral and civic capacities" and that we are able to "think beyond individual desire" (Carey, 1997b, p. 23) lest we disaggregate (perhaps the more appropriate term might be "digitize") society generally. As Grossberg (1997a) notes, a "materialist or nomadic model that argues that reality is constructed by 'anonymous' travels of people within historically articulated social spaces, places, and structures of practices" (p. 317) may well make the most sense not only as an interpretive strategy but as one with which we can understand the role of researchers striving to understand a place, to understand its people and practices, and to make a place for their own understandings.

Prediction and Partiality

It is critical that our understandings of social relations on-line are not binding and/or structuring interpretation. As Ringer (1997) stated in an examination of Weber's development of sociological method, "Sociologists must be prepared to deal with merely pretended purposes, rationalizations, displaced emotional gratifications, and plainly incomprehensible motivations" (pp. 105-106).

Ringer's words can be applied as a caution to those studying digital media generally. Steven Johnson (1997) notes, "A computer . . . is a symbolic system from the ground up" (p. 15). Another consequence of digitization and disaggregation is recombinance, editing, the ready and convenient ability by which disparate cultural symbols and elements can be placed in proximity to each other without a necessary fixed relationship (Jones, 1989). Digital media have been innovated particularly along these lines; as symbol-manipulating technologies, they have been driven by the techniques of editing. Our understandings of cultural material conveyed to us via digital media must not begin with presuppositions about rationality, linearity, or even "sense" as we may construe it, unless we are aware of, and forthcoming about, our constructions.

The more manipulable cultural material in a market system, the more economic and political controls are placed on manipulation. As a further result, economics and political economy are very important to Internet research. Hackers, we are told, perpetuate the notion that information wants to be free. That may be true, but humans like to get paid. What happens when information is simultaneously digitized and owned? And how are scholars implicated in this fashion (as I myself am)? Copyright and fair use are increasingly important issues: They will not, cannot, go away. Will we, as scholars, demand payment for our work? Likely we will, although we may not always seek it in cash; we may get it in the form of tenure and promotion, recognition and attention, or things such as release time from duties we seek to not pursue but have done so as part of "paying our dues." Internet researchers would do well to maintain self-reflexivity along the economic and political dimension as well as the epistemological. What are the politics of epistemology and the structuring of knowledge on-line, the politics of, say, directories, on-line journals, and indexes?

Marcus Breen (1997) argues that

> those of us in positions of responsibility, whether researching, teaching, producing, marketing or promoting the virtual world of digital communication, could use a political economy critique to inform our engagement with the object of our affection. This is not always an easy thing to do. Academic work especially is premised on a relationship between ourselves and the career material with which we are "employed." While we may abstractly distance ourselves from some issues, competition in the workplace tends to force us to become uncritical advocates of the material we are employed to critique. Fashion dictates our tastes, while the newly mobilized marketplace of technology directs our careers.

Breen's critique is particularly noteworthy because it can assist us to ask, In what ways do we (broadly speaking, as individuals, institutions, etc.) pay for information, and with what consequences? Surely we do not pay for it only in terms of existing currencies of exchange, in dollars and yen and rubles and dinars. We also pay for it in terms of the attention that we give to some information and not to other. It is no coincidence that the phrase "pay attention" incorporates the notion of payment. As Michael Goldhaber (1997, p. 182) points out, the resource that is scarce and desirable in cyberspace is attention. Consequently, the affective dimensions both of Internet use and of Internet research must be considered. As Grossberg (1997b) puts it, "Affective economies of mood" are a plane "on which psychic energy is organized." He goes on to say, "If desire is always focused (as the notion of cathexis suggests), mood is always dispersed. . . . It is the coloration or passion within which one's investments in, and commitments to, the world are made possible" (p. 159). Academic life has long traded in attention and been driven by affective displacements—and disbursements. Scholars often ask questions such as, How many citations are there to my work? Who is reading it? Reviewing it? Are people paying attention to it? What motivates our work? But most important for Internet research, the affective dimensions of on-line experience largely go unnuanced as the very newness of the interaction with technology leads to predictive research, no matter its methodological guise.

There is, of course, much attention (and grant monies) paid to Internet research that is predictive—in part because the Internet is a newly forming medium and in part because predictive research will find sources for funding. Such was the situation during television's early days, as it was during that of film (the Payne Fund studies serve as a classic example). But there is also much interest in research that is descriptive—again, in part because the Internet is a newly forming medium and because there is great interest in discovery and exploration of its contours. Ron Rice has written extensively about research on computer-mediated communication (CMC), and his work has provided an excellent guide for CMC researchers. In a 1989 article that provides a foundation for CMC research, Rice made a distinction between two goals of CMC research: Formative research, which "acquires information useful in designing and improving project components, and provides feedback during the design, implementation, and use of [a computer] system" (p. 448), and summative research, which "aims to summarize how [a computer] system affected those involved with the system as well as the wider social context, including intended and unintended effects, and to what extent the systems goals were achieved" (p. 449). At the time that Rice wrote that article, however, the Internet was still limited, in the main, to the minority of researchers aware of its existence. Rice noted in the article that CMC at that time was defined as "videotext, audiotext, personal computers, computer conferencing, word processing, computer bulletin boards, office information systems, and electronic and voice mail" (p. 436). Nevertheless his ideas, as an outline of how one might go about studying CMC, are still useful.

As useful is to note that Rice (1989) observed a "variety of disciplines" and "varied methodologies of these disciplines" used to "study . . . the uses and effects of computer-mediated communication systems" (p. 436). He wrote that "the insights [are] bound up in, and confounded with, the research processes applied in specific studies" (pp. 436-437). He went on to narrow his focus to the communicative aspects of computer-mediated communication, to "conversation (communication between individuals via computer systems)" (p. 437) as opposed to aspects concerning allocution, registration, and consultation. Rice's focus encompasses the Internet, but it is much more inclusive. Viewing his suggestion that research on computer-mediated communication proceeds along four dimensions (stakeholders, goals, analytical domain, and tools) from an Internet-based perspective, one can still see the practicality of the approaches he encourages.

However, one can also see the difficulties defining the Internet as a communication medium. Just as the Internet has made more concrete the concept of media convergence by being the medium of distribution for digitized media content, so too has it made clear the convergence of different forms of computer-mediated communication. The Internet is at heart an inter-networking of networks, and, consequently, it creates relationships between a variety of technologies, techniques, and ways of communicating. The Internet is a computer-mediated communication system made up of computer-mediated communication systems. How do we study it; what logics do we apply to it? The ones applied to the individual systems of which it is composed? Is there a way to reduce it to its components, to create analytically tractable elements, and if so, what are the consequences of that reduction? One approach to such reduction has been to examine the individual modes of communication—textual, hypertextual, graphical, interactive, and so on—or to examine the individual technologies and ways of communication that we have come most frequently to use—Usenet, the World Wide Web, e-mail, and the like. Although such approaches do provide insight into particular uses, they do not satisfy an appetite for a holistic understanding of the Internet. As Weber (1973) claimed,

> There is no purely "objective" scientific analysis of cultural or "social phenomena," independent of particular and "one-sided" perspectives. . . . We want to understand reality . . . in its distinctiveness—the interconnectedness and the cultural significance of its particular phenomena in their contemporary form . . . and the ground of their having historically become thus-and-not-otherwise. (pp. 170-171)

It is truly ironic that a technology of internetworking gives us great difficulty when we seek to understand its social interconnectedness. If, however, we seek only to find interconnectedness within and between the technology and its antecedents, we will likely not make the connection we truly desire, the one between life on-line and its meaning in relationship to life off-line.

Conclusion

It therefore is beneficial not only to study the Internet as an entity unto itself but, rather, to study it within the context of the particular combination of late 20th-century history and projections of 21st-century existence. What the Internet has connected is not only computer networks but ideologies and ways of life that have, thus far, seemed disconnected, perhaps even beyond connection. If we are to do a substantive, satisfying, social history of the Internet, our problem may not be the history, as it has been often when scholars have studied other media. When it comes to the history, we have it. It is written (in the electrons, generally, or magnetic particles or pits and valleys that make up floppy disks, hard drives, and CD-ROMs). It is likely not a sufficient history, insofar as we do not have, if you will pardon the expression, that which is between the electrons. Indeed, much of what has in the past provided history, the rough drafts, scribbled notes, scratched out lines, disappears with the electrons and pixels we readily manipulate to erase traces of the creative process in pursuit of an ideal end product. But many of the historical figures are still with us. It is one of the advantages of the newness of the Internet that many of the technology's founding figures are not only still alive but are quite young. One crucial aspect of Internet research should thus be to learn as much as possible from them, to engage in historical and ethnographic work, of the kind that David Bennahum, for instance, has undertaken and facilitated with the "Community Memory" project (http://memex.org/community-memory.html).

Such work will give us, at least, a sense of the time lines involved in the Internet's development. Our histories can go quite deep and tease out interesting connections, such as those between early inventors of electrical equipment. Nikola Tesla, for example, envisioned a variety of forms of "networked" communication (Jones, 1997a). Vannevar Bush, considered one of the pioneers of network technologies, worked on electrical power systems on a national scale (see Hughes, 1983), and much of his work in the 1920s (including development of a "network analyzer") prefigured later developments in Internetworking (Hillis, 1996). A particularly salient quote by Bush, for example, in hindsight presages from a technical standpoint issues related to networking protocols in nonlinear systems like that of the Internet:

> Electrical engineering, for example, having dealt with substantially linear networks throughout the greater part of its history, is now rapidly introducing these methods[,] elements the non-linearity of which is their salient feature. (Vannevar Bush quoted in Hughes, 1983, p. 377)

As Hughes (1983) reminds us, the development of the electrical power grid was closely connected to university research, and his history of the evolution of electrical power systems closely parallels, structurally, the Internet's history beginning decades later. Importantly, Hughes noted that

> the interaction between region and technology was more notable than that between nation and technology. Influences at the national level, such as legislation, affected evolving technological systems, but local geographical factors, both natural and man-made, were more direct and discernible determinants of the shape of the systems. (p. x)

Following Hughes's social history one is often struck by the resonance to social, economic, and political issues that surround Internet discourse. The Internet's roots indeed go deep, but our histories have yet to do so.

One hope that historical work can hold out is that it may provide us insight into the decision making during the Internet's development. Coupling such work with analyses such as the one Bijker (1995) undertakes to assess the history of technologies such as Bakelite, the bicycle, and the fluorescent lamp will give us additional insight into the "sociotechnical ensemble" Bijker has proposed that can enable us to "deal with questions of value-ladenness, of emancipatory and oppressive potentials, of democratization, and of the embeddedness of technology in modern culture" (p. 280). It will likely not, however, give us insight into the Internet's self-development, its social evolution, unless we are able to reformulate the social element of Bijker's "sociotechnical ensemble" to account for on-line social relations. What is sociability on the Internet? What indeed is "cybersociety," and what makes it social? That there is a group of people? That they communicate? Is the occurrence of communication "enough" for us to know that there is a "social"?

Williams, Rice, and Rogers (1988) noted that they "consider possible research methods for new media as mainly extensions of existing methods, [they] propose that the new media researcher should consider alternative methods, or even multiple methods, and . . . attempt a triangulation of methods" (p. 15). But an additional problem may be that, although our research methods may provide for triangulation, it is possible that when it comes to Internet research, our methods are not (to borrow another term from computing) *scalable.* Can our methods efficiently build on one another, or is it the case that as we apply multiple methods we are unable to achieve the sum promised by their multiple application? Or, perhaps, that our methods are not scalable is a failure of our epistemology rather than our methods: Comprehension is always less than efficient.

The Internet is, in actuality, not just a technology. Were it a technology alone, little about it would be of such general interest. The technical challenges that brought about its existence and the ones that spur its development would hold some interest. It is not the technical challenges but, rather, the social ones that have become most interesting, for those are the ones that seem to require the most demanding of social balancing acts, between compromise, competition, and standardization. As Carey (1997b) put it,

> Communication requires a mode of understanding actions and motives, not in terms of psychological dispositions or sociological conditions but as a manifestation of a basic cultural disposition to cast up experience in symbolic forms that are at once immediately pleasing and conceptually plausible, thus supplying the basis for felt identities and meaningfully apprehended realities. (p. 11)

Communication, whether on-line or off-line, is metaphorically oriented. Our attempts to both study the Internet and understand it as a medium of communication can either broaden our options for understanding the fluid and social nature of mediated communication, or it can narrow our options by focusing on the essentially digital, binary, nature of being on-line: connected versus not connected, on-line versus off-line. We are both and all of those at once (unlike the machines we use to physically access the Internet). Computers can be understood to be digital symbol manipulators, and in fact that is all they are. And we, as humans, and as researchers, must strive to be symbol perceivers and interpreters, operating in the analog realm, making digital forms (zeros and ones) that seem indistinguishable again reconstituted and recognizable.

Note

1. Cookies are files stored on a computer's hard drive by web browser software that allow web sites to silently track the user's movements from site to site. They can hold information about the user (user name, passwords, pages accessed, computer type, etc.).

References

Abbate, J. (in press). *Inventing the Internet*. Cambridge: MIT Press.

Benjamin, W. (1968). *Illuminations*. New York: Harcourt, Brace & World.

Bijker, W. E. (1995). *Of bicycles, Bakelites, and bulbs*. Cambridge: MIT Press.

Breen, M. (1997, December). Information does not equal knowledge: Theorizing the political economy of virtuality [On-line]. *Journal of Computer-Mediated Communication, 3*(3). Available: http://209.130.1.169/jcmc/vol3/issue3/breen.html

Carey, J. W. (1997a). The Chicago school and the history of mass communication research. In E. S. Munson & C. A. Warren (Eds.), *James Carey: A critical reader* (pp. 14-33). Minneapolis: University of Minnesota Press.

Carey, J. W. (1997b). Reflections on the project of (American) cultural studies. In M. Ferguson & P. Golding (Eds.), *Cultural Studies in Question* (pp. 1-24). London: Sage.

Dayan, D. (1997, December 3). [Speech at the Second Annual Conference on the Visual Construction of Reality]. Copenhagen, Denmark.

Dayan, D., & Katz, E. (1992). *Media events: The live broadcasting of history*. Cambridge, MA: Harvard University Press.

Dilthey, W. (1990). *Einleitung in die Geisteswissenschaften* [Introduction to the human sciences]. Stuttgart, Germany: Teubner.

Geertz, C. (1973). *The interpretation of cultures*. New York: Basic Books.

Goldhaber, M. (1997, December). Attention shoppers! *Wired,* pp. 182-190.

Grossberg, L. (1997a). *Bringing it all back home*. Durham, NC: Duke University Press.

Grossberg, L. (1997b). *Dancing in spite of myself*. Durham, NC: Duke University Press.

Hafner, K. (1991). *Cyberpunk: Outlaws and hackers on the computer frontier*. New York: Simon & Schuster.

Hauben, R., & Hauben, M. (1997). *Netizens*. Los Alamitos, CA: IEEE Computer Society Press.

Hillis, K. (1996). A geography of the eye: Technologies of virtual reality. In R. Shields (Ed.), *Cultures of Internet* (pp. 70-98). London: Sage.

Hughes, T. (1983). *Networks of power*. Baltimore: Johns Hopkins University Press.

Jensen, J. (1993). The consequences of vocabularies. *Journal of Communication, 43*(3), 67-74.

Jensen, J., & Pauly, J. (1997). Imagining the audience: Losses and gains in cultural studies. In M. Ferguson & P. Golding (Eds.), *Cultural studies in question* (pp. 155-169). London: Sage.

Johnson, S. (1997). *Interface culture*. New York: HarperEdge.

Jones, S. (1989). Cohesive but not coherent: Music videos, narrative and culture. *Popular Music and Society, 12*(4), 15-30.

Jones, S. (1995). Understanding community in the information age. In S. Jones (Ed.), *CyberSociety* (pp. 10-35). Thousand Oaks, CA: Sage.

Jones, S. (1997a). Communication, the Internet and electromotion. In S. Münker and A. Roesler (Eds.), *Mythos Internet* (pp. 131-146). Frankfurt, Germany: Suhrkamp Verlag.

Jones, S. (1997b). The Internet and its social landscape. In S. Jones (Ed.), *Virtual culture* (pp. 7-35). London: Sage.

Jones, S. (1997c). Reading pop: The press, the scholar and the consequences of popular cultural studies. In S. Redhead, D. Wynne, & J. O'Connor (Eds.), *The clubcultures reader* (pp. 204-216). Oxford, UK: Blackwell.

Jones, S. (1998). Information, Internet and community: Notes toward an understanding of community in the information age. In S. Jones (Ed.), *CyberSociety 2.0* (pp. 1-34), Thousand Oaks, CA: Sage.

Levy, S. (1984). *Hackers.* Garden City, NY: Anchor.

Lotfalian, M. (1996). A tale of an electronic community. In G. Marcus (Ed.), *Connected* (pp. 117-156). Chicago: University of Chicago Press.

MacKinnon, R. C. (1995). Searching for the leviathian on Usenet. In S. Jones (Ed.), *Cyber-Society: Computer-mediated communication and community* (pp. 112-136). Thousand Oaks, CA: Sage.

MacKinnon, R. C. (1997). Punishing the persona: Correctional strategies for the virtual offender. In S. Jones (Ed.), *Virtual culture* (pp. 206-235). London: Sage.

McLaughlin, M. L., Osborne, K. K., & Smith, C. B. (1995). Standards of conduct on Usenet. In S. Jones (Ed.), *CyberSociety* (pp. 90-111). Thousand Oaks, CA: Sage.

Mitra, A. (1997). Virtual commonality: Looking for India on the Internet. In S. Jones (Ed.), *Virtual culture* (pp. 55-79). London: Sage.

Negroponte, N. (1995). *Being digital.* New York: Knopf.

Newhagen, J. E., & Rafaeli, S. (1997). Why communication researchers should study the Internet: A dialogue [On-line]. *Journal of Computer-Mediated Communication, 3*(4). Available: http://www.ascusc.org/jcmc/vol1/issue4/rafaeli.html

Ong, W. J. (1996). Information and/or communication: Interactions. *Communication Research Trends, 16*(3), 3-16.

Pauly, J. J. (1991). A beginner's guide to qualitative research. *Journalism Monographs,* (Serial No. 125).

Peterson, T. (1956). *Magazines in the twentieth century.* Urbana: University of Illinois Press.

Plath, D. W. (1980). *Long engagements.* Stanford, CA: Stanford University Press.

Rice, R. E. (1989). Issues and concepts in research on computer-mediated communication systems. *Communication Yearbook, 12,* 436-476.

Rice, R. E., & Rogers, E. M. (1984). New methods and data for the study of new media. In R. E. Rice (Ed.), *The new media, communication, research, and technology* (pp. 81-99). Beverly Hills, CA: Sage.

Ringer, F. (1997). *Max Weber's methodology.* Cambridge, MA: Harvard University Press.

Schivelbusch, W. (1986). *The railway journey.* Oxford, UK: Oxford University Press.

Schwichtenberg, C. (1993). *The Madonna connection.* Boulder, CO: Westview.

Secor, L. (1998, February). Dissertations for dollars. *Lingua Franca,* pp. 8-9.

Sterling, B. (1992). *The hacker crackdown.* New York: Bantam.

Trachtenberg, A. (1986). Foreword. In W. Schivelbusch (Ed.), *The railway journey* (pp. xiii-xvi). Oxford, UK: Oxford University Press.

Vonder, S. (1998, January 26). Search sites try to find themselves. *Inter@ctive Week,* p. 51.

Weber, M. (1973). *Gesammelte aufsätze zur wissenschaftslehre* [Collected essays in social sciences] (4th ed., J. Winckelmann, Ed.). Tübingen, Germany: Mohr.

Williams, F., Rice, R. E., & Rogers, E. M. (1988). *Research methods and the new media.* New York: Free Press.

2

Complementary Explorative Data Analysis
The Reconciliation of Quantitative and Qualitative Principles

FAY SUDWEEKS
SIMEON J. SIMOFF

FOR MANY PEOPLE AROUND THE GLOBE, the Internet has become the place where they instinctively turn to for all kinds of information, particularly after the Coseil Europeen pour la Recherche Nucleaire (CERN) introduced the World Wide Web (WWW or the Web) in the late 1980s. The Internet has given birth to new research fields or has diversified existing research fields connected with human activities, including computer-mediated communication (CMC), computer-supported cooperative work (CSCW), electronic commerce, virtual communities, virtual architecture, various virtual environments, and information design. The Web phenomenon raised a number of research issues concerning the mechanisms and rules governing Internet activities, particularly the interaction of technology and society. Decision makers at different levels needed knowledge about the phenomenon, so politicians, corporate managers, educators, and developers turned their attention to the Internet research community.

In this chapter, we discuss various traditional methodologies and their strengths and weaknesses when applied to Internet-spawned research fields. We find that traditional methodologies need to be adapted to these new research environments in which communication technologies and socio-cultural norms challenge existing research assumptions and premises. We propose a complementary explorative data analysis (CEDA) framework within an Internet research schema that integrates qualitative and quantitative procedures. CEDA was inspired by the successful collaboration of the two methodologies in the field of artificial intelligence (AI). The difference is that in AI, qualitative methods still deal with quantities. They operate over their ranges and tendencies in their behavior, not over each possible value. CEDA incorporates complementary use of both methods, depending on the particular research stage or the initial assumptions that need to be taken into consideration, thereby accommodating the unique features of Internet research.

Internet Environment and Research Methodologies

The Internet research community initially endeavored to follow the major macrosteps of classical research work: (a) problem identification and formulation, (b) research design and development of research methodology, (c) data collection, (d) data analysis, and (e) communication of results. These research activities are performed in a linear fashion. Once the problem is identified, the research design becomes crucial for the success of the whole work. Earlier research, however, identified several characteristics of the Internet phenomenon that complicated the use of the classical research schema. Because the human is the central object, participant, information generator, and collector, there was an implicit assumption that the methodology developed in social sciences would be appropriate and adequate.

The majority of social science research work is conducted within the bounds of a narrow set of assumptions, beyond which the researcher rarely deviates. Underlying any research are fundamental philosophical assumptions about ontology, epistemology, and human nature (Burrell & Morgan, 1979; Doolin, 1995; Hopper & Powell, 1985).

Assumptions of an ontological nature are concerned with the physical and social reality of research questions. When applied to Internet research, on the one hand, there is an existing physical medium that supports information communication; on the other hand, around this medium, there exists a global information ether where the social reality takes place. Between the two layers there is an almost invisible connection. However, the parameters of the physical medium, such as the capacity of the links and information storage, affect the social behavior within the information ether. For example, slow links lead to a narrower bandwidth of communication and use of different expressive techniques. An ontological research assumption in this case should make explicit connection between both "realities." *Assumptions of an epistemological nature* are concerned with knowledge. In Internet research, the issue is the distinction between information and knowledge. Is any experience on the Internet a new knowledge or just a transfer of existing knowledge into a new form? For example, should virtual architectures mimic physical architectures or develop their own laws and conventions? *Assumptions of human nature* are concerned with destiny. In Internet research, the issue is the boundary of the environment. Should we consider the Internet an environment in itself or should we consider it a complementary part or an extension of our own environment?

These philosophical assumptions influence the researcher's opinion of what constitutes an acceptable research methodology. A scientist with an objective approach searches for regularities and tangible structures existing in an external world; the researcher who focuses on subjective experience chooses to understand and interpret the individual in relation to, or "being" in, the world. The positivist (or objective) epistemological approach is sometimes labeled as "hard" scientific research. The positivists vary in their research design and methodological approach, ranging from verifying to falsifying hypotheses, but the intent in both instances is based on a belief that there are immutable structures to be discovered, explored, and analyzed. The anti-positivists' (or interpretivists') methodological approach is to be immersed in situations and allow insights to emerge during the process of investigation.

When conducting Internet research, however, there are even more factors to be taken into account. One consideration is the constant and rapid change in technology. A decade ago, most Internet users were, of necessity, skilled computer programmers, or at least, they had a relatively deep understanding of network applications. With the development of point-and-click graphic interfaces, audio and video plug-ins, cableless connections, and Web development applications, the underlying technology is more complex but is a virtually closed system. The effect of this transition is a polarization of the developers and the users in the Internet population. A second consideration is the information now available. The average Internet user is often over-whelmed by the variety and vast amount of information and has difficulty processing and selecting the relevant information. A third consideration is the notion of browsing or "surfing." In contrast to the traditional linear search along shelves of books in a library, the Internet user follows a weblike nonlinear search in which most "pages" emphasize eye-catching designs and attention-grabbing movement rather than a sequential and logical presen-tation of information.

These considerations complicate classical research methodologies, so increasingly, Internet researchers are turning to methods developed in the fields of information systems and data mining. In general, the research questions of interest appear at first to guide the choice of the research design and methodological tools. At the point when the methodology needs to be selected, the qualitative versus quantitative debate begins. Both methods attempt to explain the implicit concepts hidden in the bulk of data about the investigated phenomenon. However, both methods differ in their approach to the problem.

Quantitative methodologies assume that collected data are measurable, or if they are not, it is necessary to design an experiment or computer simulation in a way that respective measurements can be taken. Once the measurements are done, the problem is to fit (in a broad sense) the data adequately. Derived dependencies are then interpreted in the context of the initial problem formulation with a possible test of the hypothesis about the nature of the data and the errors in the measurements. In qualitative methods, the interest is centered on the qualitative characteristics of the phenomenon. Rather than trying to quantify every detail, these methods try to grasp the form, the content, and some constraints of the investigated phenomenon and analyze its qualities (Lindlof, 1995).

We question, however, this neat qualitative and quantitative dichotomy. We argue that each methodology has its own set of costs and benefits, particularly when applied to Internet research, and that it is possible to tease out and match the strengths of each with particular variables of interest.

Recently, protagonists of both sides have been encroaching cautiously onto rival territory. Thus, researchers may quantify qualitative data—for example, coding concepts from interviews and surveys in a manner suitable for statistical analysis. Researchers may also qualify quantitative data—for example, using quotes from complementary dialogue to support a statistical pattern derived from data collection. Adding a little of one methodology to the other adds flavor and aesthetic appeal, but it is not essential. This is the major drawback in current attempts to develop a research schema that benefits from both methods.

Quantity and Quality:
Two Approaches to a Common Phenomenon

Quantitative and qualitative methods are quite distinct in the emphasis they place on each (Stake, 1995). In quantitative analyses, argumentation is based on a representation of the phenomenon as a finite set of variables. There, we seek systematic statistical or other functional relations between these variables. In qualitative analyses, argumentation is based on a description of the research objects or observation units rather than on approximation of a limited number of variables. In other words, in qualitative analyses, references to excerpts or cases in the data are used as clues.

In the next sections, we define distinctive steps in quantitative and qualitative research and compare the methodologies with respect to the major dimensions associated with scholarly inquiry: (a) the purpose of the inquiry, (b) the role of the researcher, (c) the acquisition of knowledge, and (d) presentation of the research.

QUANTITATIVE RESEARCH

Purpose of the Inquiry

The purpose of quantitative research is to explain observed phenomena. It was developed to provide the ability to predict and control examined concepts. Consequently, these concepts need to be quantified. To do this, the researcher needs to know the form, type, and range of the content of the data before the commencement of an experiment. The methodology is based on the model of hypothesis testing. The idea was introduced and developed in the late 1920s and early 1930s. Although in practice there are some variations, ideally, the path of quantitative research is traversed from observation to generation of theoretical explanation to further testing of the theory. Recently, the overall schema has been extended with exploratory data analysis, when hypotheses are formulated and reformulated during the analysis.

The initial step in quantitative research is the design of the experiment. The researcher specifies the goals of the research, the initial hypothesis, and the respective ranges of person responses for measuring quantified concepts.

Each range defines the structure for the data collected. The basic assumption in quantitative methodology is that observations and experiments can be *replicated*. The overall experimental schema needs to be designed in a way that ensures a higher accuracy of the estimation of these quantified values.

Role of the Investigator

The next step is to observe groups of people (study participants) and to record data. The role of the investigator is an *objective* one. The investigator acts just as an observer. In the case of a passive experiment, the researcher only records the observations without setting values to "measured variables." In the case of an active experiment, the researcher may need to intrude and set up some of the variables.

Acquisition of Knowledge

The next step is data analysis. The selection of the appropriate data analysis method depends on the initial assumptions, the nature of experimental observations, and the errors in these observations. On the basis of the numerical results of this analysis, the scientist has to provide some explanations for the observed behaviors and to *construct knowledge*. These explanations are usually in the form of an approximating model. Furthermore, either with or without refining experiments, the researcher might *generalize* these observations and propose a *theory*. Consequently, instead of trying to explain a unique event or phenomenon, the results of the research should apply to a class of cases as well. This theory could be used for building *predictive models* and become the basis for a specific research question, tested in a controlled manner to verify or falsify.

Presentation of Research

The research results are then visualized using a variety of graphing techniques designed to condense the vast amount of raw data. These presentation techniques usually expose some particular characteristics of the data structure and relationships between variables. The researcher has some degree of freedom to tweak the representation of the data to enhance the perception of the results. Usually, each technique has one or more parameters that are sensitive to noise and smoothing. For instance, the appearance of a histogram is largely controlled by the number of bars used to depict the data.

When many bars are used, the pattern of the data may look complex with fine-grained details. The reader may wonder if a simpler underlying form exists. On the other hand, the use of too few bars may obscure patterns in the data that are important to the viewer. In this case, the data may look simple with course-grained details, and the reader may wonder if important details are missing.

QUALITATIVE RESEARCH

Often, the researcher is faced with data in the form of loosely structured descriptive texts or dialogues, images, and other illustrations rather than in the form of well-structured records. This, and similar problems, has led to the development of the relatively new method of qualitative research, in which the results are obtained by other than quantification analyses.

Purpose of the Inquiry

The purpose of qualitative inquiry is to understand observed phenomena. Quantitative research begins with a theory formulated as a set of hypotheses, and the purpose of a study is to find support for or to disprove the theory. Qualitative research begins with an area of interest or a research question, and a theory emerges through systematic data collection and analysis.

The object of inquiry for the qualitative researcher is typically a case. A case is a social practice, an integrated bounded system (Smith, 1979) that may or may not be functioning well. Case study is the study of a social practice in the field of activity in which it takes place. Case research is defined as research in which the researcher has direct contact with the participants and the participants are the primary source of the data. It follows, then, that the primary methods used in case research are interviews and direct observations. Other methods, such as experiments and surveys, separate the phenomenon from its context (Yin, 1989).

Role of the Investigator

The starting point for the researcher can be either the case or the question (Stake, 1995). In the former, the case presents itself as a problem, and there is a need or a curiosity to learn more. Because there is a personal interest in the case, it is referred to as intrinsic case study. In the latter, a general problem arouses interest, and a particular case is chosen as a possible source for explanation. Because the case is an instrument to a general inquiry, it is referred to as instrumental case study.

Thus, the *role* of the investigator is *participatory* and personal. The issue on which both approaches differ most is the priority placed on the role of interpretation during this step. All research, of course, requires some form of interpretation, but whereas quantitative research advocates the suspension of interpretation during the value-free period of experimentation, qualitative research advocates actively interpreting phenomena throughout the observation period.

Acquisition of Knowledge

The next step is data interpretation. During this step, the typical qualitative researcher conceptualizes the data and *discovers knowledge.* The conceptualization process ranges from merely presenting the data as they were collected to avoid researcher bias to building a theory grounded in the phenomenon under study. These intuitive and interpretive processes are not regarded as less empirical than quantitative research. Observations and data collection are rigorously systematic, occurring in natural rather than contrived contexts.

Qualitative research is not so much generalization as extrapolation. In certain explicated respects, the results are related to broader entities. The aim is to find out what is specific and particular about the solutions adopted by these people that can be *related* to the broader population. Although the solutions adopted by the people in the case study may be regarded as isolated individual cases and as such as exceptional, some factors are very much the same for a larger population. This means it is possible to conclude indirectly (e.g., referring to other research) in which respects and to what extent the data are really exceptions, in which respects they are comparable to other solutions or population groups, and what sorts of different solutions exist.

Presentation of Research

Qualitative researchers include a great deal of the collected data to present their interpretation of the results. Research reports usually include supporting data fragments in the form of quotes from the raw data. In this case, the researcher can slant the results toward a specific interpretation by exposing particular quotes and omitting others.

Rationale for Integrated Research

Numerous attempts at integrated research over the past two decades have resulted in labels such as *triangulation, micro-macro link,* or *mixed methods* (Bryman, 1988; see also Ragin, 1987; Tschudi, 1989). The idea is to employ a combination of research methods typically used to analyze empirical results or interpretations. The rationale is that the weakness of any single method—qualitative or quantitative—is balanced by the strengths of other methods. In reality, however, the qualitative and quantitative analyses are usually distinct, mutually exclusive components of the research. One component is unstructured textual data of a phenomenon being investigated (e.g., transcripts of interviews or verbal reports from protocol studies), analyzed with an interpretive or hermeneutic method (Prein & Kuckartz, 1995). The other component is numerical data of the same phenomenon (e.g., from a content analysis or a survey questionnaire), analyzed with some statistical procedure. The result is an integrated view that narrowly focuses on a particular social phenomenon.

There is such a variety of social norms that to understand them it is necessary to identify some regularities from observations. Regular patterns are grouped together and form typologies (or categories) of human processes and behavior. The process of typification is a fundamental anthropological technique that enables us to understand our everyday world as well as to conduct scientific inquiries. It is an integral aspect of human thought in that representations of unique experiences or stimuli are encoded into an organized system that economizes and simplifies cognitive processing (Rosenman & Sudweeks, 1995).

Typologies are distinct, discrete classifications of information that help to give order to a confusing, continuous mass of heterogeneous information. In some way, this continuum of information has been divided into discrete regions where points within each such region bear qualitative similarities to each other, whereas points in different regions bear qualitative differences to each other. The construction of meaningful typologies, therefore, is the foundation of scientific inquiry.

Typification as a combined scientific methodology has its foundations in Weber's and Schutz's works (cited in Kuckartz, 1995), who were concerned with linking hermeneutic regularities in texts and standardization of information. Developing this methodology further, Kuckartz (1995) uses a case-oriented quantification model whereby typologies are developed from data rather than predefined. In terms of data analysis, this methodology corresponds to data-driven exploration in which we do not specify what we are looking for before starting to examine the case data. For example, we may parse the text in a sample of e-mail messages looking for concepts that can become the basis for the development of formal models.

Issues Specific to Internet Research

The majority of Internet CMC research is conducted in laboratories under controlled experimental conditions. These studies may not present an accurate picture of the reality of virtuality. The external validity is problematic for three reasons: (a) Study participants are an atypically captive audience; (b) groups studied in experiments tend to be unrealistically small; and (c) an almost natural inclination of experimental design is to contrast with a face-to-face standard of comparison (Rafaeli & Sudweeks, 1997, 1998). This contrast may be misleading.

The replicability of CMC field research is difficult, if not impossible, for two main reasons. On a *technological level,* the Internet is permanently changing its configuration and supporting technology. The underlying networking protocols cannot guarantee the same conditions when replicating experiments simply because each time the path of information communication is unique; thus, the time delay and consequences connected with it are different. On a *communication level,* the difficulties in replication come from the creative aspect of language use. Although the rules of grammar are finite, they are recursive and capable of producing infinite language (Chomsky, 1980). Novel sentences are constructed freely and unbounded, in whatever contingencies our thought processes can understand. Apart from standard cliques, sentences are rarely duplicated exactly, yet each variation is generally comprehended. It follows, then, that experiments involving text generation can rarely be repeated. This lack of replication is a violation of the initial assumptions for the application of statistical analysis.

Another aspect of Internet research is that it has to deal with heterogeneous sociocultural structures. The Internet is, of course, populated with people of many cultures. Culture has been defined as a complex set of behaviors and artifacts with three major dimensions: *ideas* (traditional values and beliefs); *norms* (behaviors that adjust to the environment of traditional values and beliefs); and *material culture* (artifacts produced in the environment of traditional values and beliefs; Bierstedt, 1963). On the Internet, cultural complexity appears to be an intractable problem. Global communication

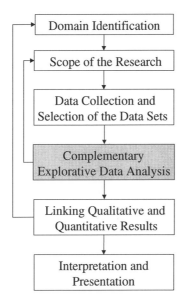

Figure 2.1. Stages of Internet Research

technologies bring together cultures that differ dramatically on each of the three dimensions.

The Internet Research Schema

Although at first glance it seems that quantitative and qualitative research are radically different, they share an important common thread. Both methods make interpretations of the phenomenon they want to examine. Both traditions create a framework for their analysis based on those interpretations. In reality, the difference between these two methods is a discursive one.

To overcome the difficulties outlined in the previous sections, we have developed an integrated methodology for Internet research (Figure 2.1). Internet research incorporates a number of separate research domains, including electronic commerce and business systems, CMC, CSCW, and distributed information systems. Therefore, the first stage is devoted to the identification of domain specifics. These specifics influence the selection of

TABLE 2.1a Quality/Quantity Matrix From a Data Point of View

Methods	Data	
	Qualitative	Quantitative
Qualitative	Survey analysis, interviews, speech acts analysis, participant observation	Qualitative reasoning, constraint reasoning
Quantitative	Data mining, cluster analysis, fuzzy data analysis, neural nets	Statistics, regression and correlation analyses, numerical simulation

TABLE 2.1b Quality/Quantity Matrix From a Methods Point of View

Methods	Data	
	Qualitative	Quantitative
Qualitative	Metaphors, ontologies, categories	Survey data
Quantitative	Text data, vocabulary, categories hierarchy	Numerical samples, coded categorical data, measurements

the appropriate research methods and the possible scope of the research. Once the scope is specified, the schema follows the traditional line of data collection.

The data collected in any of the Internet research domains are a heterogeneous combination of quantitative measurements and qualitative observations. Before the complementary explorative data analysis stage, the researcher defines the combination of methods that need to be used. Table 2.1 illustrates this heterogeneous picture in a "quality/quantity" matrix from both a data (Table 2.1a) and a methods (Table 2.1b) point of view.

Thus, CEDA can be viewed as a dynamic framework that provides valid integration of both methods. CEDA employs quantitative methods to extract

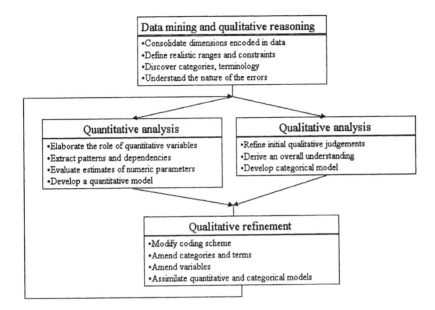

Figure 2.2. Processes in the Complementary Explorative Data Analysis (CEDA) Framework of the Internet Research Schema

reliable patterns, whereas qualitative methods are incorporated to ensure capturing of the essence of phenomena. Figure 2.2 gives a breakdown of the processes in the CEDA framework of the Internet research schema. The frameworks allows the use of different data sets in a common research cycle rather than the traditional approach of applying different analyses to the same data set.

CEDA has the potential to conduct parallel and interconnected research. This complementary analysis requires the linking of the results obtained by each of its components. The final result may lead to revision of the identified domain specifics and changes in the combination of analysis methods within the Internet research schema.

Application of the Internet Research Schema

We now provide an example of the proposed schema applied to CMC research.

DOMAIN IDENTIFICATION

A global society (or cybersociety; Jones, 1995, 1997, 1998) created by the Internet is no longer a projected vision of technocrats; it is becoming a reality. However, the global society may not be the "global village" as envisioned by McLuhan and Powers (1986), but more like virtual neighborhoods (or cybervillages). Before the Web explosion, cybervillages were defined not by geopolitical boundaries but by listserv subscriptions or chat channels. Today, even those loosely defined boundaries are blurred as cybervillages connect to a web of hyperlinks.

As the technology changes at a pace never before experienced, Internet CMC research is engaged in a catch-up situation. A modern Internet research methodology should take into account rapidly changing technology, social norms, and communication behaviors. To be able to specify and develop such a methodology, we need to identify the features specific to Internet communication research.

Communication is computer mediated. First, and obviously, Internet CMC differs from traditional face-to-face communication because the computer provides an interface between interlocutors. A common practice in Internet research is to regard face-to-face conversation as the ideal communication environment (Schudson, 1978), whereas CMC is rated as less than ideal. Experimental work has discovered a number of dysfunctional attributes of computer mediation, including flaming (Mabry, 1998; Siegel, Dubrovsky, Kiesler, & Maguire, 1986; Sproull & Kiesler, 1991) and unsociable behavior (Hiltz, Johnson, & Turoff, 1986; Matheson & Zanna, 1990), disinhibition and deindividuation effects (Hiltz & Johnson, 1989), and a lean environment (Short, Williams, & Christie, 1976; Walther, 1992). Somewhat more optimistic experimental work introduced findings on status leveling (Dubrovsky, Kiesler, & Sethna, 1991), socioemotional connections (Rice & Love, 1987), consensus formation (Dennis & Valacich, 1993), brainstorming creativity (Osborn, 1953), and collaborative productivity (Sanderson, 1996).

Communication requires technical knowledge. Each communication environment requires specific knowledge. In a face-to-face environment, we learn at a very early age not only the phonetics and grammar of the language but also, for example, the management of taking turns in conversations (Sacks, Schegloff, & Jefferson, 1978). In written communication, we add knowledge of orthography and a more formal use of language. In telephone communication, we learn how to search for telephone numbers, to press the right sequence of keys, and to engage in preliminary phatic conversation. Every Internet communicator, however, needs at least minimal technical knowledge of computers. To communicate, even with the simplest graphic mailer, the user needs to know enough of the operating system to launch the application; to compose, reply, and send a message; and to quit the application. As computer technology is being introduced more and more into elementary educational institutions, computer literacy will develop in parallel with linguistic literacy. In the meantime, however, computer literacy is a problem for the majority of current and potential Internet users and affects individual levels of interactivity.

Communication is affected by information and processing overload. Mass communication is ubiquitous, whether active or passive. We all absorb mass communication, whether it is active (television, theater, newspapers) or passive (roadside billboards, newsstand headlines, advertising on public transport). In most instances, we are able to be selective and control the amount of information absorbed. Internet communication places enormous pressures on cognitive processing. Discussion lists often generate hundreds of messages a day, and to contribute to a conversation means responding immediately before the topic shifts and the sequence is lost. On the Web, designers endeavor to engage the browser's attention by manipulating font type and size, text spacing, graphics, colors, backgrounds, video clips, sound bits, animation, and interactive gimmicks. Research has indicated that although minimal levels of novelty can stimulate and demand attention, extreme novelty leads to overstimulation, cognitive overload, distraction, and ultimately, impaired information processing.

Communication has a sense of virtual presence. Communicating with strangers on a regular basis is not new. There have been many examples of "pen pal" relationships that have lasted for many years. The sense of virtual presence in these instances, however, is not strong, because there are long delays between communication exchanges. The message exchange process on the Internet, on the other hand, can be almost instantaneous. The effect is a written correspondence that is like a conversation. Formalities, phatic introductions, signatures, and many other features of written communication are eliminated (Ong, 1982). In such a communication environment, indirect social cues are transmitted, and the virtual presence takes on qualities of a real presence. In fact, quite often, the mental distance between regular participants in discussion groups is less than with colleagues working in the same office.

SCOPE OF THE RESEARCH

Only recently are communication and cultural problems associated with a global community being investigated (e.g., Ess, 1996; Jones, 1995, 1997, 1998; Smith, McLaughlin, & Osborne, 1998; Voiskounsky, 1998). Global norms about privacy, freedom of speech, intellectual property, and standards of conduct are being developed. To understand new global communities, we address two broad aspects of mediated discussions: First, we explore communication patterns of texts, which form part of an ongoing conversation; and second, we explore the process of cohesiveness in a cross-cultural group. Specific questions of interest include the following: How does mediated communication compare with traditional interpersonal relationships? How does the mass-mediated group process work? What features of mediated communication enhance interaction and contribute to the cohesiveness of a virtual community?

DATA COLLECTION AND SELECTION OF THE DATA SETS

On the Internet, the web of computer networks provides a medium for a convergence of communication and social interaction. People congregate in global virtual neighborhoods such as discussion groups and chat rooms to engage in topics ranging from entertaining trivia to philosophical issues. In this chapter, we use qualitative data from publicly archived mediated discussions within these virtual communities. Both data sets consist of e-mail messages. Data Set A includes 3,000 e-mail messages, randomly sampled from network discussion groups between March and September 1993. Data Set B consists of 1,016 messages exchanged among a collaborative group of researchers between May 1992 and April 1994.

COMPLEMENTARY EXPLORATIVE DATA ANALYSIS

Having identified the domain, defined the scope, and collected the data, we now apply the CEDA framework (see Figure 2.3).

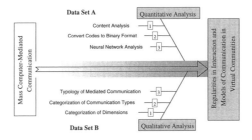

Figure 2.3. Application of the Complementary Explorative Data Analysis (CEDA) Framework

Quantitative Analysis

To understand more about global cultural norms, we focused on communication patterns in virtual communities. In particular, we were interested in features of messages that form part of an ongoing conversation—that is, messages that engage group members sufficiently to participate and respond and thus contribute to the development of group cohesiveness and consciousness.

Step 1: Content Analysis. Because the situational conditions are unknown prior to the study, variables are experientially rather than operationally defined, and some of the variables develop throughout the study. Texts of Data Set A were coded on 46 variables. Each message was described in terms of features and content, such as relevance, time, tone, purpose, and so forth. The codes were a mixture of objective and subjective ratings (see Sudweeks & Rafaeli, 1996, and Rafaeli, Sudweeks, Konstans, & Mabry, 1998, for a detailed description of the content analysis).

Step 2: Converting Codes to Binary Format. For a quantitative analysis, we chose to use a neural network because it allows a typology of features to emerge. Data analyses, such as a Euclidean cluster analysis, provide techniques for identifying correlations between particular features in a given data set, a useful indication of where the aggregation (boundaries) within a data set might appear. This form of analysis is widely recognized as providing a static view of data (a "snapshot" of typical and atypical instances) because the clusterings are based entirely on pairwise correlations. An alternative to the cluster analysis is the autoassociative neural network (ANN) in which clusterings are more dynamically created across all features synchronously. This quantitative method is modeled on human cognition. Features are drawn into particular groupings and form dynamic allegiances that can effectively overrule the original cohesion based on a simple pairwise correlation. The pattern of network activation captures complex information about dependencies between combinations of features.

ANNs are special kinds of neural networks used to simulate (and explore) associative processes. Association in these types of neural networks is achieved through the interaction of a set of simple processing elements (called *units*) connected through *weighted connections.* These connections can be positive (or *excitatory*), zero (no correlation between the connected units), or negative (*inhibitory*). The value of these connections is learned during a Hebbian training procedure (see Berthold, Sudweeks, Newton, & Coyne, 1998, for a detailed description).

To prepare the data for the ANN, codes identifying author, coder, and message number were deleted and the remaining variables converted into a binary format for processing. Each entry was split into as many mutually exclusive "features" as the entry had options. Because the main focus of interest was conversation threads in group discussions, three new entries were extracted from the original database to explore interactive threads:

1. *Reference height:* how many references were found in a sequence before this message
2. *Reference width:* how many references were found that referred to this message
3. *Reference depth:* how many references were found in a sequence after this message

Thus, as a preliminary result of the recoding of the data, we obtained a formal model of a thread in CMC (Figure 2.4). In addition to the threefold split proposed by Berthold et al. (1997, 1998) we included explicitly the time variable. Each message is completely identified by two indexes—one for its level and one for its position in time in the sequence of messages at this level. Such a model allows the comparison of the structure of discussion threads both in a static mode (e.g., their length and width at corresponding levels)

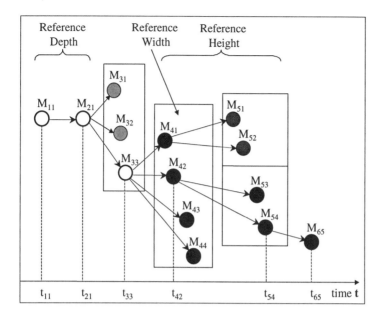

Figure 2.4. Formal Model of a Thread in Computer-Mediated Communication

and in a dynamic mode (e.g., detecting moments of time when one thread dominates another in multithread discussions, such as those that occur on bulletin boards or in MOO [multi-user domains object oriented]-based educational environments).

Step 3: Neural Network Analysis. After processing, the data consisted of 149 binary features; that is, each feature had a value of "1" (present) or "0" (not present). To identify typical features present in messages that stimulate conversation, one feature is *clamped* (forced to be present with a value of "1") to restrict the feature space of solutions. After training, the network settles on a pattern of features typically associated with the clamped feature. For example, Table 2.2 shows the frequency of features present in messages that contain "humor."

The sensitivity of associative features was then calculated. Distinguishing features of interactive messages (referenced to or referenced by another message) and noninteractive messages with their sensitivity scores are given in Tables 2.3 and 2.4 respectively.

TABLE 2.2 Frequency of Feature Activations When "Humor" Is Present

Feature description	Frequency
Medium-length message (11-25 lines)	50%
Appropriate subject line	90%
Does not contain question or request	70%
Appropriately formatted	70%
Male author	80%
Contains no abusive language	100%

TABLE 2.3 Distinguishing Features of a Typical Interactive Message

Feature Description	Sensitivity Score
Medium length (11-25 lines of text)	1
Appropriate subject line	1
Contains statement of fact	1
No question or request	1
No emoticons	2
No punctuation device to express emotion	3
Male author	2
Identifies gender by name and/or signature	3
Does not include quoted text	2
Addresses another person	1

TABLE 2.4 Distinguishing Features of a Typical Noninteractive Message

Feature description	Sensitivity Score
Does not refer to previous message	4
New topic, not referring to previous discussion	18
Does not use first person plural	1
Is not referred to by later messages	9

Qualitative Analysis

The second aspect of cultural norms in virtual communities is to identify communication features that contribute to an ongoing conversation and interaction in an environment in which many traditional features of inter-personal relationships are not present. Data Set B provides the data for qualitative analysis.

Step 1: Categorization of Dimensions. First, the messages were reviewed to identify and categorize major dimensions or regularities that occurred throughout the data. Five salient dimensions were identified:

1. *Issues:* the topics to be discussed and resolved
2. *Leadership:* the inclination to conform or reject leadership and authority
3. *Debate:* argumentativeness, criticism, or aggression among participants
4. *Relationships:* expressions or avoidance of friendship or intimacy among participants
5. *Action:* goal-directed or task-directed activity (Sudweeks & Allbritton, 1996).

Following a technique developed by Romm and Pliskin (1995), each occur-rence of a dimension was highlighted and labeled. The dimensions provided the means for observing the emergence of "turning points." Turning points, or changing patterns of regularities, indicate the development of group communication norms and standards. For example, early in the period, the focus of group discussions was on methodological issues to be resolved and on who should be responsible for coordinating the project. At a later point, the discussions became volatile, thereby introducing another dimension. The group dynamics therefore evolved to a different phase at this point.

Step 2: Categorization of Communication. The texts were reviewed again to identify not only how communication behaviors were managed but also the types of communication content. The content fell into three broad categories: (a) conceptual, (b) socioemotional, and (c) action (task oriented). The communication was managed in both a formal and informal manner.

Management of Communication. *Informal management* is the collective informal creation and enforcement of communication norms. Norms are mutually acceptable definitions of communication behaviors among indi-viduals so that interactions can be organized into an agreed-on state:

Example

We seem to be getting semiserious about this. Maybe one tentative and fairly easy way to proceed is to appoint Basil and Cyril the "leaders" (not because they talk the most, but because this is already their research interest and they have some experience in it). (May 28, 1992)

Formal management is connected with the enforcement of rules. Formally, management is needed to generate information, process knowledge, and disseminate the products of knowledge. Whereas informal management is generally performed on a collective level, formal management of communication occurs on an individual or small-group level.

Example

As this project begins to take on the prospects of developing a real finished product (i.e., the coded database), I think it might be appropriate for us to discuss the future "ownership" of that data.

Content of Communication. *Socioemotional communication* is content that deals with interpersonal relationships among the communicators. Socioemotional communication addresses the creation of relationship norms among communicators.

Example

First . . . I waded in here over the weekend, got into a barroom fight or two (there IS a certain amount of Dodge Citydom in the current situation), left, and was persuaded by Frank that I was not dealing with a crew of ogres, unemployed CIA operatives, and voyeurs. (June 26, 1992)

Conceptual communication involves the creation and prescription of shared rules to follow and involves a medium to high level of interactivity. Conceptual communication often requires that implicit communication be made explicit. Realistically, it is not always possible to have complete or full shared creation of mutual understanding of meaning, but this is what conceptual communication strives for.

Example

My reading of [this] question is not so much how CMC changes communication, but whether one can predetermine the cognitive approach by pre-selecting

TABLE 2.5 Communication Management and Content in the Development of the
             Virtual Community

Time Period	Dimensions	Communication Management	Communication Content
1	Issues, leadership	Informal	Conceptual
2	Issues, leadership, debate	Formal	Conceptual, socioemotional
3	Leadership, relationships	Informal	Socioemotional
4	Issues, leadership, action	Formal	Task oriented
5	Issues, leadership, debate, action	Formal	Task oriented
6	Relationships	Informal	Socioemotional

the form of communication. The assumption there is that various disciplines
think in very specific ways, and that each way can be matched to communication forms. (June 13, 1992)

Task communication deals with the explicit work to be accomplished. Task
communication focuses on information content of communication, whereas
conceptual communication focuses on the creation of meaning preceding the
processing of information. Task communication deals with specific activities
to be completed by members and often has to be conducted independent of
other group members. Task communication can be defined as information
exchange rather than communication.

Example

As a consequence of being the only person to answer [the] call for volunteers
to act as "Oracles" during project coding . . . my first task is to recruit others
. . . (April 16, 1993)

Step 3: Typology of Dimensions and Communication. In a third review of
the texts, the texts were divided into time periods, delineated by the turning
points identified in the first review, and the frequency of communication
types in each period was calculated. Table 2.5 shows the importance of communication styles in the development of an interactive virtual community.

Evaluation and Future Applications

We have examined the collection of data and the theoretical aspects and applicability of quantitative and qualitative analyses in Internet research. On the basis of these outcomes, we proposed an adaptive Internet research schema that combines consistently both methods. The CEDA framework can be applied to a variety of Internet research fields, including the following:

1. *Virtual communities.* Labeled initially as "virtual" to stress the absence of face-to-face physical presence, these are CMC communities that are real. These communities are established either on the basis of asynchronous e-mail message exchange or on a synchronous presence in text-based virtual environments—for example, MOOs and MUDs (multi-user domains).

2. *Internet-based distance education and on-line learning.* The communication between students and between students and educators is an essential part of current distance education. With the introduction of Internet and Web-based course delivery, communication becomes an essential part of course support. Technological support is a necessary condition for conducting successful collaborative studies, but a sufficient condition is the use of appropriate methodology. Experience from Web-mediated courses (Simoff & Maher, 1997) suggests that learning approaches taken from face-to-face courses need to be reconceptualized to take into account the unique opportunities offered by distributed computer media. The Internet research schema presented here is useful for elaborating and improving student communication in these new course environments. Applying the methodological schema to conduct research in this field will lead to the evaluation of practical specifications.

3. *Virtual organizations and intranet corporate research.* The methodological schema could be used for the analysis of the content of e-mail and multimedia communication, styles, efficiency, and productivity in traditional practices and emerging new business units—virtual organizations.

4. *Business information systems.* The methodological schema could provide results for improving the content-based information retrieval—the kernel of multimedia business systems. The research schema includes analysis of corporate e-mail, extraction of descriptive categories, compiling ontological representations of the results, and incorporation of these ontologies in the intranet search engines, thus shifting retrieval from simple keyword matching to categorical identification and category-based retrieval.

References

Berthold, M. R., Sudweeks, F., Newton, S., & Coyne, R. (1997). Clustering on the Net: Applying an autoassociative neural network to computer-mediated discussions. *Journal of Computer Mediated Communication,* 2(4). Available: http://www.ascusc.org/jcmc/vol2/issue4/ berthold.html

Berthold, M. R., Sudweeks, F., Newton, S., & Coyne, R. (1998). It makes sense: Using an autoassociative neural network to explore typicality in computer mediated discussions. In F. Sudweeks, M. McLaughlin, & S. Rafaeli (Eds.), *Network and Netplay: Virtual groups on the Internet* (pp. 191-220). Menlo Park, CA: AAAI/MIT Press.

Bierstedt, R. (1963). *The social order.* New York: McGraw-Hill.

Bryman, A. (1988). *Quantity and quality in social research.* London: Routledge.

Burrell, G., & Morgan, G. (1979). *Sociological paradigms and organisational analysis: Elements of the sociology of corporate life.* London: Heinemann.

Chomsky, N. (1980). *Rules and representations.* Oxford, UK: Basil Blackwell.

Dennis, A. R., & Valacich, J. S. (1993). Computer brainstorms: More heads are better than one. *Journal of Applied Psychology, 78*(4), 531-537.

Doolin, B. (1995). Alternative views of case research in information systems. In G. Pervan & M. Newby (Eds.), *Proceedings of the 6th Australasian Conference on Information Systems (ACIS'95)* (pp. 767-777). Perth, Australia: Curtin University of Technology.

Dubrovsky, V. J., Kiesler, S., & Sethna, B. N. (1991). The equalization phenomenon: Status effects in computer-mediated and face-to-face decision-making groups. *Human-Computer Interaction, 6,* 119-146.

Ess, C. (Ed.). (1996). *Philosophical perspectives on computer-mediated communication.* New York: SUNY Press.

Hiltz, S. R., & Johnson, K. (1989). Experiments in group decision making, 3: Disinhibition, deindividuation, and group process in pen name and real name computer conferences. *Decision Support Systems, 5,* 217-232.

Hiltz, S. R., Johnson, K., & Turoff, M. (1986). Experiments in group decision making: Communication process and outcome in face-to-face versus computerized conferences. *Human Communication Research, 13,* 225-252.

Hopper, T., & Powell, A. (1985). Making sense of research into the organizational and social aspects of management accounting: A review of its underlying assumptions. *Journal of Management Studies, 22*(5), 429-465.

Jones, S. G. (1995). *CyberSociety: Computer-mediated communication and community.* Thousand Oaks, CA: Sage.

Jones, S. G. (1997). *Virtual culture.* London: Sage.

Jones, S. G. (1998). *CyberSociety 2.0: Revisiting CMC and community.* Thousand Oaks, CA: Sage.

Kuckartz, U. (1995). Case-oriented quantification. In U. Kelle (Ed.), *Computer-aided qualitative data analysis: Theory, methods and practice.* Thousand Oaks, CA: Sage.

Lindlof, T. R. (1995). *Qualitative communication research methods.* Thousand Oaks, CA: Sage.

Mabry, E. A. (1998). Frames and flames: The structure of argumentative messages on the net. In F. Sudweeks, M. McLaughlin, & S. Rafaeli (Eds.), *Network and Netplay: Virtual groups on the Internet* (pp. 13-26). Menlo Park, CA: AAAI/MIT Press.

Matheson, K., & Zanna, M. P. (1990). Computer-mediated communications: The focus is on me. *Social Science Computer Review, 8*(1), 1-12.

McLuhan, M., & Powers, B. R. (1986). *The global village: Transformations in world life and media in the 21st century.* New York: Oxford University Press.

Ong, W. J. (1982). *Orality and literacy: The technologizing of the word.* London: Routledge.

Osborn, A. F. (1953). *Applied imagination.* New York: Scribner.

Prein, G., & Kuckartz, U. (1995). Introduction: Between quality and quantity. In U. Kelle (Ed.), *Computer-aided qualitative data analysis: Theory, methods and practice,* Thousand Oaks, CA: Sage.

Rafaeli, S., & Sudweeks, F. (1997). Net interactivity. *Journal of Computer Mediated Communication, 2*(4). Available: http://www.ascusc.org/jcmc/vol2/issue4/rafaeli.sudweeks.html

Rafaeli, S., & Sudweeks, F. (1998). Interactivity on the Nets. In F. Sudweeks, M. McLaughlin, & S. Rafaeli (Eds.), *Network and Netplay: Virtual groups on the Internet* (pp. 173-190). Menlo Park, CA: AAAI/MIT Press.

Rafaeli, S., Sudweeks, F., Konstan, J., & Mabry, E. A. (1998). ProjectH overview: A collaborative quantitative study of computer-mediated communication. In F. Sudweeks, M. McLaughlin, & S. Rafaeli (Eds.), *Network and Netplay: Virtual groups on the Internet* (pp. 265-282). Menlo Park, CA: AAAI/MIT Press.

Ragin, C. C. (1987). *The Comparative method: Moving beyond qualitative and quantitative strategies.* Berkeley: University of California Press.

Rice, R. E., & Love, G. (1987). Electronic emotion: Socioemotional content in a computer-mediated network. *Communication Research, 14,* 85-108.

Romm, C. T., & Pliskin, N. (1995). *Group development of a computer-mediated community.* Working Paper, Department of Management, University of Wollongong, Australia.

Rosenman, M. A., & Sudweeks, F. (1995). Categorization and prototypes in design. In P. Slezak, T. Caelli, & R. Clark. (Eds.), *Perspectives on cognitive science: Theories, experiments and foundations* (pp. 189-212). Norwood, NJ: Ablex.

Sacks, H., Schegloff, E. A., & Jefferson, G. (1978). A simplest systematics for the organization of turn-taking in conversation. In J. Schenkein (Ed.), *Studies in the organization of conversational interaction* (pp. 7-55). New York: Academic Press.

Sanderson, S. (1996). Cooperative and collaborative mediated research. In T. M. Harrison & T. Stephen (Eds.), *Computer networking and scholarly communication in the twenty-first-century university* (pp. 95-114). New York: SUNY Press.

Schudson, M. (1978). The ideal of conversation in the study of mass media. *Communication Research, 5*(3), 320-329.

Short, J., Williams, E., & Christie, B. (1976). *The social psychology of telecommunications.* London: Wiley.

Siegel, J., Dubrovsky, V., Kiesler, S., & Maguire, T. W. (1986). Group processes in computer-mediated communication. *Organizational Behaviour and Human Decision Processes, 37*(2), 57-187.

Simoff, S. J., & Maher, M. L. (1997). Web-mediated courses: the revolution in on-line design education. In H. Ashman, P. Thistlewaite, R. Debreceny, & A. Ellis (Eds.), *Into the mainstream: The Web in Australia* (pp. 143-154). Lismore, Australia: Southern Cross University Press. Available also on a CD AusWeb97, ISBN (Mac) 1 875 855 23 8, ISBN (Win.) 1 875 855 24 6, Produced by A. Ellis & R. Debreceny, Southern Cross University Press. Available: http://ausweb.scu.edu.au/proceedings/simoff/index.html

Smith, C. B., McLaughlin, M. L., & Osborne, K. K. (1998). From terminal ineptitude to virtual sociopathy: How conduct is regulated on Usenet. In F. Sudweeks, M. McLaughlin, & S. Rafaeli (Eds.), *Network and Netplay: Virtual groups on the Internet* (pp. 95-112). Menlo Park, CA: AAAI/MIT Press.

Smith, L. (1979). An evolving logic of participant observation, educational ethnography, and other case studies. In L. Shulman (Ed.), *Review of research in education* (pp. 316-377). Itasca, IL: Peacock.

Sproull, L., & Kiesler, S. (1991). *Connections: New ways of working in the networked organization.* Cambridge: MIT Press.

Stake, R. E. (1995). *The art of case study research.* Thousand Oaks, CA: Sage.

Sudweeks, F., & Allbritton, M. (1996). Working together apart: Communication and collaboration in a networked group. In C. D. Keen, C. Urquhart, & J. Lamp (Eds.), *Proceedings of the 7th Australasian Conference of Information Systems (ACIS96)* (Vol. 2, pp. 701-712). Tasmania, Australia: University of Tasmania.

Sudweeks, F., & Rafaeli, S. (1996). How do you get a hundred strangers to agree? Computer mediated communication and collaboration. In T. M. Harrison & T. Stephen (Eds.), *Computer networking and scholarly communication in the twenty-first-century university* (pp. 115-136). New York: SUNY Press.

Tschudi, F. (1989). Do qualitative and quantitative methods require different approaches to validity? In S. Kvale (Ed.), *Issues of validity in qualitative research* (pp. 109-134). Lund, Sweden: Studentlitteratur.

Voiskounsky, A. E. (1998). Telelogue speech. In F. Sudweeks, M. McLaughlin, & S. Rafaeli (Eds.), *Network and Netplay: Virtual groups on the Internet* (pp. 27-40). Menlo Park, CA: AAAI/MIT Press.

Walther, J. (1992). Interpersonal effects in computer-mediated interaction: A relational perspective. *Communication Research, 19*(1), 52-89.

Yin, R. K. (1989). *Case study research: Design and methods.* Newbury Park, CA: Sage.

3

Recontextualizing "Cyberspace"
Methodological Considerations
for On-line Research

LORI KENDALL

MUCH AS MY PERSONAL BIASES lead me in that direction, I would never have the audacity to suggest that all social research projects ought to include participant observation. Yet with regard to research on interactive on-line forums, I recommend just that. I do so in hopes of countering tendencies in the new and growing field of on-line research to ignore important social contexts of on-line communication and interaction. In what follows, I outline some of these social contexts and indicate their importance for understanding on-line interaction. I suggest that even when researchers ultimately seek to use other methods, participant observation can provide information important to the successful implementation of on-line research.

To facilitate discussion of the social contexts of on-line interaction, I consider both on-line and off-line contexts, addressing four different contextual realms. With regard to off-line contexts, I discuss (a) off-line organizations and conditions for participation, and (b) localized situations. With regard to on-line contexts, I consider (c) the history and cultural background of the Internet, and (d) on-line group variations, including variability of group understandings and norms. Although I thus separate my contextual considerations into discrete "realms," these realms, of course, overlap, and many of my discussions could apply to several of the sections. My division of these realms into "off-line" and "on-line" contexts also oversimplifies, because even those contextual considerations that seem to relate specifically to on-line situations have roots in off-line realities.

Some of my examples come from my research on an on-line forum known as BlueSky.[1] BlueSky is a type of interactive, text-only, on-line forum known as a mud.[2] My research on BlueSky included 3 years of on-line participant observation, thirty face-to-face interviews, participation in face-to-face gatherings, and reading of related newsgroups and e-mail lists. Many of the examples I present from this research contradict popular depictions of on-line life. As such, they highlight the degree of variation present in on-line forums and emphasize the importance of taking account of that variation.

Off-Line Organizations

On-line interaction cannot be divorced from the off-line social and political contexts within which participants live their daily lives. Various aspects of these contexts enable and constrain the ability of participants, potential participants, and nonparticipants to learn about, access, and navigate on-line forums. Once on-line, participants draw on their off-line resources, as well as understandings gained in off-line experiences, to negotiate and interpret their on-line interaction.

Several recent controversies pertaining to privacy, censorship, and related issues regarding control of on-line communication have highlighted questions regarding the role of government and/or large corporations on-line. The actions of these large institutions have significant effects on on-line environments, and this topic has received thoughtful attention from commentators and researchers. Researchers have also begun to recognize that both the desire and the ability to participate on-line depend on more than the mere availability of cheap computer equipment. Gurak (1997) identifies "issues of education and training" (p. 18) as important, but computer use and on-line participation also intersect with people's identities and cultural backgrounds. Even with available training, some people avoid computer use either because they see no value in it or because they seek to avoid the imputation of a particular identity. In this regard, several researchers have explored the effects of class, age, and gender on computer use (Haddon, 1992; Livingstone, 1992; Turkle, 1984, 1990; Wheelock, 1992). Their findings provide insights also applicable to on-line participation.

Consideration of access issues should include investigation of users' particular conditions of access and participation. Currently, many participants on on-line forums access those forums using Internet or other on-line accounts available through work or school and often participate on-line while at work (Baym, 1995; Kendall, 1998b; Rheingold, 1993; Turkle, 1995). BlueSky's daily patterns of participation reflect this, with the busiest times occurring on weekday afternoons. Most BlueSky participants are employed as computer programmers and system administrators and many log on while at work, interspersing on-line socializing with their work tasks. This pattern of participation suggests important interconnections between on-line participation, work, and social stratification, especially given the male-dominated character of these fields of employment and of BlueSky itself. On BlueSky, participation all but depends on either having a middle-class technical/ professional job or being a student. Other circumstances would not allow participation during the forum's most social times and would thus constrain people's ability to maintain a social presence in the group. With no physical presence, on-line "visibility" requires at least periodic textual contributions. (On asynchronous forums, such contributions need not occur during specific hours of the day; however, very active forums still require regular participation.)

To participate from work, mudders need jobs in which they have periods of authorized (or unauthorized but unnoticed) inactivity, and/or have some control over the timing and pace of their work. Heavy supervision would constrain employees who otherwise have computer and network access from on-line participation. Data entry clerks whose keystrokes or records production levels per hour are monitored, for instance, could not afford the time to converse on-line while at work. On the other hand, participants who log on from home must make a different kind of commitment to their on-line interaction, sacrificing other responsibilities or leisure activities. Judging from the experience of the few BlueSky participants who have recently had children, primary responsibility for the care of young children can render significant on-line participation difficult.

People's workplace situations, their use of computers for work and leisure activities, their various responsibilities and time constraints, and the availability of on-line access at work or at home constitute some of the more obvious connections between social organizations and on-line participation. These examples also point to connections between people's identities and social status and their access to on-line participation. As Haddon (1992) points out, people's continued use of computers may depend on access to groups of knowledgeable and interested others. Thus, although economic class perhaps most obviously relates to access, gender, age, and race also figure importantly in the factors enabling people's participation in on-line groups. I discuss some of these more fully in the following sections.

Localized Social Situations

In addition to taking into account larger social institutions affecting on-line participation, researchers need to consider participants' local off-line environments, as well as to explore how participants blend their on-line and off-line lives and social contacts. Individuals exist and participate in off-line social contexts both sequentially and simultaneously with their on-line participation. However, many accounts of on-line spaces, experiences, and communications ignore this, often describing on-line spaces almost wistfully as a new and discrete utopian world.

For instance, the popularity of the term *cyberspace,* with its particular science fictional resonance, reflects a tendency to view on-line forums and interaction as existing in an independent reality, separate from off-line environments, bodies, and concerns. Porter (1997) expresses this view in his statement that "the majority of one's correspondents in cyberspace, after all, have no bodies, no faces, no histories beyond what they may choose to reveal" (p. xi). In a similar vein, John Perry Barlow (1996), a well-known net personality, commentator, and writer, composed a manifesto in opposition to a U.S. law seeking to impose limits on on-line communications:[3]

> I declare the global social space we are building to be naturally independent of the tyrannies you seek to impose on us. . . . [Cyberspace] is an act of nature and it grows itself through our collective actions. . . . We are creating a world that all may enter without privilege or prejudice accorded by race, economic power, military force, or station of birth. . . . Your legal concepts of property, expression, identity, movement, and context do not apply to us. . . . Our identities have no bodies, so, unlike you, we cannot obtain order by physical coercion. (Barlow 1996)

Barlow acknowledges that his declaration was written in "grandiose" terms. However, his portrayal of cyberspace as an *organically* separate, sovereign realm resonates among many net participants. Like Porter's, his description highlights the absence of bodies in cyberspace, an absence that others have questioned (e.g., Wakeford, 1996).

Descriptions of cyberspace as a separate reality depict participants' bodies as left behind tediously typing, while their personas cavort in cyberspace. This fails to capture the complexity and diversity of relationships between on-line and off-line experiences. The degree of immersion in on-line "spaces" varies considerably, depending on myriad factors, including type of forum and participant interest. Comparisons with other media can be useful in analyzing this variation. For instance, Meyrowitz (1985) argues that television "invades" the space of the viewer, without completely displacing the reality of that physical place. Reading, on the other hand, requires fuller attention, such that "the reader tends to be removed from those physically present" (p. 124). Although Meyrowitz may overestimate the engrossment necessary for reading, his description of the dual realities created by media provides a useful perspective on forms of on-line participation like mudding. Like television programs, muds enter the participant's physical locale without completely redefining the definition of the situation within that locale. On-line interactions can at times become intensely engrossing, and some participants report experiencing physical sensations that echo the experiences of the characters that serve as their on-line representatives or analogues.[4] However, while participating in social interaction on-line, people may also participate in other on-line or off-line activities. Each participant has in any case a physical body that remains involved in experiences separate from the interactions occurring on-line.

Some researchers have suggested that this experience of simultaneously inhabiting both off-line and on-line environments results in understandings of the self as multiple (Stone, 1995; Turkle, 1995). On-line participation enables the creation of multiple personas, facilitating varying presentations of self. While this does provide evidence of identity fluidity and multiplicity, people similarly engage in different presentations of self to different audiences in other arenas of everyday life and did so prior to the existence of on-line forums. Both Goffman (1959, 1963, 1972) and Gergen (1991) document numerous pre-Internet examples of this multiplicity of identity performance. Despite the mundanity of such splits and fractures of identity, people (in the United States and similar cultures, at any rate) still tend to perceive their identities and selves as integral and continuous. (For a discussion of a more relational experience of self, see Kondo, 1990.) As I discuss more fully elsewhere (Kendall, 1998b), this has important ramifications for our understanding of our own and others' identity and for hierarchical social structures based on aspects of identity such as gender and race.

My research on BlueSky indicates that even on-line, where the performative nature of identity seems almost unavoidably obvious and where tales abound of multiplicity and fluidity, of deceptions and revelations (McRae, 1997; Reid, 1994; Rheingold, 1993; Stone, 1995; Turkle, 1995), people persist in seeking essentialized groundings for the selves they encounter on-line. On the basis of my analyses of BlueSky participants' interactions and experiences, I find that people tend to (a) perceive time and organize experience linearly, (b) privilege embodied experience over mediated experience, and (c) continually work to reincorporate their experiences of themselves and of others' selves into integrated, consistent wholes. Reaching understandings of participants' sense of self and of the meanings they give to their on-line participation requires spending time with participants to observe what they do on-line as well as what they say about what they do.

In addition to the simultaneous off-line social context of the individual's body and physical location, researchers also need to consider off-line social contexts that participants jointly create. Members of on-line groups that foster close relationships frequently go to great lengths to extend their on-line relationships into the off-line world (Bruckman, 1992; Rheingold, 1993; Turkle, 1995). Although most interaction between BlueSky participants occurs on-line, a small (in terms of time spent) but important portion of BlueSky interaction takes place off-line. People plan both business and vacation travel to enable them to meet other BlueSky participants. BlueSky relationships also extend off-line through other media. Participants exchange phone numbers and mailing addresses, and people in the same geographical area often phone each other concerning events of mutual interest or to arrange meetings. People also sometimes try to phone or write regulars who disappear from the mud for periods of time.

Off-line contacts such as these, as well as people's simultaneous off-line experience, affect their interpretations of on-line interaction. When studying groups with less off-line contact than BlueSky, researchers' access to participants' off-line experience may be limited. In such cases, scholars need to at least acknowledge the embodiment of on-line participants and keep in mind the possible effects of these off-line contexts on participant understandings of their on-line experiences.

The History and Cultural
Background of the Internet

I do not have space here to summarize the Internet's history and development, and others have done so quite adequately (e.g., Leiner et al., 1997). However, that history, with its connections to military, scientific, and academic institutions and communities, provides particular cultural contexts for on-line participation. Aspects of these contexts deserving attention in future research include (a) changing meanings and perceptions of Internet usage for various groups, (b) cultural and subcultural affiliations of Internet users, and (c) explorations of political action and affiliation on-line (see Gurak, 1997, for an example of the latter). For purposes of this discussion, however, I turn to perhaps the most obvious legacy of the Internet's history: its demographic makeup.

Reliable statistics concerning Internet users are difficult to find. Most surveys are done by commercial organizations who do not always reveal their methodology. Although various organizations and companies post demographic information on the World Wide Web, they often reserve details, and/or the most recent information, for paying customers. Keeping in mind these caveats, on-line demographics suggest some patterns of participation related to the history and ongoing cultural milieu of the Internet. (Ranges of percentages in the following represent ranges of estimates from different reports.)[5] Approximately half of Internet users are 35 or under and have at least some college experience (only 13%-18% report no college, whereas 18%-26% have some postgraduate education). More than 60% (63%-75%) hold some form of professional, technical, managerial, or other white-collar job, with incomes consistently reported as clustering in the $30,000 to $90,000 range (approximately 60%). In contrast to the relatively close agreement on these statistics, estimates of the percentage of women on-line vary dramatically, from 31% to 45%. The reasons for this range are unclear, although one survey organization suggests that the larger estimates might include greater reporting of less active users.[6]

Some observers have suggested that the proportion of underrepresented groups, including women, will increase as overall numbers of Internet participation increase. However, even if participation by women and other underrepresented groups increases, it may have little effect on the character and tone of on-line groups in which they still constitute a minority. Newcomers to on-line forums enter environments with preexisting norms and patterns of behavior. Women "newbies" joining existing forums have found themselves in unfamiliar, and sometimes hostile, territory (Brail, 1995; Camp, 1995; Kendall, 1995, 1998a). Even on those forums with mainly female constituencies (Baym, 1995; Clerc, 1995), participants understand that their forum exists in a male-dominated context and therefore feel the need to use various strategies to limit participation or to protect their regulars from hostile interlopers (Correll, 1995; Hall, 1996).

An examination of BlueSky's culture and the experience of women on BlueSky provides further evidence that mere increase in numbers need not lead to changes in the norms or expectations in on-line groups. BlueSky's group demographics reflect its beginnings (approximately 8 years ago) in an earlier era of Internet history. About one fourth of BlueSky's regulars are women, making BlueSky's percentage of women participants lower than that of the Internet overall. Both men and women agree that conversations on BlueSky frequently become insulting and obnoxious. For most women, however, obnoxiousness is not a normal expectation in friendship groups. Nor is tolerance of it usually a requirement for group membership. Many men, on the other hand, are more used to this as a feature of male group sociability. Most of the women on BlueSky have histories of participation in male-dominated groups, which helps them to deal with BlueSky's rough social ambience. However, they and any women who seek to join the group must still negotiate a stance within this potentially unfamiliar social terrain.

After several months of mostly quietly observing the conversations on BlueSky, I began participating more actively. In the following excerpt of a conversation on BlueSky, I deviate from my previously quiet comportment and attempt to respond in kind to the common style of obnoxious bantering. (My character name here is Copperhead; allia is the only other woman present.)[7]

Florin has arrived.

Shub says "Baron Florin of Shamptabarung!"

Copperhead says "hi Florin"

Florin says "shub, copperhead. who the hell is copperhead?"

Shub says "copperhead is your future wife, Florin."

Copperhead WHULPs at the thought of being Florin's wife

Florin says "bah. every woman on this earth bleeds from the crotch at the thought of being my wife."

Florin isn't sure whether it's GOOD or BAD, but that's what they DO.

allia thinks every woman on this earth gets a yeast infection at the thought of
   being florin's wife.
Florin SILENCE, UNSHORN HUSSY
Shub wondered why they all bleed from the crotch . . .
Florin says "because their WOMBS are FERTILE"
Florin must PROCREATE
Copperhead says "uh-oh"
Copperhead hands Florin a Petri dish
Florin says "well, if you're nasty looking, CH, i'll just hand ya sperm in a petri
   dish. i understand."
Florin won't deny any woman the chance to bear his offspring; he only denies
   them the chance to touch his Captain Happy, when they're unacceptable.

Like many forms of bantering among groups of young males, this conversation revolves around sexual references and insults. As a woman newly entering the group, I have a limited set of choices regarding how to deal with this masculine pattern of interaction. As Fine (1987) suggests,

> Women who wish to be part of a male-dominated group typically must accept
> patterns of male bonding and must be able to decode male behavior patterns.
> They must be willing to engage in coarse joking, teasing, and accept male-based
> informal structure of the occupation—in other words, become "one of the
> boys." While some women find this behavioral pattern congenial, others do not,
> and they become outcasts or marginal members of the group. (p. 131)

In this regard, my performance in the above constitutes an attempt to become "one of the boys"—that is, to perform a masculine identity. My efforts partly fail because of people's previous knowledge of my female identity (as evidenced by their references to my female body and status as potential wife). On the other hand, my performance partly succeeds, in that the other participants accept my behavior as normal. My own obnoxiousness, while out of character with my previous demeanor, fits into the conversation without apparently causing anyone to change their definition of the situation or their understanding of my identity. This suggests that participants may consider continuity more important with regard to the norms of the group than with regard to individual identities. This puts considerable pressure on newcomers to conform to expected behaviors in existing forums.

   On-line demographics, and on-line participants' knowledge of these demographics, also influence people's assumptions about who they will meet on-line. Despite the oft-cited degree of anonymity on-line, this suggests that anonymity does not equal an absence of identity but, rather, carries with it a set of assumptions about identity which hold "until proven otherwise." As I discuss elsewhere (Kendall, 1998b), BlueSky participants suggest that race does not matter on-line, but their discussions of race highlight the degree to which their assumptions about race (and about to whom race "matters") reflect dominant off-line discourse about race.

For instance, Anguish, a Korean American BlueSky participant, reveals her view that social interaction, both on-line and off, is steeped in a racial context specifically determined by the dominant white racial group.

> Anguish whispers "I think most people assume most everyone else is white [on-line], and for the most part, they'd be right. When people find out I'm Asian, there is a little surprise, but not much"
>
> Copperhead whispers "hmm. do you think people "act white" here in some way?"
>
> Anguish whispers "is there a way of acting otherwise? irl and on-line, I think people act white mostly. I've acted "not-white," but only among other not-whites."
>
> Copperhead whispers "huh, that's interesting; can you tell me how that differs for you?"
>
> Anguish whispers "well, I act in the ways I was taught to by my parents, i.e., Korean customs. An intrinsic part of that is language. The language here [on BlueSky] is English."

Anguish's assertion that "people act white mostly" highlights the assumptions that people make in interpreting "generic" or anonymous personas. Her statement that everybody always "acts white" both on-line and off suggests that rules for identity performances are set by more powerful groups. Rules for racial performances are also set within particular social contexts; thus, Anguish considers herself to be "acting Korean" only when speaking Korean around other Koreans or Korean Americans.

On-line anonymity does not represent an absence of identity, providing instead a set of assumed identity facts. Anonymous participants are assumed to be white and male until proven otherwise (hence, reports from several participants that female characters receive more questions regarding their "true" identity than do males). The strength of these assumptions varies from person to person, and participants can manipulate others' assumptions in various ways. But in any case, on-line forums do not provide contextless spaces free from expectations about identity or from challenges to identity claims. Instead, participants actively interpret, evaluate, and react to others' on-line presentations and do not recognize all such performances as equally valid or real. Despite arguments that on-line interaction can flatten hierarchies and "drastically call into question the gender system of the dominant culture" (Poster, 1995, p. 31), gender and other identity hierarchies continue to constitute a significant context for on-line interaction. Participants clearly can and do reproduce off-line power relationships in their on-line interaction. On-line forums, by limiting available cues, enable experimentation and play with identity. For some, this may provide new perspectives on identity. However, participant knowledge of the history and demographics of the Internet imposes limitations on the range of identities that they will interpret as real. Because on-line interaction in and of itself does not necessarily disrupt understandings of identity, we need to ask when, for whom, and under what circumstances such disruptions do occur.

On-Line Group Variations

Given that racial and other identity performances occur within specific social situations, researchers must consider the social dynamics of particular groups. This requires attention to differences between on-line groups. Most researchers recognize differences between types of on-line forums, understanding that factors such as synchronicity versus asynchronicity (muds vs. newsgroups, for instance) and public availability versus various forms of controlled access (registration on muds or newsgroup moderation) affect the interactions that occur in particular groups. Even among forums of the same type, there are significant variations in purpose, level of participation, acceptable behaviors, and so on. Smith (1997), for instance, maps out differences between Usenet newsgroups in terms of average message size, thread length, number of cross-postings, and other similar features.

However, some commentators, apparently seeking to broadly identify effects of computer mediation on social interaction, lump together disparate subcultural groups and participants in the linguistic formulation of "the Net." This usage makes sense for superficial references to on-line communication generally but becomes problematic when used to make more analytical generalizations. For instance, Porter (1997) describes "the culture that the Net embodies" as "a product of the peculiar conditions of virtual acquaintance that prevail on-line" (p. xi). This presumes that all on-line interaction occurs within a single, homogeneous cultural context, separate from the cultures and subcultures of participants who contribute to it. As I discuss above, the specific conditions and history of the Internet's development do lead to particular cultural tendencies on-line. However, broad synthesizing descriptions of on-line culture overstate both the Internet's homogeneity and its independence from off-line contexts. They also tend toward technological determinism.

Some researchers also overgeneralize regarding particular types of forums, relying on superficial characterizations or ignoring significant variation to support a particular interpretation of on-line interaction. For instance, even while acknowledging the use of muds for different purposes, including pedagogical, professional meetings, game playing, and so on, several researchers characterize all muds as forums for "role-playing" (Porter, 1997; Poster, 1995; Turkle, 1995). Many mudders themselves would object to this as trivializing their experience. In addition, such a characterization relegates mud interaction to a sphere of meaning separate from everyday norms and assumptions regarding sociability and identity continuity.

Although many muds encourage role-playing, others do not, and the types of role-playing also vary. Some role-playing muds derive their scenarios from popular science fiction or fantasy works. Participants on these muds engage in elaborate character and scene development and liken their participation to interactive theater. On other muds, participants role-play around a loosely defined theme, such as anthropomorphic animal characters. In these cases, a participant may invent a character (a talking tool-using cat, for instance) and role-play aspects of that character but may then converse with friends about off-line life rather than enacting elaborate on-line dramas. In either of these cases, participants may understand the meanings of their on-line actions as "keyed" differently from everyday life and thus differentiate their role-playing from their "true" selves (Goffman, 1972).

On BlueSky, people do not role-play, expecting that others will represent themselves more or less as they appear off-line. Participants share information about their off-line lives, and some tend to sneer at role-playing muds where people act as if the mud were a reality separate from other aspects of life. BlueSky participants view the mud as a means of communication that enables them to "hang out" with a group of friends and acquaintances. Although they compare BlueSky with a bar or pub, they do so to explain a style of interaction that preexists the analogy, rather than to set up a theme to which they will conform their on-line behavior.

This stance toward on-line interaction emphasizes identity continuity and interpersonal responsibility and contrasts with representations by participants and researchers who emphasize the flexibility of identity in on-line interaction. Turkle (1995) quotes a participant as saying, "You can be whoever you want to be. You can completely redefine yourself if you want" (p. 84). Turkle goes on to characterize most muds as anonymous, indicating that "you are known only by the name you give your characters" (p. 85). This is far from the case on BlueSky, where people generally have only one character and are known not just by their character name but by their known personality characteristics, their shared history with others in the group, and often by data concerning their off-line lives. Although certainly all of these pieces of information could be hidden by participants wishing to enjoy anonymity on-line, the degree of tolerance of anonymity varies greatly from forum to forum. BlueSky participants regularly question (and often harass) newbies who refuse to reveal data about their off-line identities, as in the following exchange:

Guest1 arrives from the south.

Beryl eyes guest1

Guest1 waves.

Beryl says "speak up, guest, who are you?"

Guest1 says "Guest1."

Ulysses says "specify"

Guest1 says "What do you mean?"

Beryl says "who are you? do you not speak english?"

Guest1 says "In what sense?"

Beryl says "if i were to walk up to you in a bar and say "Hi" and asked who you were, what would you say?"

Guest1 smiles. . . . then I would say I'm a stranger . . . looking around for something interesting.

Beryl says "yikes; nothing interesting here"

Guest1 chuckles.

Ulysses says "or, more to the point, if you walked up to a group of friends talking amongst themselves at a bar and tried to join their conversation, what would you say if they wanted to know why you wanted to join their conversation"

Beryl nods to Uly

Beryl says "Uly has it exactly"

By evoking the analogy of friends in a bar, Ulysses and Beryl describe BlueSky regulars as people who know each other's identities. They contrast this with Guest1, whose anonymity and cagey behavior they consider rude and suspicious. Even Guest1 would probably acknowledge that such behavior would be unconscionably rude in a similar setting off-line.

BlueSky participants' suspicion of anonymity provides a striking contrast to many reports of life on-line. BlueSky may of course be atypical of on-line groups. However, the attitudes of those on BlueSky demonstrate that researchers cannot take for granted that similar forums will have similar norms regarding issues such as anonymity and identity continuity. In particular, because most on-line groups are relatively new, and many participants new to them, researchers need to familiarize themselves with the various social, political, cultural, and identity contexts of the groups they seek to study. Rather than describing *the* culture of "the Net," scholars need to explore the various existing, emerging, and overlapping culture*s*.

Methodological Implications

Nobody lives only in cyberspace. The various social contexts I have identified herein demonstrate some of the ways in which off-line realities impinge on and intertwine with on-line interaction. The necessity of considering these contexts suggests some methodological implications for scholars conducting social research on-line.

For instance, the distinction that BlueSky participants make between regulars and anonymous guests suggests that researcher emphasis on anonymity may stem from an oversampling of newbies. Newbies tend to congregate (sometimes in large groups) in the most public and easy-to-find areas of muds. (Often, the "room" first accessed on entering a mud becomes a favorite hangout spot; regulars who seek a quieter place to convene with friends build their own rooms, which allows them to control access.) This makes popular "public" rooms easy sources of multiple interactions for observation. However, the population of the busiest room does not necessarily represent the population of the mud as a whole.

Insufficient time spent on a particular forum can also lead a researcher to overestimate the anonymity of that forum. For studying interactive forums, especially synchronous forums such as chat groups and muds, participant observation (whether or not used with other methods) may provide the most accurate observations. Spending time with other participants and getting to know the particular norms and understandings of the group allows researchers to build trust and to learn to interpret participants' identity performances in the same way that participants themselves do. In many such forums, shared history of time spent together as well as repetition of on-line performances and stories about that shared history compensate for the relative paucity of interactional cues available on-line. Researchers who instead make brief visits to forums to solicit respondents for interviews or surveys may find that people respond to these relatively anonymous strategies on the part of researchers by self-selecting for a preference for anonymity on-line. It can also be difficult to evaluate the honesty of responses to such surveys and interviews when administered on-line.

Many researchers appear, in fact, to be unaware of a strong bias against survey research among those on-line participants connected in some fashion to computer or "hacker" cultures. *The Hacker's Dictionary,* a book compiling a large body of on-line jargon and cultural references, defines "social science number" as "a statistic that is content-free, or nearly so. A measure derived via methods of questionable validity from data of a dubious and vague nature" (Raymond, 1991, p. 327). In the case of my own research, mudder suspicion of survey research was compounded by a recent rash of poorly thought out and badly executed surveys appearing in the mudding newsgroups, often apparently conceived by mudding college students hoping to glean a term paper out of their favorite pastime. Had I in fact attempted to do survey research about mudding, it is unlikely that I would have received sufficient responses, and the validity of those responses would have been seriously suspect. Researchers need to be aware of these kinds of attitudes within specific on-line groups so that they can either take steps to ensure better responses, or reconsider their choice of methodology.

Participant observation allows researchers to gain a better understanding of participants' ranges of identity performances and the meaning those performances have for them. The ability to access off-line environments provides particularly useful information about the connections between on-line and off-line interaction, but such access may not always be feasible. Nevertheless, the fact that researchers cannot assume congruence between on-line and off-line identity performances should not lead them to sever on-line identities from off-line bodies and realities.

Finally, using participant observation to take account of the various social contexts of on-line interaction can highlight the politics of identity. Participants come to on-line forums from different positions of power within society, which affects both their own actions on-line and their interpretations of others' actions. Considering these power differences, as well as comparing participants' descriptions of their on-line behavior with actual examples of that behavior, enables researchers to critically evaluate statements by participants concerning the effects of their on-line participation.

Notes

1. I have changed all names from my research, including the name of the forum and people's on-line pseudonyms.

2. Mud originally stood for multi-user dungeon (based on the original multi-user dungeons-and-dragons-type game called MUD). Some mud participants ("mudders") distance muds from their gaming history by referring to them as multi-user "dimensions" or "domains" and others cease to use MUD as an acronym, instead using "mud" as both noun and verb. People connect to mud programs through Internet accounts. They then communicate through typed text with other people currently connected to that mud. Of the hundreds of muds available on-line, many provide gaming spaces for adventure or "hack-and-slash" games. Others operate as social spaces, as locations for professional meetings, or for pedagogical purposes. Although participants have programmed various toys and games for use within BlueSky, it functions primarily as a social meeting space.

3. The "Communications Decency Act" (CDA), passed by the U.S. Senate in 1996, attempted to restrict dissemination of sexually explicit content over the Internet. Its passage provoked widespread on-line protest. The Center for Democracy and Technology provides a good source of information about the CDA, its potential impact, and the various protests and measures against it at http://www.cdt.org.

4. Personal communication with T. L. Taylor, based on her research on on-line graphical multi-user virtual environments.

5. I obtained these figures from an on-line search I conducted on November 28, 1997. Since conditions of on-line survey administration may exacerbate self-select and self-report biases (see my discussion of on-line biases against survey research later in text), I do not consider these statistics particularly reliable. So far as I know, only the Nielsen study purports to have taken a probability sample. However, the percentages are relatively consistent from report to report and fit expectations based on Internet history and attitudes toward computers in the United States. My aim is to give an idea of the range of responses reported in these studies and suggest likely patterns of Internet participation. Because different surveys asked their questions differently, my figures in text are approximations only. It is worth noting that although an earlier search turned up a few studies that looked at race, in this search I was unable to find *any* statistics on race, ethnicity, or nationality. Following is a partial list of sites I reviewed:

http://www2.chaicenter.org/otn/aboutinternet/Demographics-Nielsen.html

http://www3.mids.org/ids/index.html

http://www2000.ogsm.vanderbilt.edu/surveys/cn.questions.html (this site provides a detailed critique of the Nielsen study)

http://thehost.com/demo.htm

http://www.scruznet.com/%7Eplugin01/Demo.html (no longer available)

http://www. cyberatlas.com/market/demographics/index.html

http://www.cc.gatech.edu/gvu/user_surveys/survey-1997-04

http://www.ora.com/research/users/results.html

6. The GVU 7th WWW User Survey (http://www.cc.gatech.edu/gvu/user_surveys/ survey-1997-04) states, "Much of the difference between results can be explained by inspecting the definition of a user and possible age limitations placed upon the users. Our numbers, by the very nature of our sampling method, represent active Web users, whereas other numbers may more accurately reflect very casual users (i.e., they have used the Internet at least once in the past 6 months, etc.)."

7. In the excerpt, each person's name precedes his or her text. Participants use different commands to vary their communication, producing some lines as "speech" and others as "actions" or "thoughts." This results in a much greater used of the third person than occurs in face-to-face communication. I am able to identify people's off-line identities because most BlueSky regulars have met each other off-line, and I also have met many of them. (The word *whulp* in the excerpt is BlueSky slang for *vomit.*)

References

Barlow, J. P. (1996). A declaration of the independence of cyberspace. Available: http://www.eff.org/pub/Publications/John_Perry_Barlow/barlow_0296.declaration [1998, May 11]

Baym, N. K. (1995). The emergence of community in computer-mediated communication. In S. G. Jones (Ed.), *CyberSociety: Computer-mediated communication and community* (pp. 138-163). Thousand Oaks, CA: Sage.

Brail, S. (1995). The price of admission: Harassment and free speech in the wild, wild west. In L. Cherny & E. R. Weise (Eds.), *Wired_women* (pp. 141-157). Seattle, WA: Seal Press.

Bruckman, A. S. (1992). Identity Workshop. Available: ftp://ftp.lambda.moo.mud.org/pub/MOO/papers [1998, May 11]

Camp, L. J. (1995). We are geeks, and we are not guys: The Systers mailing list. In L. Cherny & E. R. Weise (Eds.), *Wired_women* (pp. 114-125). Seattle, WA: Seal Press.

Clerc, S. (1995). Estrogen brigades and "big tits" threads: Media fandom on-line and off. In L. Cherny & E. R. Weise (Eds.), *Wired_women* (pp. 73-97). Seattle, WA: Seal Press.

Correll, S. (1995). The ethnography of an electronic bar: The Lesbian Cafe. *Journal of Contemporary Ethnography, 24*(3), 270-298.

Fine, G. A. (1987). One of the boys: Women in male-dominated settings. In M. S. Kimmel (Ed.), *Changing men: New directions in research on men and masculinity.* Newbury Park, CA: Sage.

Gergen, K. J. (1991). *The saturated self: Dilemmas of identity in contemporary life.* New York: Basic Books.

Goffman, E. (1959). *The presentation of self in everyday life.* New York: Anchor.

Goffman, E. (1963). *Stigma: Notes on the management of spoiled identity.* New York: Simon & Schuster.

Goffman, E. (1974). *Frame analysis: An essay on the organization of experience.* Cambridge, MA: Harvard University Press.

Gurak, L. J. (1997). *Persuasion and privacy in cyberspace: The on-line protests over Lotus Marketplace and the Clipper Chip.* New Haven, CT: Yale University Press.

Haddon, L. (1992). Explaining ICT consumption: The case of the home computer. In R. Silverstone & E. Hirsch (Eds.), *Consuming technologies: Media and information in domestic spaces.* London: Routledge.

Hall, K. (1996). Cyberfeminism. In S. C. Herring (Ed.), *Computer-mediated communication: Linguistic, social and cross-cultural perspectives* (pp. 147-172). Amsterdam: John Benjamins.

Kendall, L. (1995). MUDder? I hardly know 'er! Adventures of a feminist MUDder. In L. Cherny & E. R. Weise (Eds.), *Wired_women* (pp. 207-223). Seattle, WA: Seal Press.

Kendall, L. (1998a). Are you male or female? The performance of gender on muds. In J. Howard & J. O'Brien (Eds.), *Everyday inequalities: Critical inquiries* (pp. 131-153). London: Basil Blackwell.

Kendall, L. (1998b). Meaning and identity in "Cyberspace": The performance of gender, class and race on-line. *Symbolic Interaction, 21*(2), 129-153.

Kondo, D. K. (1990). *Crafting selves: Power, gender and discourses of identity in a Japanese workplace.* Chicago: University of Chicago Press.

Leiner, B. M., Cerf, V. G., Clark, D. D., Kahn, R. E., Kleinrock, L., Lynch, D. C., Postel, J., Roberts, L. G., & Wolff, S. (1997). The past and future history of the Internet. *Communications of the ACM, 40*(2), 102-108.

Livingstone, S. (1992). The meaning of domestic technologies: A personal construct analysis of familial gender relations. In R. Silverstone & E. Hirsch (Eds.), *Consuming technologies: Media and information in domestic spaces.* London: Routledge.

McRae, S. (1997). Flesh made word: Sex, text and the virtual body. In D. Porter (Ed.), *Internet culture* (pp. 73-86). New York: Routledge.

Meyrowitz, J. (1985). *No sense of place: The impact of electronic media on social behavior.* New York: Oxford Press.

Porter, D. (1997). Introduction. In D. Porter (Ed.), *Internet culture* (pp. xi-xviii). New York: Routledge.

Poster, M. (1995). *The second media age.* Cambridge, MA: Polity Press.

Raymond, E. S. (1991). *The new hacker's dictionary.* Cambridge: MIT Press.

Reid, E. (1994). *Cultural formations in text-based virtual realities.* Master's thesis, Department of English, University of Melbourne, Australia.

Rheingold, H. (1993). *The virtual community: Homesteading on the electronic frontier.* Reading, MA: Addison-Wesley.

Smith, M. (1997). *Measuring and mapping the social structure of Usenet.* Paper presented at the 17th Annual International Sunbelt Social Network Conference, San Diego, California, February 13-16, 1997. Available: http://www.sscnet.ucla.edu/soc/csoc/papers/sunbelt97

Stone, A. R. (1995). *The war of desire and technology at the close of the mechanical age.* Cambridge: MIT Press.

Turkle, S. (1984). *The second self: Computers and the human spirit.* New York: Simon & Schuster.

Turkle, S. (1990). Epistemological pluralism—styles and voices within the computer culture. *Signs, 16*(1), 128-157.

Turkle, S. (1995). *Life on the screen: Identity in the age of the Internet.* New York: Simon & Schuster.

Wakeford, N. (1996). Sexualised bodies in cyberspace. In S. Chernaik, M. Deegan, & A. Gibson (Eds.), *Beyond the book: Theory, culture, and the politics of cyberspace.* Oxford, UK: Office for the Humanities Communication, Humanities Computing Unit, Oxford University Computing Services.

Wheelock, J. (1992). Personal computers, gender and an institutional model of the household. In R. Silverstone & E. Hirsch (Eds.), *Consuming technologies: Media and information in domestic spaces.* London: Routledge.

4

Studying On-Line Social Networks

LAURA GARTON
CAROLINE HAYTHORNTHWAITE
BARRY WELLMAN

The Social Network Approach

When a computer network connects people or organizations, it is a social network. Just as a computer network is a set of machines connected by a set of cables, a social network is a set of people (or organizations or other social entities) connected by a set of social relations, such as friendship, co-working, or information exchange. Much research into how people use computer-mediated communication (CMC) has concentrated on how individual users interface with their computers, how two persons interact on-line, or how small groups function on-line. As widespread communication via computer networks develops, analysts need to go beyond studying single

AUTHORS' NOTE: This chapter first appeared in 1997 in *JCMC (Journal of Computer Mediated Communication)* Vol. 3, Issue 1. The chapter is reprinted here with permission of the editors. Research for this chapter has been supported by the Social Science and Humanities Research Council of Canada and the Information Technology Research center, and Industry Canada. We appreciate the advice of Joanne Marshall and Marilyn Mantei and the assistance of Keith Hampton and Alexandra Marin in preparing the figures.

users, two-person ties, and small groups to examining the computer-supported social networks (CSSNs) that flourish in areas as diverse as the workplace (e.g., Fulk & Steinfield, 1990; Wellman et al., 1996) and virtual communities (e.g., Wellman & Gulia, in press). This chapter describes the use of the social network approach for understanding the interplay between computer networks, CMC, and social processes.

Social network analysis focuses on patterns of relations between and among people, organizations, states, and so on (Berkowitz, 1982; Wasserman & Faust, 1994; Wellman, 1988b). This research approach has rapidly developed in the past 20 years, principally in sociology and communication science. The International Network for Social Network Analysis (INSNA) is a multidisciplinary scholarly organization that publishes a refereed journal, *Social Networks,* and an informal journal, *Connections.*

Social network analysts seek to describe networks of relations as fully as possible, tease out the prominent patterns in such networks, trace the flow of information (and other resources) through them, and discover what effects these relations and networks have on people and organizations. They treat the description of relational patterns as interesting in its own right—for example, Is there a core and periphery?—and examine how involvement in such social networks helps to explain the behavior and attitudes of network members—for example, Do peripheral people send more e-mail and do they feel more involved? They use a variety of techniques to discover a network's densely knit clusters and to look for similar role relations. When social network analysts study two-person ties, they interpret their functioning in the light of the two persons' relations with other network members. This is quite different from the standard CMC assumption that relations can be studied as totally separate units of analysis. "To discover how A, who is in touch with B and C, is affected by the relation between B and C . . . demands the use of the social network concept" (Barnes, 1972, p. 3).

There are times when the social network itself is the focus of attention. If we term network members *egos* and *alters,* then each *tie* gives egos not only direct access to their alters but also indirect access to all those network members to whom their alters are connected. Indirect ties link in compound relations (e.g., friend of a friend) that fit network members into larger social systems. The social network approach facilitates the study of how information flows through direct and indirect network ties, how people acquire resources, and how coalitions and cleavages operate.

Although a good deal of CMC research has investigated group interaction on-line, a group is only one kind of social network, one that is tightly bound and densely knit. Not all relations fit neatly into tightly bounded solidarities. Indeed, limiting descriptions to groups and hierarchies oversimplifies the complex social networks that computer networks support. If Novell had not trademarked it already, we would more properly speak of "netware" and not "groupware" to describe the software, hardware, and peopleware combination that supports CMC.

COMPARISON WITH OTHER APPROACHES TO THE STUDY OF CMC

Much CMC research concentrates on how the technical attributes of different communication media might affect what can be conveyed via each medium. These characteristics include the richness of cues that a medium conveys (e.g., whether a medium conveys text or whether it includes visual and auditory cues), the visibility or anonymity of the participants (e.g., video mail vs. voice mail; whether communications identify the sender by name, gender, title), and the timing of exchanges (e.g., synchronous or asynchronous communication). A reduction in cues has been cited as responsible for uninhibited exchanges (e.g., flaming), more egalitarian participation across gender and status, increased participation of peripheral workers, decreased status effects, and lengthier decision processes (Eveland, 1993; Eveland & Bikson, 1988; Finholt & Sproull, 1990; Garton & Wellman, 1995; Huff, Sproull, & Kiesler, 1989; Rice, 1994; Sproull & Kiesler, 1991).

Studies of group communication are somewhat closer to the social network approach because they recognize that the use of CMC is subject to group and organizational influences (Contractor & Eisenberg, 1990; Poole & DeSanctis, 1990). The group communication approach includes CMC theories such as social influence (Fulk, Steinfield, & Schmitz, 1990), social information processing (Fulk, Schmitz, Steinfield, & Power, 1987), symbolic interactionism (Trevino, Daft, & Lengel, 1990), critical mass (Markus, 1990), and adaptive structuration (Poole & DeSanctis, 1990). These theoretical approaches recognize that group norms contribute to the development of a critical mass and influence the particular form of local usage (Connolly & Thorn, 1990; Markus, 1990, 1994a, 1994b; Markus, Bikson, El-Shinnawy, & Soe, 1992). Yet this focus on the group leads analysts away from some of the most powerful social implications of CMC in computer networks: its potential to support interaction in unbounded, sparsely knit social networks (see also discussions in Haythornthwaite, 1996b; Rice, 1994; Rice, Grant, Schmitz, & Torobin, 1990).

Units of Analysis

Social network analysis reflects a shift from the individualism common in the social sciences toward a structural analysis. This method suggests a redefinition of the fundamental units of analysis and the development of new analytic methods. The unit is now the relation—for example, kinship relations among persons, communication links among officers of an organization, friendship structure within a small group. The interesting feature of a relation is its pattern: It has neither age, sex, religion, income, nor attitudes, although these may be attributes of the individuals among whom the relation exists: "A structuralist may ask whether and to what degree friendship is transitive. He [or she] may examine the logical consistency of a set of kin rules, the circularity of hierarchy, or the cliquishness of friendship" (Levine & Mullins, 1978, p. 17).

Social network analysts look beyond the specific attributes of individuals to consider relations and exchanges among social actors. Analysts ask about exchanges that create and sustain work and social relations. The types of resources can be many and varied; they can be tangibles, such as goods and services, or intangibles, such as influence or social support (Wellman, 1992b). In a CMC context, the resources are those that can be communicated to others via textual, graphical, animated, audio, or video-based media—for example, sharing information (news or data), discussing work, giving emotional support, or providing companionship (Haythornthwaite, Wellman, & Mantei, 1995).

RELATIONS

Relations (sometimes called strands) are characterized by content, direction, and strength. The content of a relation refers to the resource exchanged. In a CMC context, pairs exchange different kinds of information, such as communication about administrative, personal, work-related, or social matters. CMC relations include sending a data file or a computer program as well as providing emotional support or arranging a meeting. With the rise of electronic commerce (e.g., Web-based order entry systems, electronic banking), information exchanged via CMCs may also correspond to exchanges of money, goods, or services in the "real" world.

A relation can be directed or undirected. For example, one person may give social support to a second person. There are two relations here: giving support and receiving support. Alternately, actors may share an undirected friendship relation; that is, they both maintain the relation, and there is no specific direction to it. However, although they both share friendship, the relation may be unbalanced: One actor may claim a close friendship and the other a weaker friendship, or communication may be initiated more frequently by one actor than the other. Thus, although the relation is shared, its expression may be asymmetrical.

Relations also differ in strength. Such strength can be operationalized in a number of ways (Marsden & Campbell, 1984; Wellman & Wortley, 1990). With respect to communication, pairs may communicate throughout the workday, once a day, weekly, or yearly. They may exchange large or small amounts of social capital: money, goods, or services. They may supply important or trivial information. Such aspects of relations measure different types of relational strength. The types of relations important in CMC research have included the exchange of complex or difficult information (Fish, Kraut, Root, & Rice, 1992); emotional support (Fish et al., 1992; Haythornthwaite et al., 1995; Rice & Love, 1987); uncertain or equivocal communication (Daft & Lengel, 1986; Van de Ven, Delbecq, & Koenig, 1976); and communication to generate ideas, create consensus (Kiesler & Sproull, 1992; McGrath, 1984, 1990, 1991), support work, foster sociable relations (Garton & Wellman, 1995; Haythornthwaite, 1996a; Haythornthwaite & Wellman, in press), or support virtual community (Wellman & Gulia, in press).

TIES

A tie connects a pair of actors by one or more relations. Pairs may maintain a tie based on one relation only (e.g., as members of the same organization), or they may maintain a multiplex tie, based on many relations, such as sharing information, giving financial support, and attending conferences together. Thus, ties also vary in content, direction, and strength. Ties are often referred to as weak or strong, although the definition of what is weak or strong may vary in particular contexts (Marsden & Campbell, 1984). Weak ties are generally infrequently maintained, nonintimate connections—for example, between co-workers who share no joint tasks or friendship relations. Strong ties include combinations of intimacy, self-disclosure, provision of reciprocal services, frequent contact, and kinship, as between close friends or colleagues.

Both strong and weak ties play roles in resource exchange networks. Pairs who maintain strong ties are more likely to share what resources they have (Festinger, Schacter, & Back, 1950; Lin & Westcott, 1991; Wellman &

Wortley, 1990). However, what they have to share can be limited by the resources entering the networks to which they belong (Burt, 1992; Espinoza, in press; Liebow, 1967; McPherson & Smith-Lovin, 1986, 1987; Stack, 1974). Weakly tied persons, although less likely to share resources, provide access to more diverse types of resources because each person operates in different social networks and has access to different resources. The cross-cutting "strength of weak ties" also integrates local clusters into larger social systems (Granovetter, 1974, 1982).

The strength of weak ties has been explored in research suggesting that CMC reduces the social overhead associated with contacting people who are not well-known to message senders—that is, people to whom they are weakly electronically tied (Constant, Sproull, & Kiesler, 1996; Feldman, 1987; Pickering & King, 1995). Thus, an electronic tie combined with an organizational tie is sufficient to allow the flow of information between people who may never have met face-to-face. Connectivity among previously unacquainted people is a well-established finding in the CMC research literature (Garton & Wellman, 1995). Examples of this form of connectivity are documented in studies of large international organizations (Constant, Kiesler, & Sproull, 1994; Constant et al., 1996), as well as in dispersed occupational communities, such as oceanographers (Hesse, Sproull, Kiesler, & Walsh, 1993); "invisible colleges" of academics in the same field (Hiltz & Turoff, 1993; Pliskin & Romm, 1994, p. 22); members of the computer underground (Meyer, 1989); and Internet friends (Katz & Aspden, 1997).

MULTIPLEXITY

The more relations (or strands) in a tie, the more multiplex (or multi-stranded) is the tie. Social network analysts have found that multiplex ties are more intimate, voluntary, supportive, and durable (Wellman, 1992b; Wellman & Wortley, 1990) and are maintained through more media (Haythornthwaite, 1996a; Haythornthwaite & Wellman, in press). Yet some analysts have feared that e-mail, the Internet, and other reduced-cues CMCs are unable to sustain broadly based, multiplex relations (see the review in Wellman et al., 1996; see also Garton & Wellman, 1995). These fears are extended by the boutique approach to on-line offerings, which fosters a specialization of ties within any one of thousands of topic-oriented newsgroups (Kling, 1996; Kollock & Smith,1996). However, this tendency toward

specialization is counterbalanced by the ease of forwarding on-line communication to multiple others. Through personal distribution lists, Internet
participants can sustain broad, multiplex, supportive ties (Wellman, 1997;
Wellman & Gulia, in press). As yet, there has been little research into the
extent to which specialized, on-line, single relations grow into multiplex ties
over time. However, recent results by Katz and Aspden (1997) suggest that
on-line friendships at least lead to more multiplex use of media: Of the 81
respondents who reported making friends on-line, 60% reported meeting
face-to-face with one or more of these friends.

COMPOSITION

The composition of a relation or a tie is derived from the social attributes
of both participants: For example, is the tie between different- or same-sex
dyads, between a supervisor and an underling, or between two peers? CMC
tends to underplay the social cues of participants by focusing on the content
of messages rather than on the attributes of senders and receivers. By
reducing the impact of social cues, CMC supports a wider range of participants and participation. Hence, CMC in organizations may help to transcend
hierarchical or other forms of status barriers (Eveland & Bikson, 1988;
Sproull & Kiesler, 1991) and to increase involvement of spatially and
organizationally peripheral persons in social networks (Constant et al., 1994;
Huff et al., 1989).

Beyond the Tie: Social Networks

TWO VIEWS:
EGO-CENTERED AND WHOLE NETWORKS

A set of relations or ties reveals a social network. By examining patterns
of relations or ties, analysts are able to describe social networks. Typically,
analysts approach social networks in two ways. One approach considers the
relations reported by a focal individual. These ego-centered (or "personal")
networks provide Ptolemaic views of their networks from the perspective of
the persons (egos) at the centers of their network. Members of the network
are defined by their specific relations with ego. Analysts can build a picture
of the network by counting the number of relations, the diversity of relations,

and the links between alters named in the network. This ego-centered approach is particularly useful when the population is large or the boundaries of the population are hard to define (Laumann, Marsden, & Prensky, 1983; Wellman, 1982). For example, Wellman and associates (Wellman, 1988a; Wellman & Wortley, 1990) used ego-centered network analysis to explore how a sense of community is maintained through ties, rather than through geographical proximity, among Toronto residents. They built a picture of the typical person as having about a dozen active ties outside his or her household and workplace, including "at least 4 ties with socially close intimates, enough to fill the dinner table and at least 3 ties with persons routinely contacted three times a week or more" (Wellman, Carrington, & Hall, 1988, p. 140). This approach was also used by Granovetter (1973) to explore what types of actors in people's networks provided information important for finding new jobs and by Lee (1969) to explore how individuals found information about access to abortions. It is well suited to the study of how people use CMC to maintain wide-ranging relations on the Internet.

The second, more Copernican, approach considers a whole network based on some specific criterion of population boundaries, such as a formal organization, department, club, or kinship group. This approach considers both the occurrence and nonoccurrence of relations among all members of a population. A whole network describes the ties that all members of a population maintain with all others in that group. Ideally, this approach requires responses from all members on their relations with all others in the same environment, such as the extent of e-mail and video communication in a workgroup (Haythornthwaite, Wellman, & Mantei, 1995). Although methods are available for handling incomplete data sets (see Stork & Richards, 1992), this requirement places limits on the size of networks that can be examined. The number of possible ties is equal to the size of the population (N) multiplied by ($N - 1$) and divided by 2 if the tie is undirected. For a population of size 20, there are 380 links for each specific relation.

In CMC research, ego-centered and whole-network views provide two ways of examining the communication links among people. Ego-centered network analysis can show the range and breadth of connectivity for individuals and identify those who have access to diverse pools of information and resources. Whole-network analysis can identify those members of the network who are less connected by CMC as well as those who emerge as central figures or who act as bridges between different groups. These roles and positions emerge through analysis of the network data rather than through prior categorization.

NETWORK CHARACTERISTICS

Range

Social networks can vary in their range: that is, in their size and heterogeneity. Larger social networks have more heterogeneity in the social characteristics of network members and more complexity in the structure of these networks (Wellman & Potter, in press). Small, homogeneous networks are characteristic of traditional workgroups and village communities; they are good for conserving existing resources. These networks are often the norm against which pundits unfavorably compare computer-supported cooperative work networks and virtual communities (e.g., Slouka, 1995; Stoll, 1995) or praise CSSNs for unlocking social relations from traditional molds (e.g., Barlow, Birkets, Kelly, & Slouka, 1995; Rheingold, 1993; see also the review in Wellman & Gulia, in press). Yet large, heterogeneous networks (such as those often found on-line) are good for obtaining new resources.

Centrality

In the CMC context, it may be important to examine who is central or isolated in networks maintained by different media. Thus, the manager who does not adopt e-mail becomes an isolate in the e-mail network while retaining a central role in the organizational network. Information exchanged via e-mail will not reach this manager, and information exchanged in face-to-face executive meetings will not reach lower-level workers. In a situation such as this, another person may play a broker role, bridging between the e-mail network and the face-to-face executive network and conveying information from one network to the other. Social network analysis has developed measures of centrality that can be used to identify (a) network members who have the most connections to others (referred to as having the highest *degree*) or (b) those whose departure would cause the network to fall apart (referred to as the *cut-points,* because their departure cuts the network apart; see Freeman, 1979; Bonacich, 1987; Wasserman & Faust 1994).

Roles

Similarities in the behaviors of different network members suggest the presence of a network role. Teachers fill the same network role with respect to students: giving instruction, giving advice, giving work, receiving completed work, and assigning grades. Regularities in the patterns of relations (known as *structural equivalence*) across networks or across behaviors within a network allow the empirical identification of network roles. For example, the "technological gatekeeper" (Allen, 1977) is a role that may be filled by any member of a network according to what resources he or she brings to the network. At the same time, the role is not identified by a title and cannot be found on organization charts.

Partitioning Networks

GROUPS

In social network analysis, a group is an empirically discovered structure. By examining the pattern of relations among members of a population, groups emerge as highly interconnected sets of actors known as cliques and clusters. In network analytic language, they are densely knit (most of the possible ties exist) and tightly bounded—that is, most of the relevant ties stay within the defined network (see Scott, 1991; Wasserman & Faust, 1994; Wellman, 1997). Social network analysts want to know who belongs to a group, as well as the types and patterns of relations that define and sustain such a group.

Network density is one of the most widely used measures of social network structure—that is, the number of actually occurring relations or ties as a proportion of the number of theoretically possible relations or ties. Densely knit networks (i.e., groups) have considerable direct communication among all members: This is the classic case of a small village or workgroup. Much traditional groupware has been designed for such workgroups. By contrast, few members of sparsely knit networks communicate directly and frequently with each other. As in the Internet, sparsely knit networks provide people with considerable room to act autonomously and to switch between relations. However, the resulting lack of mutual communication means that a person must work harder to maintain each relation separately; the group that would keep things going is not present.

By examining relations to identify network groups, CMC researchers can track the beginnings of what may become more formal groups or identify coalitions and alliances that influence others and affect social outcomes. They can link research findings on commonly held beliefs to the regular patterns of interactions among people using CMC. By identifying the group prior to its formalization, social network analysis can be used to follow the growth of CMC network phenomena. For already defined e-mail groups, the social network approach can be used to examine what specific kinds of exchanges define the groups. For example, on-line groups may be formed initially based on socioeconomic characteristics and the vague notion of access to information, such as *SeniorNet* for senior citizens (Furlong, 1989) or *Systers* for female computer scientists (Sproull & Faraj, 1995). Analysts can examine these e-mail or bulletin board networks for the kinds of information exchange that sustain the network.

The social network approach can also be used to see where relations and ties cross media lines. Which kinds of groups maintain ties via multiple media, and which communicate only by means of a single medium? For example, a luncheon group might coordinate meeting times through e-mail and coordinate food delivery by phone, with final consumption face-to-face. Other network groups, such as remotely located technicians, might exchange information about only one topic and use only one medium, such as e-mail.

Positional Analysis

In addition to partitioning social network members by groups, analysts also partition members by similarities in the set of relations they maintain. Such members occupy similar *positions* within an organization, community, or other type of social network (Burt, 1992; Wasserman & Faust, 1994). Those who share empirically identified positions are likely to share similar access to informational resources. Some central positions have greater access to diverse sources of information, whereas other positions may have a limited pool of new ideas or information on which to draw. For example, why assume that managers always give orders and subordinates always take them when an analysis of e-mail traffic may show otherwise? Thus, our study (of university computer scientists) found that faculty did not always give orders and students did not always receive orders. The actual practice was more a function of specific work collaborations among network members (Haythornthwaite, 1996a; Haythornthwaite & Wellman, in press).

One social network method, *blockmodeling,* inductively uncovers such underlying role structures by juxtaposing multiple indicators of relations in analytic matrices (Boorman & White, 1976; Wasserman & Faust, 1994; White, Boorman, & Breiger, 1976). It might place in one block all those in the *structurally equivalent* position of giving (and not receiving) orders, even if these order givers have no ties to each other. A second block might consist of those who only receive orders, and a third block might consist of those who both give and receive orders. This is but a simplified example of blockmodeling: Blockmodeling can partition social network members while simultaneously taking into account role relations such as giving or receiving orders, socializing, collaborating, and giving or receiving information.

NETWORKS OF NETWORKS

The "web [network] of group affiliations" (Simmel, 1922) identifies the range of opportunities as well as the constraints within which people operate. Hence, the study of relations does not end with the identification of groups (or blocks). The concept of networks is scalable on a whole-network level to a "network of networks" (Craven & Wellman, 1973): network groups connected to other network groups by actors sharing membership in these groups. This operates in a number of ways. People are usually members of a number of different social networks, each based on different types of relations and, perhaps, different communication media. For example, a scholar may belong to one network of CMC researchers and also belong to a network of friends. This person's membership in these two networks links the two networks: There is now a path between CMC researchers and the scholar's friends.

Not only do people link groups, but groups link people; there is a "duality of persons and groups" (Breiger, 1974, p. 181). The group of CMC researchers brings together people who are themselves members of different groups. Their interpersonal relations are also intergroup relations (Figure 4.1). For example, the ties of this chapter's coauthors links the University of Illinois with the University of Toronto and the disciplines of information science and sociology. Such cross-cutting ties structure flows of information, coordination, and other resources and help to integrate social systems.

Recognizing the nature of the Internet as a network of networks opens up interesting questions for CMC research:

1. There are questions about the multiplexity of CSSNs. For example, what types of interest groups maintain their single-stranded makeup, and which change to maintain more multiplex ties.

2. There are questions about overlap of membership in specialized CSSNs, such as the extent of similarities in newsgroup memberships (Schwartz & Wood, 1993; Smith, in press).

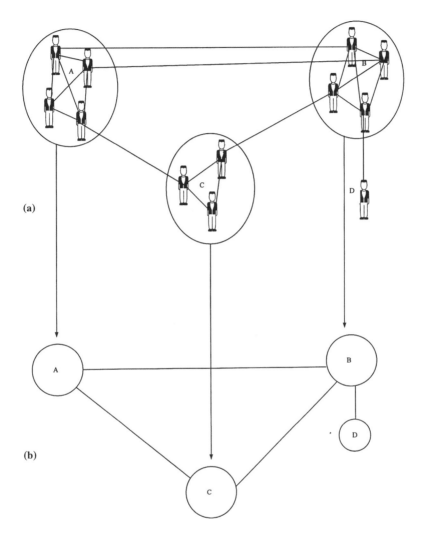

Figure 4.1. A Network of Networks: (a) Ties Between Individuals and (b) Ties Between Network Clusters

3. There are questions about how comembership affects the resources flowing into and out of specialized CSSNs. For example, how does the composition of a newsgroup affect the types of information flowing to this group? From what other groups are messages forwarded, and how different are they in content from the newsgroup's self-definition?

4. There are questions about how CSSNs link organizations. Just as trade and airline traffic flow differentially among countries, Internet traffic flows differentially among universities and other organizations (Schwartz, 1992). To what extent are such flows correlated with the existing power and size of organizations, or does the Internet diminish differences between the core and the social (or spatial) periphery?

PLACING CMC IN CONTEXT

The preceding discussion has largely focused on a computer network as the only arena of activity. Yet this is a trap, deliberately walked into for heuristic purposes. Computer networks are only one method of maintaining ties, and social networks are not restricted to one medium. Ties may be maintained by face-to-face contact, meetings, telephone, e-mail, writing, and other means of communication. When examining CMCs, it is often useful to distinguish between the types of resource exchange occurring by way of a particular medium and the resource exchange occurring between actors in a social network who happen to be using these media. We suggest adding to the term *computer-supported social networks,* the notion of *computer-assisted social networks* (CASNs) to acknowledge that social networks often use both computer and noncomputerized media to sustain relations and ties.

Collecting Network Data for CMC Studies

SELECTING A SAMPLE

Ego-Centered Networks

Social network analysts gather relational data at different levels of analysis, such as for individuals, ties, clusters, or whole networks (Wasserman & Faust, 1994). In an ego-centered network study, a set of people (selected on the basis of some sampling criteria) are asked questions to generate a list of people (alters) who are the members of their personal social network. For example, a person may be asked to report on the people her or she goes to for advice about work matters and the people he or she goes to for advice about personal matters. When the naming of alters is not restricted to a specific group, ego-centered approaches can help identify the different social pools on which people draw for different resources (e.g., Wellman, 1982; Wellman & Wortley, 1990).

Ego-centered social network studies have almost never collected information about all the relations that people have with all the 1,500 or so members (Kochen, 1989) of their social network. Such an effort would be prohibitively expensive; one heroic researcher took a year to identify all the interactions in the networks of only two persons (Boissevain, 1974). Thus, studies purporting to be of "the social network" engage in literary reduction at best. What they really do is observe people's specified relations with a sample of their network members—for example, socially close network members who provide social support.

Software logging may make it technically feasible for scholars to collect data about all those with whom a person is in contact on-line, although substantial coding and privacy invasion questions remain for dealing with the content of these communications. With more resources, the U.S. Federal Bureau of Investigation routinely uses who-to-whom mail covers, wiretaps, and e-mail logs to discover all those with whom a person is communicating and to identify organized crime clusters (Davis, 1981), and espionage agencies routinely do the same thing with traffic analyses of who sends messages to whom.

Whole Networks

In a whole-network study, people are often given a roster of all the people in a specific group and asked to identify a connection of some specific content. Every person in the group is surveyed about every other person, giving an overall snapshot of the structure of relations, revealing disconnections as well as connections. This approach is particularly useful to identify the relative positioning of members in a network as well as the partitioning of subgroups (Haythornthwaite, 1996a; Haythornthwaite et al., 1995; Haythornthwaite & Wellman, in press). It is also feasible to automate the collection of who-to-whom on-line contact data within a group.

Before collecting data about either ego-centered or whole networks, researchers must consider where they are going to draw the boundaries or limitations of the sample. Because indirect as well as direct relations can become data, the boundary expands exponentially. For example, people can also be asked to report on relations among the alters named in their network (Wellman, 1979; Wellman et al., 1988). Or the alters can be asked for their own list of network members to reveal indirect relations between different networks (Shulman, 1972). Such data about alter-alter relations can provide information about the interconnectivity of the network, indicating how quickly information might flow among network members, how well the network might coordinate its activity, and how much social control it might exert. One "small-world" study investigated the number of steps or ties it took for a person sending a note to an unknown person in an entirely different geographic and social location. The links quickly extended well beyond the original network into the friends of friends and then to their friends. This study suggested that it took no more than six links for information to flow through the United States (Milgram, 1967; see also Rapoport, 1979; White, 1970).

COLLECTING DATA

Information about social networks is gathered by questionnaires, interviews, diaries, observations, and more recently, through computer monitoring. In both whole and ego-centered network studies of CMC, people are often asked to identify the frequency of communication with others as well as the medium of interaction. Questions may refer to a specific relational content such as "socialize with" or "give advice to" within a given time frame. In our studies of communication patterns, respondents were asked to think about each member of their team and to identify the means of communication for each type of relation. For example, they were asked to give an account of their work communication with each person in unscheduled face-to-face meetings, scheduled face-to-face meetings, by telephone, fax, e-mail, paper letters or memos, audioconferencing, and videoconferencing (see Table 4.1 for an example of the questionnaire format used in our research; Haythornthwaite, 1996a; Haythornthwaite et al., 1995).

To capture as much information as possible, respondents are often asked to recall behavior that took place over a broad time frame. If the time frame is too long or the amount of information too detailed, reliability and accuracy are jeopardized. This can be a problem for some network communication studies in which respondents are expected to recall not only the content of the interaction but also the frequency and the media of communication. There is some concern among social network analysts that data based on recall, although widely used, may be less reliable than data gathered by observation (Bernard, Killworth, Kronenfield, & Sailer, 1984; Bernard, Killworth, & Sailor, 1981). Although people are able to rank the relative frequency of communication with others (Romney & Faust, 1982) results may be biased because not all interactions are equally memorable (Christensen, Sullaway, & King, 1983). However, accuracy is not the only concern. Data gathered by

TABLE 4.1 Communication Patterns Survey

For each question, please indicate in the appropriate box the number of times you have interacted with each person over the LAST TWO WEEKS (Monday March 8th to Monday March 22nd). At the end of each question, please provide some example of the question asked (not for each person, just as an example of the interaction).

	1	2	3	4	5	6	7	8	9	10
1. Overall how often did you interact with this person on work-related activities?										
In unscheduled face-to-face meetings?										
In scheduled face-to-face meetings?										
By telephone?										
By electronic mail?										
By paper letters or memos?										
By tele-(audio)conferencing?										
By videoconferencing?										

Please give one or two typical examples.

self-reporting may tap into a different meaning of a communication episode than data gathered by observation. Thus, recall may be better for perceptions of media use, whereas observation or electronic data gathering may be better for measuring actual use. Recall may also be better when comparing across media (e.g., face-to-face vs. e-mail) when electronic data gathering is possible for only one of the media studied.

Most network researchers agree that the best approach is to use a combination of methods, including questionnaires, interviews, observation, and artifacts (Rogers, 1987). In addition to survey questionnaires, our own research has made use of qualitative data gathered through in-depth interviews and observations. Software applications such as NUD•IST are useful to organize ethnographic data and to investigate patterns among persons, activities, and attitudes toward new media. This process provides a way for integrating the analysis of social networks of persons and offices with cognitive networks of meaning.

Social network questionnaires need not be restricted to asking about relations between people, because researchers can also examine intersections between people and their group memberships. In some cases, the research question is to discover the cross-cutting pattern of memberships in electronic newsgroups or distribution lists (Breiger, 1974; Finholt & Sproull, 1990; Kiesler & Sproull, 1988). Or investigators may want to find out how CMC has changed the overall structure of membership in face-to-face as well as in electronic committees (Eveland & Bikson, 1988). On-line groups attract those with similar interests, and friends may be drawn from these types of focused affiliations (Feld, 1981). CMC's potential for bringing diversity into group membership may be countered by its efficiency as a tool for finding and maintaining relations with others who share similar narrow sets of attitudes and behaviors. Network data can reveal the structure of these person-group relations and the implications for social behaviors.

People linked to people and groups are not the only sources of network data. Network analysts also look at other types of structural arrangements. Electronic text, including CMC, can be analyzed for patterns of relations between words or phrases (Carley, 1996; Danowski, 1982; Rice & Danowski, 1993). This type of data reveals cognitive maps and identifies people who hold similar conceptual orientations. It has been used to help identify emerging scientific fields and the diffusion of new ideas and innovations (Carley & Wendt, 1991; Valente, 1995).

Gathering data electronically replaces issues of accuracy and reliability with issues of data management, interpretation, and privacy. Electronic monitoring can routinely collect information on whole networks or selected subsamples. Time frames are flexible, and any form of computerized communication is potential data. Constraints are the amount of server storage space and the ingenuity of researchers and programmers in their study design. All commands entered into a system are available for monitoring, making it possible to gather information on the form of media used, the frequency of use, the timing and direction of messaging, the subject of the message, and even the content of the message itself.

The amount of information that can be gathered through automated means can be so overwhelming as to pose challenges for interpretation and analysis. Moreover, it is difficult to assess the relative importance of electronic interactions captured in a log, causing researchers to look for other ways to separate trivial communication from significant interactions. In some cases, the "subject header" is captured along with the who-to-whom data. However, headers may be misleading because they often remain in place long after a topic has been abandoned in the to-and-fro of messaging. Full texts of a message offer more possibilities for sorting out issues of significance and interpretation, but even within a message, there may be a sentence or phrase that carries specific meanings known only to the sender and receiver.

Because electronic data can be collected unobtrusively, it is more difficult for people to maintain control over what information is gathered and how it will be used in the future. Sensitive topics may be avoided when people know their mail is being monitored. Capturing electronic communication can reveal alliances and information that may jeopardize employment or work relations. To alleviate these concerns researchers can randomly assign codes so that individuals cannot be identified (Rice, 1994). However, privacy protections are often less prevalent and less comprehensive in private organizations than public or government institutions (Rice & Rogers, 1984). This issue is important for studies of institutional intranets, but even more important for researchers who want to study a larger public on the Internet. How will people know when they are the subjects of a study in on-line public fora when the researchers do not identify themselves? Must researchers identify themselves if they are only participating in the electronic equivalent of hanging out on street corners or doughnut shops where they would never think of wearing large signs identifying themselves as "researchers"?

How Are Network Data Analyzed?

EGO-CENTERED ANALYSIS

Ego-centered data are often analyzed using standard computer packages for statistical analysis (e.g., SAS, SPSS). If the aim is tie-level analysis, then all ties from all networks are analyzed as if they were from one grand sample of ties. For example, our research group recently found that work role and friendship level each independently predicted the multiplexity of computer scientists' ties, on-line as well as off-line (Haythornthwaite, 1996a; Haythornthwaite & Wellman, in press). If the aim is network-level analysis, summary measures of each network's composition can be calculated using these packages; for example, the percentage who give social support, the percentage who are women, mean frequency of contact, or median multiplexity (Wellman, 1992a). In such ego-centered network analysis, information about network members, such as their age or gender, are most conveniently stored in the same data set as information about the tie between that network member and the ego at the center of a network. Such operations can provide information that, for example, networks with more contact (or higher percentages of women) tend to be more multiplex. Merge procedures can link tie or network data with information about the ego at the center of a network, facilitating the analysis of questions such as, Do supervisors (or women) have more multiplex (or supportive) social networks?

The whole-network analytic procedures described below can be used to analyze the structure of each ego-centered network. However, this is laborious to do for large samples of egos, because existing software requires that an analytic run must be performed separately for each ego. For manageable samples, the resultant structural data can be merged (via SAS or SPSS) with the data sets describing each ego's attributes (e.g., gender) and the composition of each ego-centered network (e.g., median multiplexity).

WHOLE-NETWORK ANALYSIS

Whole-network studies examine the structure of social networks (including groups or blocks), as well as the networks' composition, functioning, and links to external environments.

For example, our research group is interested in assessing the role of e-mail and desktop videoconferencing within the context of overall communication. This has meant examining such questions as the following:

1. Who talks to whom (the composition of ties)?
2. About what (the content of ties and relations, the composition of ties)?
3. Which media do they use to talk (a) to whom and (b) about what?
4. How do ties and relations maintained by CMC change over time?
5. How do interpersonal relations such as friendship, work role, and organizational position affect CMC?
6. How does CMC differ from face-to-face communication in terms of (a) who uses it and (b) what people communicate about?
7. Does CMC describe different social networks than do face-to-face communications?

Several microcomputer programs have been especially designed to analyze social network structure: UCINET, Multinet, Negopy, Krackplot, and Gradap, with the combination of UCINET and Krackplot being the most widely used. To use these applications, data often must be transformed into a matrix with rows and columns representing the units of analysis. These

TABLE 4.2 Data Matrix of Overall Work Interaction at Time 1 Formatted for Entry Into the UCINET Program

	Sec1	*SatC*	*HqC*	*VP*	*TDir*	*IDir*	*PubR*	*Pres*	*FinC*
Data:	0	6	42	10	5	23	7	27	7
	10	0	15	10	0	0	0	0	1
	125	59	0	24	30	46	74	126	95
	21	46	21	0	11	9	7	20	12
	18	0	22	3	0	8	1	46	12
	20	1	12	12	20	0	19	5	6
	4	0	11	3	4	8	0	5	0
	40	2	20	50	10	8	1	0	10
	10	7	75	14	6	5	20	5	0

dl $N = 9$
Matrix labels: Overall_Work_Interaction_Time1

units can be people, events, groups, or other entities related to one another. In a person-by-person whole-network study, the columns and rows represent the respondents. In a directed matrix, rows represent the initiators and columns the receivers of specific relations. For example, Person B gives advice to Person D, but Person D may not reciprocate.

Each relation is represented by one matrix. For example, in our whole-network study of members of a distributed workgroup, we constructed one matrix for frequency of "overall work interaction" by totaling members' communication by each medium. Individual matrices are constructed for separate media. In a longitudinal study, there are matrices for each time period as well as for each relation. Managing data in matrix format can be a challenge if there are many different relations or, as in the case of communication media studies, several types of media for each relation (e.g., communication about work projects conveyed via e-mail, face-to-face meetings, and phone).

Table 4.2 shows how data can be formatted for entry into the UCINET program. The first line specifies the number of nodes: in this case, the number of people included in the study ($N = 9$). The second line specifies the label associated with each person, and the third line the label for the matrix itself. The data that follows gives the number of times each respondent communicated with every other respondent about work-related matters over a 2-week period. Rows show a network member's communication with others; columns show the communication from others. For example, the first row is Sec1's communication with each of the other members of the network—with

Sec1 (i.e., with oneself and therefore the value is 0), SatC, HqC, VP, TDir, IDir, PubR, Pres, and FinC; the second row is SatC's communication with others, and so on. The first column is other members' reported communication with Sec1 and so on. The zeros along the diagonals are placeholders for individuals' communication with themselves. Although these may have meaning for some relations, they are not usually used in analyses.

Analysis of interaction frequency identifies the connections between people. The pattern of connections can be used to build network models of resource flow and influence, to assess overall density of interactions between all members of the network, or to examine frequency of exchange of resources from and to specific actors in the network. Subgroups such as cliques can be identified through partitioning the network into clusters of relative interaction density. Communication positions such as "isolate," "bridge," or "star" emerge from an analysis of matrix data.

Visual representations of relational matrices can be generated by establishing coordinates through multidimensional scaling and importing these into a drawing program such as Krackplot (Krackhardt, Blythe, & McGrath, 1994). They can also be generated from within Krackplot by importing raw matrix data from UCINET (Borgatti & Freeman, 1996) or another compatible program. Visual representations of a network help identify the overall structure of positions and changes over time.

For example, in our study of media use within an organizational context, we were interested in whether the introduction of a desktop videoconferencing system would produce new patterns of communication and increase collaboration between geographically distributed workgroups. We collected data on work relations and media use both before and at 6-month intervals after the implementation of the system, referred to here as CMS (computer-mediated systems). Seven members of the organization, including the president, worked from headquarters. The vice president and his office coordinator operated from a satellite office 100 km away. The following sociograms were generated by Krackplot and depict the organizational communication structure at different times over the 20-month study. In these visual representations, people are displayed as points and arranged in relation to the relative frequency of their interaction. People who communicated more with each other are placed closer together. The connecting lines indicate communication direction and frequency level (above average).

The sociograms of work interaction (by all media) before and after the introduction of CMS (Figures 4.2 and 4.3) indicate that few changes took place in the overall structure of communication patterns. The headquarters

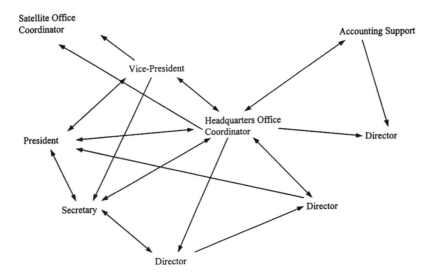

Figure 4.2. Work Interaction by All Media Prior to the Introduction of CMS

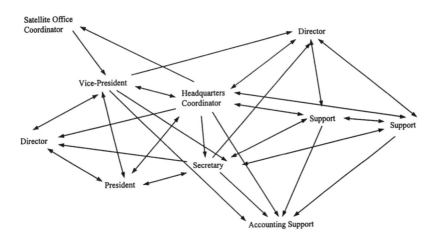

Figure 4.3. Work Interaction by All Media 18 Months After the Introduction of CMS

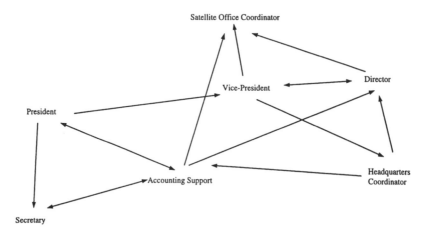

Figure 4.4. Work Interaction by CMS 6 Months After Introduction

office coordinator remained a central communication star despite changes in staff and job descriptions. Furthermore, the satellite office coordinator remained a relative isolate, connected to the others primarily through a link with the vice president. This interpretation of the sociograms is reinforced by statements made in interviews with individual organizational members. They reported a continued preference to organize their work activities with others who were physically proximate despite the addition of CMS. The exception was the vice president, who reported increased connectivity with all members of the organization and in particular with the president.

Figures 4.4 and 4.5 are sociograms showing the work-related communication networks that operated via CMS. The data are drawn from an electronic log of all interactions on CMS by all members of the organization over 18 months.

In Figure 4.4, the vice president and president are directly connected via CMS with an above-average use in the direction from the president to the vice president. In interviews, both parties reported that CMS was helpful in supporting collaboration and decision making. The system saved the vice president travel time between sites. More important, it allowed him to take part in unscheduled meetings as well as spontaneous consultations. The satellite office coordinator was also pleased with the system because there was no pressure from headquarters to take on more work responsibilities, yet CMS provided an added visibility within the workgroup.

Eighteen months after the initial implementation of CMS, there were changes in the relative positions and links between organizational members

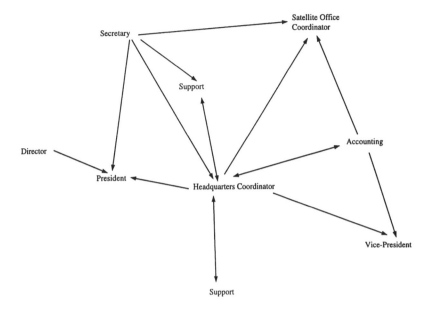

Figure 4.5. Work Interaction by CMS 18 Months After Introduction

who used the system to communicate about work (see Figure 4.5). For example, the vice president and president were no longer directly connected or even close to each other in their use of the system. CMS had blurred boundaries between the two office sites, which made it more difficult for the vice president to unobtrusively control frequency and timing of interruptions by others. Because work between sites could be handled without visual synchronicity, CMS had become less useful as a tool for collaboration. However, CMS was used among members of the support staff. This group did not distribute work to each other and consequently did not report CMS interaction as disruptive or problematic. Media use in this case study depended on the nature of the relation between the users as well as on the features of the technology and the distribution of tasks.

Sociograms such as these provide snapshots of organizational interaction structures that can indicate how static or dynamic these structures are over time. From these types of diagrams, we can visually identify emergent positions and clusters of interaction. The nature and content of relations may be part of the initial construction of the sociogram or determined later through surveys and interviews with members of the network. Visual depictions of whole networks can highlight both linkages and nonlinkages, revealing "structural holes" (Burt, 1992). By examining these patterns of mediated and unmediated interaction, we gain an added perspective on communication structures that underpin explicit work processes as well as those that support affective, less instrumental behaviors.

Conclusion

Because computer networks often are social networks, the social network approach gives important leverage for understanding what goes on in CMC—how CMC affects the structure and functioning of social systems (be they organizations, workgroups, or friendship circles) and how social structures affect the way CMC is used.

Initial studies of CMC developed from studies of human-computer interactions. Such studies focused on how individuals interfaced with various forms of groupware: software and hardware adapted for CMC and work at a distance (Johnson-Lenz & Johnson-Lenz, 1994). The obvious analytic expansion beyond the individual has been to the tie—that is, how two persons interact through CMC. Not only is this a natural expansion, it is analytically tractable, and it has fit the expertise of those social scientists who have pioneered CMC research: psychologists and psychologically inclined communication scientists and information scientists.

A need for new ways of analyzing CMC has developed with the spread of computer networks and the realization that social interactions on-line are not simply scaled-up individuals and ties. Analysts want to know how third parties affect communications, how relations off-line affect relations on-line, and how CMC intersects with the structure and functioning of social systems. For example, have organizations flattened their hierarchy, are virtual communities rebuilding social trust on-line, and have personal attributes become less relevant on the Internet where "nobody knows you are a dog" (to quote a legendary *New Yorker* cartoon)? Given the network nature of CMC, the social network approach is a useful way to address such questions.

References

Allen, T. J. (1977). *Managing the flow of technology: Technology transfer and the dissemination of technological information within the R&D organization.* Cambridge: MIT Press.

Barlow, J. P., Birkets, S., Kelly, K., & Slouka, M. (1995, August). What are we doing on-line. *Harper's*, pp. 35-46.

Barnes, J. A. (1972). *Social networks.* Reading, MA: Addison-Wesley.

Berkowitz, S. D. (1982). *An introduction to structural analysis: The network approach to social research.* Toronto: Butterworth.

Bernard, H. R., Killworth, P., Kronenfeld, D., & Sailer, L. (1984). The problem of informant accuracy: The validity of retrospective data. *Annual Review of Anthropology, 13,* 495-517.

Bernard, H. R., Killworth, P., & Sailer, L. (1981). Summary of research on informant accuracy in network data and the reverse small world problem. *Connections, 4*(2), 11-25.

Boissevain, J. (1974). *Friends of friends: Networks, manipulators, and coalitions.* Oxford, UK: Blackwell.

Bonacich, P. (1987). Power and centrality: A family of measures. *American Journal of Sociology, 92,* 1170-1182.

Boorman, S., & White, H. (1976). Social structure from multiple networks II: Role structures. *American Journal of Sociology, 81,* 1384-1446.

Borgatti, E., & Freeman, L. (1996). UCINET IV 1.64. Natick, MA: Analytic Technologies.

Breiger, R. (1974). The duality of persons and groups. *Social Forces, 53,* 181-190.

Burt, R. (1992). *Structural holes.* Chicago: University of Chicago Press.

Carley, K. (1996). Communicating new ideas: The potential impact of information and telecommunication technology. *Technology in Society, 18*(2), 219-230.

Carley, K., & Wendt, K. (1991). Electronic mail and scientific communication. *Knowledge, 12*(4), 406-440.

Christensen, A., Sullaway, M., & King, C. (1983). Systematic error in behavioral reports of dyadic interaction: Egocentric bias and content effects. *Behavioral Assessment, 5,* 131-142.

Connolly, T., & Thorn, B. K. (1990). Discretionary data bases: Theory, data and implications. In J. Fulk & C. W. Steinfield (Eds.), *Organizations and communication technology* (pp. 219-234). Newbury Park, CA: Sage.

Constant, D., Kiesler, S., & Sproull, L. (1994). What's mine is ours, or is it? A study of attitudes about information sharing. *Information Systems Research, 5*(4), 400-421.

Constant, D., Sproull, L., & Kiesler, S. (1996). The kindness of strangers: The usefulness of electronic weak ties for technical advice. *Organization Science, 7*(2), 119-135.

Contractor, N. S., & Eisenberg, E. M. (1990). Communication networks and new media in organizations. In J. Fulk & C.W. Steinfield (Eds.), *Organizations and communication technology* (pp. 143-172). Newbury Park, CA: Sage.

Craven, P., & Wellman, B. (1973). The network city. *Sociological Inquiry, 43*(1), 57-88.

Daft, R. L., & Lengel, R. H. (1986). Organizational information requirements, media richness and structural design. *Management Science, 32,* 554-571.

Danowski, J. A. (1982). Computer-mediated communication: A network based content analysis using a CBBS conference. *Communication Yearbook, 6,* 905-924.

Davis, R. H. (1981). Social network analysis: An aid in conspiracy investigations. *FBI Law Enforcement Bulletin, 50*(12), 11-19.

Dimitrova, D., & Salaff, J. (1998). Telework as Social Innovation: How remote employees work together. In P. Jackson & J. van der Wielen (Eds.), *Teleworking: International perspectives. From teleworking to the virtual organisation* (pp. 261-280). London: Routledge.

Espinoza, V. (in press). Social networks among the urban poor: Inequality and integration in a Latin American city. In B. Wellman (Ed.), *Networks in the global village.* Boulder, CO: Westwood.

Eveland, J. D. (1993, September). Uses and limitations of communication network analysis in the evaluation of CSCW applications. Paper presented at the Third European Conference on Computer-Supported Cooperative Work, Milan, Italy.

Eveland, J. D., & Bikson, T. (1988). Work group structures and computer support. *ACM Transactions on Office Information Systems, 6,* 354-379.

Feld, S. (1981). The focused organization of social ties. *American Journal of Sociology, 86,* 1015-1035.

Feldman, M. (1987). Constraints on communication and electronic mail. *Office: Technology and People, 3*(2), 83-101.

Festinger, L., Schacter, S., & Back, K. W. (1950). *Social pressure in informal groups.* Stanford, CA: Stanford University Press.

Finholt, T., & Sproull, L. S. (1990). Electronic groups at work. *Organization Science, 1*(1), 41-64.

Fish, R. S., Kraut, R. E., Root, R. W., & Rice, R. E. (1992). Evaluating video as a technology for informal communication. In P. Bauersfeld, J. Bennet, & G. Lynch (Eds.), *Striking a balance: CHI '92 conference proceedings* (pp. 37-48). New York: ACM Press.

Freeman, L. (1979). Centrality in social networks: Conceptual clarification. *Social Networks, 1,* 215-239.

Fulk, J., Schmitz, J., & Steinfield, C. (1990). A social influence model of technology use. In J. Fulk & C. Steinfield (Eds.), *Organizations and communication technology* (pp. 117-140). Newbury Park, CA: Sage.

Fulk, J., & Steinfield, C. W. (Eds.). (1990). *Organizations and communication technology.* Newbury Park, CA: Sage.

Fulk, J., Steinfield, C., Schmitz, J., & Power, J. G. (1987). A social information processing model of media use in organizations. *Communication Research, 14*(5), 529-552.

Furlong, M. S. (1989). An electronic community for older adults: The SeniorNet network. *Journal of Communication, 39*(3), 145-153.

Garton, L., & Wellman, B. (1995). Social impacts of electronic mail in organizations: A review of the research literature. *Communication Yearbook, 18,* 434-453.

Granovetter, M. (1973). The strength of weak ties. *American Journal of Sociology, 78,* 1360-1380.

Granovetter, M. (1974). *Getting a job.* Cambridge, MA: Harvard University Press.

Granovetter, M. (1982). The strength of weak ties: A network theory revisited. In P. Marsden & N. Lin (Eds.), *Social structure and network analysis* (pp. 105-130). Beverly Hills, CA: Sage.

Haythornthwaite, C. (1996a). *Media use in support of communication networks in an academic research environment.* Unpublished doctoral dissertation, University of Toronto, Toronto.

Haythornthwaite, C. (1996b). Social network analysis: An approach and technique for the study of information exchange. *Library and Information Science Research, 18,* 323-342.

Haythornthwaite, C., & Wellman, B. (in press). Work, friendship and media use for information exchange in a networked organization. *Journal of the American Society for Information Science.*

Haythornthwaite, C., Wellman, B., & Mantei, M. (1995). Work relationships and media use: A social network analysis. *Group Decision and Negotiation, 4*(3), 193-211.

Hesse, B. W., Sproull, L. S., Kiesler, S. B., & Walsh, J. P. (1993). Returns to science: Computer networks in oceanography. *Communications of the ACM, 36*(8), 90-101.

Hiltz, S. R., & Turoff, M. (1993). *The network nation* (2nd ed.). Cambridge: MIT Press.

Huff, C., Sproull, L., & Kiesler, S. (1989). Computer communication and organizational commitment: Tracing the relationship in a city government. *Journal of Applied Social Psychology, 19,* 1371-1391.

Johnson-Lenz, P., & Johnson-Lenz, T. (1994). Groupware for a small planet. In P. Lloyd (Ed.), *Groupware for the 21st century* (pp. 269-285). Westport, CT: Praeger.

Katz, J., & Aspden, P. (1997). A nation of strangers? *Communications of the ACM, 40*(12), 81-86.

Kiesler, S., & Sproull, L. (1988). *Technological and social change in organizational communication environments.* Carnegie Mellon University, Department of Social and Decision Sciences.

Kiesler, S., & Sproull, L. (1992). Group decision making and communication technology. *Organizational Behavior and Human Decision Processes, 52,* 96-123.

Kling, R. (1996). Social relationships in electronic forums: Hangouts, salons, workplaces and communities. In R. Kling (Ed.), *Computerization and controversy: Value conflicts and social choices* (2nd ed., pp. 426-454). San Diego, CA: Academic Press.

Kochen, M. (Ed.). (1989). *The small world.* Norwood, NJ: Ablex.

Kollock, P., & Smith, M. A. (1996). Managing the virtual commons: Cooperation and conflict in computer communities. In S. Herring (Ed.), *Computer-mediated communication* (pp. 109-128). Amsterdam: John Benjamins.

Krackhardt, D., Blythe, J., & McGrath, C. (1994). KrackPlot 3.0: An improved network drawing program. *Connections, 17*(2), 53-55.

Laumann, E., Marsden, P., & Prensky, D. (1983). The boundary specification problem in network analysis. In R. Burt & M. Minor (Eds.), *Applied network analysis* (pp. 18-34). Beverly Hills, CA: Sage.

Lee, N. (1969). *The search for an abortionist.* Chicago: University of Chicago Press.

Levine, J., & Mullins, N. (1978). Structuralist analysis of data in sociology. *Connections, 7,* 16-23.

Liebow, E. (1967). *Tally's corner.* Boston: Little Brown.

Lin, N., & Westcott, J. (1991). Marital engagement/disengagement, social networks, and mental health. In J. Eckenrode (Ed.), *The social context of coping* (pp. 213-237). New York: Plenum.

Markus, M. L. (1990). Toward a "critical mass" theory of interactive media. In J. Fulk & C. W. Steinfield (Eds.), *Organizations and communication technology* (pp. 194-218). Newbury Park, CA: Sage.

Markus, M. L. (1994a). Electronic mail as the medium of managerial choice. *Organization Science, 5*(4), 502-527.

Markus, M. L. (1994b). Finding a happy medium: Explaining the negative impacts of electronic communication on social life at work. *ACM Transactions on Information Systems, 12*(2), 119-149.

Markus, M. L., Bikson, T., El-Shinnawy, M., & Soe, L. (1992). Fragments of your communication: E-mail, v-mail, and fax. *The Information Society, 8,* 207-226.

Marsden, P., & Campbell, K. E. (1984). Measuring tie strength. *Social Forces, 63,* 482-501.

McGrath, J. (1984). *Groups: Interaction and performance.* Englewood Cliffs, NJ: Prentice Hall.

McGrath, J. E. (1990). Time matters in groups. In J. Galegher, R. E. Kraut, & C. Egido (Eds.), *Intellectual teamwork: Social and technological foundations of cooperative work* (pp. 23-61). Hillsdale, NJ: Lawrence Erlbaum.

McGrath, J. E. (1991). Time, interaction and performance (TIP): A theory of groups. *Small Groups Research, 22,* 147-174.

McPherson, J. M., & Smith-Lovin, L. (1986). Sex segregation in voluntary associations. *American Sociological Review, 51*(1), 61-79.

McPherson, J. M., & Smith-Lovin, L. (1987). Homophily in voluntary organizations. *American Sociological Review, 52,* 370-379.

Meyer, G. R. (1989). *The social organization of the computer underground.* Unpublished master's thesis, Northern Illinois University, De Kalb.

Milgram, S. (1967, March). The small-world problem. *Psychology Today, 1,* 62-67.

Pickering, J. M., & King, J. L. (1995). Hardwiring weak ties: Interorganizational computer-mediated communication, occupational communities, and organizational change. *Organizational Science, 6*(4), 479-486.

Pliskin, N., & Romm, C. T. (1994). *Empowerment effects of electronic group communication: A case study.* University of Wollongong, Department of Management, Faculty of Commerce.

Poole, M. S., & DeSanctis, G. (1990). Understanding the use of group decision support systems: The theory of adaptive structuration. In J. Fulk & C. W. Steinfield (Eds.), *Organizations and communication technology* (pp. 173-193). Newbury Park, CA: Sage.

Rapoport, A. (1979). Some problems relating to randomly constructed biased networks. In P. Holland & S. Leinhardt (Eds.), *Perspectives on social network research* (pp. 119-136). New York: Academic Press.

Rheingold, H. (1993). *The virtual community: Homesteading on the electronic frontier.* Reading, MA: Addison-Wesley.

Rice, R. (1994). Network analysis and computer-mediated communication systems. In S. Wasserman & J. Galaskiewicz (Eds.), *Advances in social network analysis* (pp. 167-203). Thousand Oaks, CA: Sage.

Rice, R., Grant, A., Schmitz, J., & Torobin, J. (1990). Individual and network influences on the adoption and perceived outcomes of electronic messaging. *Social Networks, 12,* 27-55.

Rice, R., & Love, G. (1987). Electronic emotion: Socioemotional content in a computer-mediated communication network. *Communication Research, 14*(1), 85-108.

Rice, R., & Rogers, E. (1984). New methods and data for the study of new media. In R. Rice & Associates (Eds.), *The new media: Communication, research, and technology* (pp. 81-99). Beverly Hills, CA: Sage.

Rice, R. E., & Danowski, J. A. (1993). Is it really just like a fancy answering machine? Comparing semantic networks of different types of voice mail users. *Journal of Business Communication, 30*(4), 369-397.

Rogers, E. (1987, February). *Progress, problems and prospects for network research: Investigating relationships in the age of electronic communication technologies.* Paper presented at the Sunbelt Social Networks Conference, Clearwater Beach, FL.

Romney, A. K., & Faust, K. (1982). Predicting the structure of a communications network from recalled data. *Social Networks, 4,* 285-304.

Schwartz, M. (1992, Spring). How big is the Internet? *Internet Society News,* 3-5.

Schwartz, M., & Wood, D. C. M. (1993). Discovering shared interests using graph analysis. *Communications of the ACM, 36,* 78-89.

Scott, J. (1991). *Social network analysis.* London: Sage.

Shulman, N. (1972). *Urban social networks.* Unpublished doctoral dissertation, Department of Sociology, University of Toronto.

Simmel, G. (1922). The web of group affiliations. In K. Wolff (Ed.), *Conflict and the web of group affiliations* (pp. 125-195). Glencoe, IL: Free Press.

Slouka, M. (1995). *War of the worlds: Cyberspace and the high-tech assault on reality.* New York: Basic Books.

Smith, M. A. (in press). Measuring the social structure of the Usenet. In P. Kollock & M. A. Smith (Eds.), *Communities in cyberspace.* London: Routledge.

Sproull, L., & Faraj, S. (1995). Atheism, sex and databases: The net as social technology. In B. Kahin & J. Keller (Eds.), *Public access to the Internet* (pp. 62-81). Cambridge: MIT Press.

Sproull, L., & Kiesler, S. (1991). *Connections: New ways of working in the networked organization.* Boston: MIT Press.

Stack, C. (1974). *All our kin.* New York: Harper & Row.

Stoll, C. (1995). *Silicon snake oil: Second thoughts on the information highway.* New York: Doubleday.

Stork, D., & Richards, W. (1992). Nonrespondents in communication network studies. *Group and Organization Management, 17,* 193-209.

5

Cybertalk and the Method of Instances

NORMAN K. DENZIN

The internet is where my problems blossomed, and maybe with other avenues, it can be where I find some healing.

New male reader/member, alt.recovery.codependency newsgroup [a.r.c.], September 5, 1996

ALT.RECOVERY.CODEPENDENCY (a.r.c.) is an on-line Internet newsgroup that draws on the tenets of the Adult Children of Alcoholics (ACOA) and the Co-Dependents Anonymous (CoDA) movements.[1] In this chapter, I use the method of instances, a common analytic strategy in conversation analysis (Psathas, 1995), to interpret the gendered "narratives of self" posted in this newsgroup.[2] I take a critical interpretive, poststructural approach to these materials and their meanings (see Denzin, 1997, p. 250). I hope to demonstrate the utility of the method of instances for the study of cybertalk, especially the talk that occurs in on-line 12-step groups.

In 1994, Alt.recovery.codependency was one of "more than 5,000 discussion groups, or newsgroups, housed on the Internet" (Hahn & Stout, 1994; Walstrom, 1996), forming "what is commonly called the Usenet" (Parks & Floyd, 1996, p. 80). The Internet users who participate in these discussion groups post messages disseminated "to all Internet sites carrying the news-group. Others may respond to a particular message, thereby creating a 'thread' or connected series of messages, or they may read without respond-ing (called 'lurking')" (Parks & Floyd, 1996, p. 80; also cited in Walstrom, 1996, p. 1).

Elsewhere (Denzin, 1998), I have examined how this new information technology, Usenet, has created a site for the production of new emotional self-stories, stories that might not otherwise be told. My concerns here deal with analytic approaches to this form of textuality. Cybernarratives are grounded in the everyday lives and biographies of the women and men who write them, yet they circulate in the anonymous, privatized territories of cyberspace. The life on the screen (Turkle, 1995) that occurs for this, or any other newsgroup, involves struggles over identity, meaning, and the self. A politics of gendered identity is enacted in these sites, a politics that intersects with technology, the personal computer, and embodied, biographical identi-ties (Bardini & Horvath, 1995, p. 44).

This intersection creates a competent computer user who learns how to talk and write within the preferred languages and representational formats of a particular group, in this case a.r.c. These interactions are shaped by the prevailing cultures of family, therapy, illness (addiction), and recovery (Kaminer, 1992; Rice, 1996) that circulate in the international cyberspace recovery movement. The increasing medicalization of illness in American culture (Conrad & Schneider, 1992, pp. 106-107) has shaped the concept of the dysfunctional, alcoholic family. Persons in such families are seen as suffering from the disease of codependency (see below).

Once the technology was available, this disease model of the alcoholic and nonalcoholic family quickly spread to the Internet. The cybertalk in a.r.c. joins three dominant discourses from this larger medical meaning system, the discourses on addiction, therapy, and family (Denzin, 1993, p. viii). We all now have a disease of our own (Rice, 1996, p. 210), the disease of codependency, which requires a liberation psychotherapy for its treatment. Alt.recovery.codependency is one place where this therapy occurs. Virtual reality (VR) thus serves to help repair the ruptures that occur in the real world (RW). This is talking therapy turned into the exchange of written words whose meanings are constantly being deferred as they are read, debated, and discussed.

I will offer intensive analyses of two complex threads, the first from a series of exchanges in late 1994, one month after the group went on-line. The second thread is taken from September 2 through September 5, 1996.[3] I compare and contrast these two threads (Thread 1—"Choices, Holidays, and Gifts," and Thread 2—"Help Me Understand Something") using the method of instances.

Life on the Net

Internet life in moderated and nonmoderated newsgroups is cyclical—and this in a double sense (see below).[4] First, as in a conversation, exchanges follow the comment-response cycle, woven into a thread. One person makes a statement, another person comments, and then another person comments, perhaps on the comments of the second person, and so on. Second, over any given time, a small number of topics, formed into threads, constitutes the life on the screen of this particular newsgroup. (Moderated newsgroups clear out their files on a regular schedule, usually every 2-3 weeks.) A reader's entry into a group is thus shaped by what is on the screen at any given time. The appeal of the group to a reader may differ markedly over any extended time period. And the public face of the group may be drastically different from Time 1 to Time 2.

This is what I discovered in the two threads analyzed below. Each thread gives a different picture of a.r.c. In Thread 1, women control the discourse. In Thread 2, a male, acting as a moderator, attempts to control the discourse. Thread 2 supports the argument (Balsamo, 1994, p. 142; Kramarae, 1995, p. 54) that men tend to control talk on the net, whereas Thread 1 leads to the opposite conclusion.

THE METHOD OF INSTANCES

But it is premature and perhaps incorrect to phrase the problem this way. The initial empirical concern is not *with who* controls the discourse over any period of time. Rather, the question involves *how* control is exercised in any given sequence. Once this "how" question is provisionally answered, the second question involving how "power" is socially distributed in terms of race, class, or gender becomes relevant. Following Psathas (1995, p. 50), the initial (and primary) focus is on the use of the "method of instances." This method takes each instance of a phenomenon as an occurrence that evidences the operation of a set of cultural understandings currently available for use by cultural members.

An analogy may help. In discourse analysis,

> No utterance is representative of other utterances, though of course it shares structural features with them; a discourse analyst studies utterances in order to understand how the potential of the linguistic system can be activated when it intersects at its moment of use with a social system. (Fiske, 1994, p. 195)

This is the argument for the method of instances. The analyst examines those moments when an utterance intersects with another utterance, giving rise to an instance of the system in action.

Psathas (1995) clarifies the meaning of an instance: "An instance of something is an occurrence . . . an event whose features and structures can be examined to discover how it is organized" (p. 50). An occurrence is evidence that "the machinery for its production is culturally available . . . [for example] the machinery of turn-taking in conversation" (pp. 50-51).

An intersection of utterances is established referentially, within the historical context of the ongoing discourse. That is, an intersection occurs when one speaker-writer directly or indirectly refers to the utterance of another speaker or indexes that utterance through a gloss (see below). Clearly, the intersection does not have to be immediate. It does not have to be directly tied to what has just occurred within the thread. Intersections are often located within the framework of an extended discourse that has developed around a set of particular topics, with particular speakers—in which case, the writer "indexically" references this larger system, its speakers, and their utterances. In such moments, the speaker may bring personal experience into the text, thereby enlarging the frame of the discourse.

The analyst's task is to understand how this instance and its intersections works, to show what rules of interpretation are operating, to map and illuminate the structure of the interpretive event itself. The analyst inspects the actual course of the interaction "by observing what happens first, second, next, etc., by noticing what preceded it; and by examining what is actually done and said by the participants" (Psathas, 1995, p. 51). Questions of meaning are referred back to the actual course of interaction, where it can be shown how a given utterance is acted on and hence given meaning. The pragmatic maxim obtains here (Peirce, 1905). The meaning of an action is given in the consequences produced by it, including the ability to explain past experience and predict future consequences. In the arena of cybertalk, meaning is given in the responses one speaker-writer makes to another.

However, cybertalk, like everyday conversation, is not always linear. In extended sequences of talk (Psathas, 1995, p. 21), speakers depart from the turn-taking model of greetings, questions and answers, and closings.

Through personal embellishment, and by looping backward and forward in time, speakers create the context for extended utterances such as stories or confessions. Nonetheless, as Psathas notes, extended sequences emerge from turn-by-turn talk, "are locally occasioned by it, and upon their completion, turn-by-turn talk is reengaged. Stories are thus sequentially implicative for further talk" (p. 21).

Interpretation moves through two stages. In Stage 1, the analyst examines how these meaningful utterances are directly and indirectly connected to one another as interactional accomplishments within a particular interpretive frame. Here, the focus is on the form, not the content, of the event—for example, the use of taking turns, compliments and responses, greeting exchanges, closings, and so on. In Stage 2, the content of the event, as it operates within the interpretive frame, is examined—for example, a request for help within the frame of a.r.c. There is an attempt to show how these occurrences in this context articulate matters of power, biography, self, gender, race, class, and ethnicity.

Whether the particular utterance occurs again is irrelevant. The question of sampling from a population is also not an issue, for it is never possible to say in advance what an instance is a sample of (Psathas, 1995, p. 50). Indeed, collections of instances "cannot be assembled in advance of an analysis of at least one [instance], because it cannot be known in advance what features delineate each case as a 'next one like the last' " (Psathas, 1995, p. 50). Thus, large samples of Internet talk are of little use until the analyst has exhausted the method of instances.

This means there is little concern for empirical generalization. Psathas is clear on this point. The goal is not an abstract or empirical generalization; rather, the aim is "concerned with providing analyses that meet the criteria of unique adequacy" (p. 50). Each analysis must be fitted to the case at hand; each "must be studied to provide an analysis *uniquely adequate* for that particular phenomenon" (p. 51).

ADEQUATE INTERPRETATIONS AND INTERPRETIVE CRITERIA

A uniquely adequate interpretation of a cybertext proceeds on the basis of the following understandings. It reads such events, threads, and extended sequences as places where an information technology interacts with a biographically specific individual. The message that is written is a performance text, an attempt by one person to make connections to another person or to his or her text. This performance text, the thread, is messy and dialogical, tangled up in the writer's (and reader's) imagined interpretations of the other's text.

This written text, however, is not intentional speech, although it is often read as if it were. Barthes (1985) reminds us that speech is "always fresh, innocent, and theatrical" (pp. 3-5). Unlike direct spoken speech, cyberwriting, before it is sent, can be spell checked, edited, rearranged, even inflected with emoticons. But once received, written, or transcribed, speech is dead; it's theatricality is destroyed. It is a mistake to read cyberwriting as if it reflects a direct connection to the conscious meanings and intentions of the writer. Although the writer is conscious of his or her thoughts when writing, written speech, Derrida argues (1981, p. 22), is not a mirror to the self. The "conscious text is thus not a transcription because there is no text present elsewhere as an unconscious one to be transposed or transported" (Derrida, 1978, p. 211).

Yet like everyday talk, cybertext discourse is contextual, immediate, and grounded in the concrete specifics of the interactional situation. It joins people in tiny little worlds of concrete experience. The dialogues that occur in these spaces cannot be repeated. They are always first-time occurrences; each attempt at repetition creates a new experience. Hence, meaning cannot be fixed in the printed text. No text or utterance can be repeated without a change in meaning and in context. The reproduction of the text is a new, unrepeatable event in the life of the text (Bakhtin, 1986, p. 106).

To summarize: A performance-based approach to cybertext discourse seeks always to map the ambiguities and areas of misunderstanding that arise in such transactions. It seeks dense, deep readings of particular texts. The power or authority of a given interpretation is determined by the nature of the critical understandings it produces.

These understandings are based on glimpses and slices of the culture in action. Any given practice that is studied is significant because it is an instance of a cultural practice that happened in a particular time and place. This practice cannot be generalized to other practices; its importance is that it instantiates a cultural practice, a cultural performance (storytelling), and a set of shifting, conflicting cultural meanings (Fiske, 1994, p. 195).

This approach to interpretation rejects a normative epistemology that presumes that what is normal is what is most representative in a larger population. A normative epistemology directs generalizations to this "normal" population. This stance pays little attention to the processes that produce an instance in the first place. Furthermore, it ignores the "nonrepresentative" and marginal formations that can exist in any social structure (see Baym, 1995b, p. 49; Turkle, 1995, pp. 128-130). Consider now two selected texts from a.r.c. But first a brief aside on history.

History

The ACOA and CoDA movements are connected to the languages and literatures of the 12-Step groups (AA, Al-Anon, and Alateen).[10] In addition, they accept the disease concept of alcoholism; a.r.c. (1996) states, "We come to see parental alcoholism . . . for what it is: a disease that infected you as a child and continues to affect you as an adult" (p. 15). This disease concept is generalized to the lived experiences of nonalcoholics. "As an addict, I probably have multiple addictions: . . . work, money, control, food, sexual, approval" (p. 15).

Alt.recovery.codependency started in early 1994. The reason for its existence was given as this: "to create a supportive, loving and safe environment for those of us who consider ourselves to be codependent and wish to interact with others in similar situations" (a.r.c., 1996, p. 3). In this space, the individual begins to experience recovery. This occurs through a process wherein people share their "experience, strength and hope with others" (p. 3). Through this sharing, they are able to aid in their "own recovery and to help others make progress on their journey to recovery" (p. 3). Recovery now becomes a process of letting go of a painful past that is damaging a person's life today: "Recovery . . . loosely describes the methods we utilize in order to . . . let go of the pain in our past and present so that we may fully live our lives today" (p. 5). There are different paths to recovery: physicians, friends in recovery, therapists, inner-child work, and 12-step groups.

a.r.c. (1996) has few rules concerning postings; any subject relating to codependency is relevant, including topics that "deal with our relationships with other people . . . spouses, children, family of origin, friends, employers, co-workers, most importantly ourselves" (p. 7). There are, however, several guidelines defining the netiquette of a.r.c.: (a) do not reproduce entire copyrighted documents; (b) avoid posting private e-mail correspondence; (c) if dissatisfied with a particular person, take what you like from his or her posting and leave the rest; (d) if persons respond to your posting on group mail, inform them privately that you do not like this; (e) avoid sending notes void of substance (p. 8). Persons are invited to just jump in and post, and those who want to maintain anonymity can use first only or false names, or an anon ID. Posting can occur by using anonymous server (anon.penet.fi and anon.twwells. com). Lurking is encouraged (p. 9).

Discourse centers on the "inner-child" work, discovering the child within us. According to Melody Beattie (1987), a leader of the codependency movement, many of us ignore this inner child, and this causes us trouble. The gendered talk that occurs in this newsgroup does not connect to an oral tradition of group storytelling, as is the case for Alcoholics Anonymous (Denzin, 1993, p. 246). A number of canonical texts are referenced, however, including AA's *Alcoholics Anonymous* (1955) and the works of Bradshaw (1990) and Beattie (1987). A monthly list of codependency videos is posted, as is an updated list of codependency sayings and slogans ("You have a right to choose relationships," " 'To let go' does not mean to stop caring.").

Thread 1: "Choices"

Consider the following anonymous postings between persons using the names Jacki and Liz. The postings occurred between December 9 and 16, 1994, under the headings of "Choices, Holidays, and Gifts."

CHOICES

On December 9, Liz wrote to Jacki, connecting to Jacki's discussion of her past, finding a link to her own childhood. She discusses the pain involved in working on the inner child:

> Your post reminded me of how I struggled also with the idea of my childhood having effects that lasted past the time of childhood . . . It was/can still be hard to allow myself to accept that it affected my experiences outside the family home as I was growing up.

Jacki agrees:

> It's funny, cuz all my life and still to this day when I look back on the time when my parents were still married I think of my family as a normal middle class family with no problems. I still look back through that glass ball and think how can that be, I can't seem to make the connection of the abuse with what I perceived as a normal family. . . . After my parents divorced the abuse was more apparent. It came in the form of neglect and abandonment and that is something

matter—essentially a family viewpoint, and a highly dysfunctional one at that—to your supervisor for reinforcement. Your brothers behavior is typical of a codep in recovery. YOURS is typical of a dysfunctional family member struggling to scapegoat the recovering member who has broken ties with an obviously toxic family environment.

To ". . . behavior approved for recovering codependents?" Richard answers, "Lady, we don't approve shit! Each person follows the 12-Steps as best they can for their personal recovery. Your attempt to recruit support in turning a recovering persons back into a sick family is in itself insane."

To "Lucia . . . MSW . . . ," Richard takes exception:

The attempt to introduce yourself with the presentation of credentials is inappropriate to the NG [newsgroup]. We do not welcome professional healers and helpers here. The approach and reasonings used above confirm this as a wide tradition. We, I personally, are unimpressed with your credentials. Further, I am negatively impressed with the illness presented in your post. It is truly frightening that you are in the professional recovery field. Richard

Thus, does Richard directly attack Lucia. Fixing meaning in the printed text, sharing little of his personal experience with her, Richard positions himself as a spokesperson for the newsgroup. His responses border on flaming ("saves me the chore of doing [reaming] again"; "Lady, we don't approve shit!"). Richard reads his way into the unnamed brother's social situation and then positions Lucia against the brother and the family ("For the good of the family?"). He then suggests that Lucia has a dysfunctional family and uses the CoDA language of toxic environment and scapegoating to explain what she is doing to her brother. Richard then challenges Lucia's credentials and tells her that "we do not welcome professional healers . . . here." This suggests a difference between lay and professional healers. Richard sides with the lay healing traditions, using the phrase "truly frightening" to describe his reactions to her presence in the professional recovery field. Four days later Lucia responded to Richard.

LUCIA REPOSTS TO RICHARD

Lucia corrects misspellings in her original posting and responds directly to Richard's harsh evaluations of her situation. He counters each of her comments, as if they were in Internet relay chat (IRC):

Richard: "Brother's keeper?"

Lucia: "No. but I was puzzled."

Richard: "Not my point. I see a lot of putting your brother in the position of a patient."

Lucia: "I figured that out already."

Richard: "I believe its critical to examine your motives."

Lucia: "Excellent! Saves me the chore of doing again?"

Richard: "You're not hearing what I am saying!"

Lucia: "Mister! I don't want him to come back to a sick family! I'm not asking for reinforcement. I'm trying to figure out where to go from here. I am working on acceptance."

Richard: "If I misunderstood your intentions, I apologize. However, your original post was, upon review, an attempt at solicitation for a position already formed. This is not what we call recovery. Perhaps you do not understand our traditions (traditions are posted as ACOA Bill of Rights). It is truly frightening that you are in the professional field of recovery."

Lucia: "It is truly frightening that you read a sincere request with suspicion."

Richard: "Call em like you see em. I did."

One can almost visualize Lucia and Richard in the same room, perhaps at an ACOA or CoDA meeting, shouting at each other. The emotionality is electric. Lucia gets in Richard's face and refuses to back down: "Mister!"; "I'm not asking for reinforcement." In defending her position, which has surely moved and changed since the original posting, Lucia reveals an attempt to help her brother get distance from her sick family. (This understanding was not evident in the original call for help.) Yet Richard will not give her the benefit of this change, insisting that she is still sick, thereby emphasizing his version of what recovery is all about. She retorts, suggesting that his inability to read a sincere request for help without suspicion is "truly frightening."

This is more than an IRC give-and-take. A woman with professional credentials is challenging a man, a professed lay expert who is attempting to control the grounds, terms, and language of recovery. Richard is acting as if he were the gatekeeper to the recovery process, as that process is structured by ACOA and CoDA. Lucia proposes an alternative reading of this language, an alternative that Richard rejects. A gendered conflict occurs; a battle over recovery identities is fought. Lucia will not accept the labels Richard wants to apply to her, and she will not grant Richard the power he claims.

Later that day, Lucia again posts to the entire group, thereby ending the thread, which has become an extended sequence. Her posting is titled, Epilogue:

> Thanks to those who have posted, and to those who will post as they see my original post. To those who have, or will accuse of me being the problem: If you recall, my original post asked for HELP. Accusations do not help anyone. If put downs are what you consider help, thanks, but no thanks. But don't worry, you have not totally dashed my hopes for learning what I need to do. Based on my survey of responses, turns out yours are in the minority. I guess I can use a little advice I hear often: if it don't apply, let it fly.
>
> At this point, I am respecting my brother's wishes. I was going to reply, but after my initial reaction, I decided it would be easier this way. We still have some business to complete, and it would be better to do it quick and without conflict from anyone. I can guarantee we won't get his new address—I'd be surprised if he did . . . I have no idea how I'll respond when he decides to open up lines of communication. That's where I'm at. An extra thanks to those who gave/will give their insights. Lucia.

INSCRIBING LUCIA'S ILLNESS

And so ends, for the time being at least, Lucia's foray into this particular on-line recovery group. Her epilogue divides the persons who responded into two groups, the accusers and the nonaccusers. Still, she takes something from the accusers, as seen in her decision not to respond to her brother. But she is firm; put-downs are not help, not what she thinks recovery is all about.

Thus, by entering a.r.c.'s virtual reality, Lucia receives advice on how to handle problems in the so-called real world. This is talking therapy in the form of a written text. The written word becomes an instance of the illness that requires therapy.

Return to Jacki and Liz: two women talking about mothers and childhood. Same newsgroup—a.r.c. But the talk is different. No one attempts to control the discourse. Gender in its masculinized versions does not operate. No men are present. Experiences as mothers, wives, and daughters are shared; common problems are taken up. Pathologies and illness are not inscribed in the talk. Rather, each woman addresses a specific (or general) problem or issue, which is then loosely interpreted from within the ACOA and CoDA frameworks. The talk is taken to be symptomatic of what persons in recovery say to one another, including how they describe themselves and their situations.

The talk is not read as an example of pathology. This is in stark contrast to Richard's using Lucia's talk as an instance of her illness.

Conclusion

When the self-help industry went on-line, few could have imagined the uses to which this new information technology would be put. Of course, in retrospect, it all makes perfect sense, and nothing seems at all odd about an on-line 12-Step Recovery Shopping Network, hanging out at the 12 Steps Cyberspace Cafe, belonging to any one of several Usenet recovery groups, from Sex Offenders Anonymous to Smokers Anonymous to CoDA to ACOA to that old standby, AA. Kaminer (1992, p. 165) reminds us that we cannot imagine America without its self-help groups. And we cannot imagine an America that is not in love with technology. Cyberspace and the recovery movement were meant for each other—cyber-recovery.

Ten years of personal computers on the job, in the home, and in schools has prepared millions of Americans for the cyber-recovery movement. Any computer-literate child over the age of 6 can participate in this conversation. The method of instances represents one way to read this discourse. This interpretive strategy focuses on the intersection of utterances and extended conversational exchanges. It attempts to make visible the cultural apparatuses and biographical histories that allow such talk to be produced and understood. It understands meaning to be a public, interactional, pragmatic accomplishment. In these moves, the method of instances goes beyond other more text-based approaches to cybertalk, and herein lies its value.

Notes

1. The decade of the 1990s has been a time of renewed public concerning self-help groups (Kaminer, 1992), personal health (Rice, 1996), drugs, drinking, and the problems of alcohol consumption in American society (Conrad & Schneider, 1992, p. 109). A new temperance movement (Pittman, 1991), paralleling the outbreak of a national war on drugs, is one manifestation of this concern. As David Pittman (1991, p. 775) observes, for the third time in the 20th century the United States is in the midst of a war on drugs. The first war occurred during those years bounded by Prohibition, 1914 to 1933, the second overlapped with the Vietnam War years, 1965 to 1972, and the third has just begun. Other indicators of this renewed public concern can

be seen in the many new recovery groups that have appeared in the last decade, including the Adult Children of Alcoholics (ACOA) and the Co-Dependents Anonymous (CoDA) movements.

2. See Denzin (1998) for an extended treatment of these and related issues as they are articulated in this particular newsgroup.

3. I was a passive, lurking observer. I never identified myself to the group, nor did I obtain permission to quote from postings, thereby violating many of Schrum's (1995) ethical injunctions for electronic research.

4. In a moderated newsgroup, all messages are screened by a moderator for content, and only those deemed appropriate for the group are posted (MacKinnon, 1995, p. 132).

5. Hammersley's (1992, pp. 67-72) version of these criteria for validity rests on a subtle realism; "An account is valid or true if it represents accurately some feature of the phenomena that it is intended to describe, explain or theorise" (p. 69). True or valid accounts are plausible, credible, and relevant. The constructivists (e.g., Guba & Lincoln, 1989; Lincoln & Guba, 1985) offer an important departure from the postpositivists. They argue for quality criteria that translate internal and external validity, reliability, and objectivity into trustworthiness and authenticity. These criteria are different from those employed by critical theorists, who stress action, praxis, and the historical situatedness of findings. In contrast, feminist scholarship, in the empiricist, standpoint, and cultural studies traditions, works, respectively, within the traditional positivist, postpositivist, and postmodern (and poststructural) models of evaluation. Ethnic, critical theory, and cultural studies models of inquiry are similarly so aligned. As one moves from the postpositivist to the postmodern and poststructural positions, increased importance is attached to antifoundational criteria such as emotionality, caring, subjective understanding, dialogic texts, and the formation of long-term trusting relationships with those studied.

6. Historically, these have been female-based movements, ACOA being an offshoot of Alanon, the spousal (mostly wives) side of Alcoholics Anonymous (see Asher, 1992; Rudy, 1991). The participation of males in ACOA and CoDA has dramatically increased in the last decade; however, in 1994, the ratio of females to males was still approximately 2:1 (see Rice, 1996, p. 223). In late 1994, women outnumbered men 7:1 in the on-line a.r.c. conversations. Kaminer (1992, pp. 88-89) argues that CoDA is disproportionately female (but see Rice, 1996, p. 44). The welcoming document inviting the reader into a.r.c. is apparently written by a person who uses the name deedee.

7. The user can also go shopping (http://www.network12.com); recent posting (May 13, 1998) announces, "Visit Network 12 Recovery Stores, Recovery Gift Supliers, Distributors, and Vendors Where a Wide Array of Recovery Gifts Are Available."

8. Adjacency pairs are at least two turns in length (hello-good-bye), have at least two parts, with at least two speakers, where the sequences are immediate next turns (Psathas, 1995, p. 18). Internet relay chat (IRC), "that mode of Internet talk in which people are able to communicate synchronistically on different 'channels' from disparate locations" (Baym, 1995a, p. 151), most closely approximates these features of the adjacency pair.

9. Stories are narratives, tellings with beginnings, middles, and ends. Stories begin with an initial situation. A sequence of events leads to the disturbance, or reversal, of this situation. The revelation of character and setting are made possible by this disturbance. A personification of characters (protagonists, antagonists, and witnesses) also occurs. The resolution of this predicament leads to stories in which there is regression, progression, or no change in the main character's situation (Polkinghorne, 1988, p. 15; 1995).

10. a.r.c. (1996, p. 6) states, "The three most common twelve step programs pertinent to those of us dealing with codependency are Codependents Anonymous CoDA), Al-Anon, and Al-Anon, Adult Children of Alcoholics . . . [see] Melody Beattie's Codependent's Guide To The Twelve Steps."

References

Alcoholics Anonymous. (1955). *Alcoholics Anonymous: The story of how many thousands of men and women have recovered from alcoholism* (Rev. ed.). New York: Author.

alt.recovery.codependency. (1996). Frequently asked questions and general information about the Usenet Newsgroup alt.recovery.codependency. Available: http://www.infinet.com/deedee/arc.html [March 17, 1996]

Asher, R. M. (1992). *Women with alcoholic husbands: Ambivalence and the trap of codependency.* Chapel Hill: University of North Carolina Press.

Aycock, A., & Buchignani, N. (1995). The e-mail murders: Reflections on "dead" letters. In S. G. Jones (Ed.), *CyberSociety: Computer-mediated communication and community* (pp. 184-231). Thousand Oaks, CA: Sage.

Bakhtin, M. M. (1986). *Speech genres and other late essays.* Austin: University of Texas Press.

Balsamo, A. (1994). Feminism and the incurably informed. In M. Dery (Ed.), *Flame wars: The discourse of cyberculture* (pp. 125-156). Durham, NC: Duke University Press.

Bardini, T., & Horvath, A. T. (1995). The social construction of the personal computer user. *Journal of Communication, 45,* 40-65.

Barthes, R. (1985). *The grain of the voice: Interviews: 1962-1980* (L. Coverdale, Trans.). New York: Hill & Wang.

Baym, N. K. (1995a). The emergence of community in computer-mediated communication. In S. G. Jones (Ed.), *CyberSociety: Computer-mediated communication and community* (pp. 138-163). Thousand Oaks, CA: Sage.

Baym, N. K. (1995b). From practice to culture on Usenet. In S. L. Star (Ed.), *The cultures of computing* (pp. 29-52). Cambridge, MA: Blackwell.

Beattie, M. (1987). *Codependent no more.* New York: HarperCollins.

Bradshaw, J. (1990). *Homecoming: Reclaiming and championing your inner child.* New York: Bantam.

Conrad, P., & Schneider, J. W. (1992). *Deviance and medicalization: From badness to sickness* (expanded ed.). Philadelphia: Temple University Press.

Denzin, N. K. (1993). *The alcoholic society.* New Brunswick, NJ: Transaction Publishers.

Denzin, N. K. (1997). *Interpretive ethnography: Ethnographic practices for the 21st century.* Thousand Oaks, CA: Sage.

Denzin, N. K. (1998). In search of the inner child: Co-dependency and gender in a cyberspace community. In G. Bendelow & S. J. Williams (Eds.), *Emotions in social life* (pp. 97-119). London: Routledge.

Derrida, J. (1976). *Of grammatology.* Baltimore, MD: Johns Hopkins University Press.

Derrida, J. (1978). *Writing and difference.* Chicago: University of Chicago Press.

Derrida, J. (1981). *Positions* (A. Bass, Trans., annotated by). Chicago: University of Chicago Press.

Dery, M. (1994). Flame wars. In M. Dery (Ed.), *Flame wars: The discourse of cyberculture* (pp. 1-10). Durham, NC: Duke University Press.

Ellis, C., & Flaherty, M. G. (1992). An agenda for the interpretation of lived experience. In C. Ellis & M. G. Flaherty (Eds.), *Investigating subjectivity: Research on lived experience* (pp. 1-16). Newbury Park, CA: Sage.

Fiske, J. (1994). Audiencing: Cultural practice and cultural studies. In N. K. Denzin & Y. S. Lincoln (Eds.), *Handbook of qualitative research* (pp. 189-198). Thousand Oaks, CA: Sage.

Guba, E., & Lincoln, Y. S. (1989). *Fourth generation evaluation.* Newbury Park, CA: Sage.

Hahn, H., & Stout, R. (1994). *The Internet complete reference.* Berkeley, CA: Osborne McGraw-Hill.

Hammersley, M. (1992). *What's wrong with ethnography?* London: Routledge.

became the foundation of critical scholarship to parallel the development of paradigmatic methodologies in neighboring disciplines, especially in linguistic and historical research. The marshaling of evidence through warranting assumptions generated by particular models of texts became the cornerstone of literary and rhetorical analysis—for example, if the structure of a tragedy (a generic model of a text) implies a plot in which a hero experiences a precipitous and calamitous downfall, then Shakespeare's Macbeth is a tragic figure. In this type of critical argument, the words of the primary text provide the evidence for literary and rhetorical analysis.

For most researchers in recent years, however, the concept of a text has changed dramatically. Beginning with semiotic research in the 1960s, new conceptions of texts altered the way critics habitually worked. Notions of intertextuality became current. Readers were understood to constitute the texts they read. The meaning of texts was reunderstood in ways that deconstructed prior interpretations of them. Now, with the explosion of interest in the Internet, researchers have to include hypertextual features and graphical elements (even cartoons) in their paradigms of texts.

Although literary critics may avoid the methodological implications of the World Wide Web (WWW), it is not an option for rhetoricians. Rhetoric is, at a minimum, the study of the available means of persuasion. The WWW is a site of increasing significance as a "means of persuasion" in our society. Consider the growing business and pedagogical uses of the WWW; we have to recognize it as an "available means of persuasion." As a consequence, contemporary rhetoricians need to employ a mode of analysis that can handle the sounds and images of the multimedia hypertexts that populate the Web.

As a guide to what follows, I offer the following chart, which shows a contrast between the traditional mode of rhetorical analysis and the emerging mode I call *configuring:*

Traditional Justifications		Emerging Justifications	
Logical Analysis	(model *of* data type) WARRANT [Template] ↓	(model *for* experience) WARRANT [analog to data] ↓	Analogical Analysis
Assimilates	Printed Texts DATA Object of Analysis ↓	Hypertexts DATA Subject of analysis ↓	Accommodates
Logical Inference	COMMENTARY	COMMENTARY	Analogical Inference

In the left-hand column, we see an inference pattern used in traditional rhetorical analyses (if we assume this warrant, given this data, then we can draw this conclusion). The warrant is a model of the data being analyzed, and when used as a template, it justifies an evaluation of it. In the right-hand column we see an analogous or configural patterning, which is increasingly used in rhetorical analyses of multimedia (these data suggest an analogy to similar data, which allows us to understand it as a configuration of a particular experience). The "logical" mode of the left-hand column, in effect, takes a particular instance of a text and uses it as a template on which to judge other texts (this text is an instance of a textual genre, the classic of which is *X*). The "analogical" mode of analysis accommodates novel data (e.g., of hypertexts) by allowing it to suggest explicitly or implicitly an analogy to experiences that have a recognizable shape (reading this particular hypertext is like taking a journey through space).

Traditional Rhetorical Research

The tradition of rhetorical analysis, beginning with Aristotle (1991), asks us to examine the elements of ethos, pathos, and logos in a communication. Following Aristotle, rhetoricians commonly focused their analyses on "the rhetorical triangle," modifying and extending its applications (see Figure 6.3).

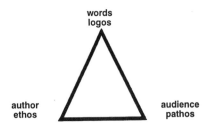

Figure 6.3. The Rhetorical Triangle

The rhetorical triangle is a simple model of a communication situation and extended versions of it have been developed by various rhetorical theorists, for instance, Kenneth Burke's (1969) pentad. A contemporary version would feature the following components with dynamic feedback loops (see Figure 6.4).

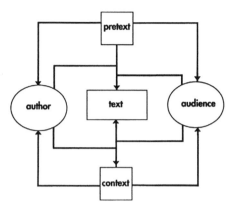

Figure 6.4. A Contemporary Version of the Rhetorical Triangle

During the modern period, the model of communication used in rhetorical analysis has been, for the most part, "text oriented."[1] In this model, the text is treated as an object—that is, as a set of facts that can be described and thus used as evidence in arguments about its meaning, manner, and significance.[2] The features of texts in this systematic view of them are often construed as devices aimed at disposing audiences to believe or do what the text's author invites. Disciplinary protocols established in graduate training usually govern such analyses. In addition, specific approaches to or methods of analysis are learned as the identifying marks of different schools of thought.[3]

Conducted during the second half of the 20th century, this type of analysis is "justificatory" in Stephen Toulmin's (1976) terms.[4] Justificatory arguments are based on specific methods for describing facts. However, a researcher's ability to describe the features of a text depends on the model of the text used. The clearest instance of this aspect of research is in linguistic or semiotic analyses in which textual features are identified by "markers" in the language. Once the linguistic or semiotic markers have been identified, larger textual patterns can be discerned. Most "formal" analyses of texts are loose variants of the same systematic "modeling."

Models *of* and Models *for* Experience

Justificatory analyses rely on models *of* texts as guidelines. This works quite well in contexts where texts can be judged in the light of generic typologies

Figure 6.5. The Panopticon

and conventional expectations but not as well in instances where innovation and imagination dominate and audiences expect to be entertained by novel arrangements or surprising juxtapositions. To accommodate the kinds of multimedia texts that one finds on the WWW, we need to depart from the logical use of a model *of* a text and employ a model *for* a text.

In *Models and Metaphors,* Max Black (1962) distinguishes between scale models (such as the model cars and airplanes that kids build) and analogue models (such as analogies between minds and computers). Scale models rely for their usefulness on identity. The more the scale model mirrors what it models, the better the model. On the other hand, analogue models do not necessarily resemble what they are models *for;* they rely not on identity but on isomorphism—that is, on a similarity of form or structure. It is in this sense that Foucault (1977) illustrates the experience of discipline by providing us with Jeremy Bentham's architectural design (scale model) for a prison, the panopticon, and then using it metaphorically (as an analogue model) for institutions with analogous forms of surveillance (see Figure 6.5).

It's not that the sort of discipline one might find in the army or at school takes place in institutions that look exactly like Bentham's prison but that the structure of surveillance is similar: The persons so structured feel as if they may be observed at any moment and punished for deviance from established norms. In Foucault's (1977) account of discipline, the image of Bentham's prison is a metaphor (which is at root an analogy) for discipline. Foucault's metaphoric use of Bentham's scale model articulates the paranoid state of mind we experience when we feel "under surveillance." Foucault gives us a model *for* understanding experience (an analogue) rather than a model *of* experience (a scaled-down representation). To take a simpler example, a Nike ad that shows Michael Jordan dunking a basketball is not intended to be a model *of* dunking a basketball. It is not a training tape that illustrates the proper way of dunking a basketball. Rather, it is a model *for* a certain style of playing basketball—with a particular élan characteristic of players like Jordan. Hence, the slogan: Be Like Mike!

Models *for* experience are configurations. When they warrant an argument, it changes the type of evidence the argument offers in support of its claims. Before I delineate this newer mode of analysis, let me point to some of the parameters of arguments that employ models *of* experience as their warranting assumptions.

The Parameters of Traditional Modes of Research Argumentation in Rhetorical and Literary Criticism

Justificatory arguments in criticism—whether as formulations of literary or rhetorical analyses—are deliberately restrictive because a model *of* a text is chosen as the warranting assumption out of an array of possible models.[5] Part of their efficacy is their selectivity. However, when the evidence gathered is not "hard" (see next section), the logic of the procedure results in an "evaluative" argument with a template character. Texts are matched against a general model *of* textuality and judged adequate or inadequate depending on the values assigned to the model.

Davida Charney (1996), the author of "Empiricism Is Not a Four-Letter Word," is a rhetorical theorist who has developed a "cognitive model of reading for Hypertext" on the basis of which she proposes specific criteria for their design. In "The Effect of Hypertext on Processes of Reading and Writing" (Charney, 1995), she draws on studies of the reading process undertaken by cognitive psychologists and offers a model *of* the ideal hypertext, one designed for the delivery of information to its potential readers. Her ideal hypertext is structured to enable a particular reading process by way of "appropriate paths" for its potential readers. This is contrasted to a "romantic view of hypertext that aims at enabling imaginative leaps and connections between disparate texts, facts, and images" and "thus puts enormous technological and creative effort at the service of preserving what might be quite rare and ephemeral associations" (p. 259).

Although the template or justificatory mode exemplified by Charney is useful in analyzing hypertexts designed to communicate information, many Web sites are not, strictly speaking, informational and come closer to the type she describes, somewhat disparagingly, as "romantic." Michael Joyce's (1987) "Afternoon," for example, is a hypertext in which the reader is invited to develop his or her own paths through the text. Joyce's hypertext is a fiction, but other uses of StorySpace that are designed to communicate ideas and information allow readers to choose their own paths. There are also sites best described as "Artspaces," for example *Lingua Elettrica* (http://no.va.com.au/) described as

> a web and gallery installation exploring language and its displacement through technology and online communication. . . . it is a dynamic, evolving zone, that integrates virtual processing systems and the physical space of the installation at Artspace to create a system which seeks and is fuelled by information both locally and remotely.

At this site, images are predominant and words are "framed" by the images that contextualize them. Charney's (1995) template, however logically applied, would not be an appropriate approach to this site. To get a sense of what is going on as you navigate *Lingua Elettrica,* you are helped by metaphors such as "evolving zone" or by regarding it as a system that is only "fueled" by information that it then displaces. These analogies suggest that navigating the site has dreamlike effects.

It will be helpful for our purposes to use Michael Joyce's (1995, pp. 41-42) distinction between exploratory and constructive hypertexts. The exploratory (or expository) hypertext is a "delivery or presentational technology" that provides ready access to information. By contrast, constructive hypertexts allow writers to invent and/or map relationships between bits of information to suit their own needs. To avoid being too simplistic, we can add a third type to suggest the middle of a spectrum—a hypertext that is a "reading" (an interpretation or fiction that blends the exploratory and the constructive). Having proposed a spectrum, we nonetheless need to simultaneously acknowledge that any Web site may be a combination of many types in it. We also need to acknowledge that, in many instances, none of the types will fit all the Web pages that can be surveyed.

In this section, we have been considering "assimilative" or "logical" modes of analysis. Let us consider what happens when texts are viewed from an "accommodative" or "analogical" perspective.

Changing Conceptions of Evidence

A purely accommodative perspective, one that involved no preconceptions of what a text is, would be impossible. Granting this point, analysts do approach hypertexts with the attitude that they cannot be easily assimilated into preconceptions of what they should be. The contrast I draw is between the kinds of attention we give to the phenomenon we experience. On the one hand, we can seek in an experience confirmations of our typologies and schemata. On the other, we can look for the discrepancies between the models we typically use to filter experience and the phenomena at hand.[6] From a disciplinary perspective, a shift from assimilation to accommodation can be understood as a shift from a model *of* to a model *for* experience, although some might identify it, misleadingly, as a "paradigm shift." On a less grand scale, we can say that the technical vocabularies we use as researchers to assimilate the overwhelming crush of data we encounter often need to be modified to accommodate changes in our cultural environments.

Returning to the domain of rhetoric, we can say that the main element in an accommodative approach to texts disposes us to modify the "paradigmatic" conceptions of textuality we bring to the experience of reading a text. From a practical point of view, this is tantamount to conceiving experiences such as surfing as "reading" texts. Many critics do not regard surfing the WWW as an experience parallel to reading printed texts because hypertexts do not conform to conceptions of texts developed in print environments. However, from a cognitive point of view, surfing is a form of reading, although one that differs significantly from the more customary experience of deriving meaning from printed pages.

To illustrate the differences, we can say that surfing or hyper-reading[7] is characterized by the following:

Filtering: a higher degree of selectivity in reading

Skimming: less text actually read

Pecking: a less linear sequencing of passages read

Imposing: the reader's cognitive frameworks override the text's

Filming: the ". . . but I saw the film" response that implies that significant meaning is derived more from graphical than from verbal elements of the text

Trespassing: loosening of textual boundaries

De-authorizing: lessening sense of authorship and authorly intention

Fragmenting: breaking texts into notes rather than regarding them as essays, articles, or books

Critics such as Stephen Bernhardt (1993) describe reading from the
computer screen in ways that complement the aspects of hyper-reading I
delineate. In his "The Shape of Text to Come," Bernhardt suggests 10
features of texts constructed to be read on-line: situationally embedded,
interactive, functionally mapped, modular, navigable, hierarchically embedded, spacious, graphically rich, customizable, and publishable (p. 151).
Whatever the categories we use to describe reading on-line, they are not
likely to match up well with the desires for meaning advanced by more
traditional critics. In many quarters, the differences between hyper-reading
and the reading of print identified above are perceived as losses; Sven
Birkerts's (1994) *The Gutenberg Elegies: The Fate of Reading in an Electronic Age* comes readily to mind. Nonetheless, if the hypertextual WWW is
to be a subject of rhetorical analysis (if not literary analysis), these differences must be taken into account.

In such an account, it needs to be noted that the techniques used in reading
the Web outlined above do not produce "hard facts" in a regular manner; that
is, "hyper-reading" does not produce consistent results. Quite to the contrary.
Skimming, filtering, pecking, imposing, transgressing, and fragmenting activities are not likely to produce the sort of stable, shareable descriptions of
the reading experience that has characterized disciplinary research into
printed texts. Furthermore, hyper-reading has a much more profoundly
graphical dimension than print reading. In many instances, the graphical
elements of hypertexts carry the meaning of the site.

The differences between hyper-reading and print reading are significant.
Of paramount importance is the difference in the ways the act of reading the
Web (surfing) constitutes the features of texts to make them available as
evidence in analytical arguments. Even if the difference is simply the degree
to which the reader is free to structure the features of the text, it needs to be
noted that differences in degrees can result in radical metamorphoses (e.g.,
water freezing). Critics not only need to modify their conceptions of texts if
they take the WWW as a subject of analysis, but a new mode of analysis is
required to accommodate "constructive" hypertextual readings.

Configuring as a Mode of Rhetorical Analysis

We can see a new mode of research emerging by implication in the theories advanced by poststructural and postmodern thinkers such as Foucault (the panopticon), Haraway (the cyborg), Virilio (video games), and Baudrillard (the simulacra of the Gulf war).

As I mentioned above, Michel Foucault's (1977) use of the panopticon in his *Discipline and Punish* is an example of a configuration. In this work, the panopticon functions as a metaphor for a particular experience of discipline. Foucault's use of it is not restricted to the exact figure of Jeremy Bentham's panopticon. It is not a model *of* a discipline. Rather, it is a concrete rendering of an experience to which a reader can relate his or her experience only by analogy. Although few readers of *Discipline and Punish* have been institutionalized in buildings "architected" like Bentham's, most recognize the experience that Foucault configures. Thus, the expression, "panoptic surveillance," can evocatively reinterpret for them experiences of their own education.

Donna Haraway's (1985) use of the figure of the cyborg in her famous "Cyborg Manifesto" configures contemporary experiences of technology in a way that parallels Foucault's use of the panopticon. She describes a cyborg as a hybrid of machine and organism that is simultaneously a social reality and a creature of fiction. Haraway's (1991) analogy to the images of cyborgs that we see in films or imagine while reading science fiction enables us to understand that the boundaries between the artificial and the natural have been "breached" (p. 152) in ways that affect us personally. In *War and Cinema,* Paul Virilio (1989) draws out the parallels between cinematic techniques and "military ways of seeing." Jean Baudrillard (1994), the author of *Simulacra and Simulation,* provides a theoretical basis for using configurations in the analysis of culture.

Another example of the configural mode of research can be seen in the work of technocultural critics such as Constance Penley, Andrew Ross (Penley & Ross, 1991), and Stuart Moulthrop (1994). These critics, who in general follow the lead of thinkers such as Haraway, Foucault, and Baudrillard, take the media as their subject of analysis. In doing so, their conception of textuality is necessarily expanded. This is evident in " 'Penguin in Bondage': A Graphic Tale of Japanese Comic Books" by Sandra Buckley, which appears in Penley and Ross's (1991) *Technoculture.* Buckley takes as her subject of analysis a pornographic video game, and her essay's effect depends heavily on the illustrations from the software packet presented in the print volume. Although the essay itself reads like a traditional critique of literature, the graphics play an unusually significant role as evidence in it. Although a more dramatic instance than most, this essay demonstrates the changing relationships between graphics and "text" in cultural criticism. When nonprint media (television, film, compact discs, software) are the subjects of analysis, reading becomes viewing, and graphical aspects of texts become evidence in arguments about them.

Rhetorical Analyses That Employ Configuring

Edward R. Tufte's (1997) *Visual Explanations* examines the various ways in which we use graphical material to analyze complex phenomena. His work gives us an array of the "visual techniques for depicting quantities": statistical tables, charts, scales, models, maps, and so on. It helps us understand that graphical elements of texts can constitute "explanations" of phenomena—for example, when scientific data about weather patterns are represented in computer simulations in ways that allow us to anticipate the actual weather.

Although the use of supercomputers in the Department of Atmospheric Sciences at the University of Illinois to develop visualizations of weather-related data may seem far removed from literary and rhetorical issues, as models *for* experience, they help us understand the significance of analogies used in research methodologies. The differences between a model *for* and a model *of* experience, discussed earlier, are applicable to the weather experiments to which Tufte (1997) refers. In the instances when a supercomputer develops a graphic representation from data gathered during an actual storm, it provides a model *of* that storm. However, when a similar model *of* a potential storm is used to anticipate future weather conditions, it is a model *for* a possible storm.

Such analyses are "configurations." As a mode of analysis, configuring is a "figuring out" through analogies, an attempt to describe in general the contour of similar interactions that suggests how specific instances work. Unlike using a model *of* experience as a template, configuring is a purely heuristic gesture that makes no claim to be representational. It draws an outline of interactions metaphorically. To put the matter as simply as possible, a configuration offers an analogy from one realm of experience to suggest the shape that an experience might take in another (Sosnoski, 1994, p. xxxi). Configuring is a style of thinking whose domain is largely rhetorical. It is often used (e.g., in ads) to persuade persons to believe or do or experience something in a particular way. It is often used in the construction of the Web pages we commonly read/view on our computer screens.

We can probably credit Ted Nelson (1987), the inventor of the term *hypertext,* for this turn of events. His early proposals, which came under the rubric of the "Xanadu Project," involved a configuration; that is, he proposed a model *for* a world-wide network of texts, not a model *of* it. Following suit, early work on hypertext theory (e.g., *Hypermedia and Literary Studies,* Delany & Landow, 1991) introduced the notion of configuring when theorists advocated metaphoric devices to show readers how to navigate the pathways through their links.

Since the explosion of interest in hypertexts, many of its literary and rhetorical theorists have drawn on developments in contemporary literary theory that imply an analogical approach rather than a strictly logical approach. Greg Ulmer (1995), referring to Derrida's work, writes,

> My hypothesis is that a discourse of immanent critique may be constructed for an electronic rhetoric (for use in video, computer, and interactive practice) by combining the mise-en-abyme with the two compositional modes that have dominated audiovisual texts—montage and mise-en-scene." (p. 137)

Following the lead of George Landow (1992) and others who borrowed from poststructuralist theory, Jay Bolter's (1991) influential *Writing Space* configures writers as "dwellers."

Influenced by thinkers such as Haraway, Virilio, and Bolter, critics of technology such as Cynthia Selfe undertake configural analyses of various computer related "texts." "The Politics of the Interface" (Selfe & Selfe, 1994), coauthored with Richard Selfe, is an argument that works by drawing analogies. The article begins with an anecdote about being detained at the Mexican border that allows them to "see how teachers of English who use computers are often involved in establishing and maintaining borders themselves" (p. 483). This analogy leads them to examine the "borders" that interfaces inscribe both culturally and socially: desktops, offices, file cabinets, and so on, all evoking American cultural contexts. They note that computer interfaces are "sites within which the ideological and material legacies of racism, sexism, and colonialism are continuously written and re-written along with more positive cultural legacies" (p. 484). In subtle ways, the "rhetoric of technology" inscribes "cultural information passed along in the maps of computer interfaces" (p. 485), which sometimes undermines the ideas that educators advance in computer classrooms. Of course, a very similar analysis probably persuaded a corporation to design an interface to attract this target market, and the interface itself probably attracted persons whose cultural and social backgrounds it reflected. Rhetorically speaking, however, the configurations that such interfaces invite are potentially harmful cultural communications, which the Selfe (Selfe & Selfe, 1994) analysis makes abundantly clear. Lest I seem to imply that cultural critique is the only kind of insight that configurations can provide, let me turn to a different type of analysis.

An exemplary instance of configuring occurs in a recent article by Joe Janangelo (1998) titled "Joseph Cornell and Hypertexts." In this essay, Janangelo analyzes several student hypertexts, assuming that their composition is analogous to the collage techniques characteristic of Joseph Cornell's artwork. Through the lens of this analogy, he describes his experience of the hypertexts at issue. This essay exhibits the characteristics of a configural analysis wherein readers are invited to experience the hypertexts under discussion through the lens of the analogous experience of viewing Cornell's artwork. The analogy warrants a way of relating the features of the text to each other. Cornell's collage technique is not offered as a model *for* all hypertexts but as an ad hoc means of viewing the ones to hand.

Conclusion

Owing to the ratios between sounds, images, and words in multimedia texts, rhetorical research will increasingly be in the mode of configuring. Changes in reading strategies associated with the WWW make it undesirable to unilaterally employ a template model in the analysis of its hypertexts.[8] Unlike the print environment where the structure of an essay or a speech would be expected to follow a particular pattern, Web pages bear only some resemblances to each other. Moreover, rapid changes in technology make it problematic to use templates to assess Web pages "across the board." In contrast to justifications, rhetorical analyses of Web sites will more and more often be ad hoc and ephemeral. They will no doubt entail reconceptions of "evidence" and cope with the interconnected sites that do not always provide boundaries to their own textuality.

To summarize the implications of the newer modes of rhetorical analysis, we can say that configuring modifies traditional or modern argumentation in the following ways:

- The warranting analogies or configurations project possible rather than actual relationships to experience and suggest ways that texts may be navigated (structured) that are random and ad hoc.

- A subject rather than an object is investigated (analogies to possible experiences are "intersubjective" relationships).

- The dynamics of the reading process are factored into the constitution of "data" to a greater degree.

- The visual dimension of "reading" assumes a more significant role in deriving meaning from texts (cf. Ellen Esrock's, 1994, work on the visual aspects of reading).

We can anticipate that advances in virtual reality technology will further change the modes of argumentation in rhetorical study. The likelihood is that rhetorical research will accommodate virtual reality scenarios. One possibility is that not only will the subjects of study be represented graphically or configurally but also dynamically—that is, in motion sequences. We will no doubt soon be plagued by questions such as, Is a virtual reality scenario a model *of* a model *for* or a model *for* a model *of?*

Notes

1. I use the expression "traditional" to refer to the rhetorical tradition as it is commonly understood to have been developed from Aristotle (1991), the expression "modern" to refer to the period from the late 19th century to the 1960s, and the expression "contemporary" to refer to developments from the late 1960s. This periodization of the history of rhetoric demarcates two shifts in the model of the communication situation underlying rhetorical research: first from an Aristotlean conception to a more flexible model influenced by 20th-century developments in linguistics, anthropology, psychology, and semiotics and second to the period when poststructuralist and postmodern critiques of the previous models have made substantial inroads on rhetorical thinking. The late 1960s is usually considered to be the watershed moment, in particular the Johns Hopkins symposium in 1966 during which Paul de Man met Jacques Derrida and whose proceedings introduced Americans to poststucturalism.

2. My reference here is to rhetorical analysis as it has been conducted in departments of English literature. Acknowledging that communications departments also employ rhetorical analysis, I can testify only to the ways rhetorical analysis has been developed in English literature departments.

3. Poststructuralist approaches to textual analysis are more common in literary circles than in rhetorical ones. However, instances of rhetorical analysis that can be termed *deconstructive,* for example, are nonetheless still structured as justificatory arguments whose warranting assumptions (derived from the work of de Man, Derrida, or others) justify the claims being made by determining the relevance of the "evidence" brought to bear on the claims made.

4. Stephen Toulmin's *Uses of Argument* became a leading analytic tool in rhetorical analyses shortly after its publication in 1958.

5. A similar phenomenon occurs in literary criticism. Many disciplines in the humanities depend on interpretation, and their mode of argumentation generally is employed to justify particular interpretive claims. In a spectrum analysis of disciplinary warrants, the warrants used to justify interpretive claims are restrictive models-*of* texts that have a template character. However, many interpretations de facto depend more on "figures" than on "concepts" as their warranting assumptions. For example, various schools of interpretation or criticism employ conceptual warrants with a high degree of metaphoricity. Perhaps the most famous metaphorical warrant is the one that stipulates that a text is "organic." Other familiar ones are "the unconscious is a language," "texts are silent," and so on.

6. This distinction was proposed by Jean Piaget (1963).

7. I draw this description of surfing from my "Hyper-readers and their Reading Engines" (Sosnoski, in press) where I elaborate on the various features enumerated here.

8. It may be that in a few years, software products such as FrontPage will provide a predominate structure to Web sites, and matching them against design templates will be commonplace in rhetorical analysis; but given the extent to which such templates are likely to be redesigned by software makers rushing to introduce the most recent technical innovations, it seems unlikely that any format pattern will ever be as durable as the arrangements of informal logic that have traditionally dominated argument analysis. Yet it can be argued that the essays themselves, more often than not, violated the recommended logical structures—and that more supple and flexible modes of analysis are long overdue.

References

Aristotle. (1991). *Rhetoric* (George Kennedy, Trans.). New York: Oxford University Press.

Baudrillard, J. (1994). *Simulacra and simulation.* Ann Arbor: University of Michigan Press.

Bernhardt, S. A. (1993). The shape of text to come: The texture of print on screens. *College Composition and Communication, 44,* 151-175.

Birkerts, S. (1994). *The Gutenberg elegies: The fate of reading in an electronic age.* Boston: Faber & Faber.

Black, M. (1962). *Models and metaphors: Studies in language and philosophy.* Ithaca, NY: Cornell University Press.

Bolter, J. (1991). *Writing space: The computer, hypertext, and the history of writing.* Hillsdale, NJ: Lawrence Erlbaum.

Buckley, S. (1991). "Penguin in bondage": A graphic tale of Japanese comic books. In C. Penley & A. Ross (Eds.), *Technoculture.* Minneapolis: University of Minnesota Press.

Burke, K. (1969). *A grammar of motives.* Berkeley: University of California Press.

Charney, D. (1995). The effect of hypertext on processes of reading and writing. In C. Selfe & S. Hilligoss (Eds.), *Literacy and computers.* New York: Modern Language Association.

Charney, D. (1996). Empiricism is not a four-letter word. *College Composition and Communication, 47*(4), 567-593.

Delany, P., & Landow, G. (Eds.). (1991). *Hypermedia and literary studies.* Cambridge: MIT Press.

Esrock, E. J. (1994). *The reader's eye: Visual imaging as reader response.* Baltimore: Johns Hopkins University Press.

Foucault, M. (1977). *Discipline and punish: The birth of the prison* (A. Sheridan, Trans.). New York: Pantheon.

Haraway, D. (1985). A cyborg manifesto: Science, technology, and socialist feminism in the 1980s. *Socialist Review, 15*(80), 65-107.

Haraway, D. (1991). *Simians, cyborgs, and women: The reinvention of nature.* New York: Routledge.

Janangelo, J. (1998). Joseph Cornell and hypertext. *College Composition and Communication, 49*(1), 24-43.

Joyce, M. (1987). *Afternoon, a story.* Cambridge, MA: Eastgate.

Joyce, M. (1995). *Of two minds: Hypertext, pedagogy, and poetics.* Ann Arbor: University of Michigan Press.

Landow, G. (1992). *Hypertext: The convergence of contemporary theory and technology.* Baltimore: Johns Hopkins University Press.

Moulthrop, S. (1994). Paragnosis, or the story of cyberspace. *Works and Days, 12*(23/24), 33-55.

Nelson, T. H. (1987). *Computer lib/dream machines.* Redmond, WA: Tempus.

Penley, C., & Ross, A. (Eds.). (1991). *Technoculture.* Minneapolis: University of Minnesota Press.

Piaget, J. (1963). *The psychology of intelligence.* Paterson, NJ: Littlefield, Adams.

Selfe, C. L., & Selfe, R. J. (1994). The politics of the interface: Power and its exercise in electronic contact zones. *College Composition and Communication, 45*(4), 480-505.

Sosnoski, J. (1994). *Token professionals and master critics: A critique of orthodoxy in literary studies.* Albany: SUNY Press.

Sosnoski, J. (1995). *Modern skeletons in postmodern closets: A cultural studies alternative.* Charlottesville: University Press of Virginia.

Sosnoski, J. (in press). Hyper-readers and their reading engines: Passions, politics and 21st century technologies. In G. E. Hawisher & C. L. Selfe (Eds.), *Passions, politics, and 21st century technologies.* Urbana: University of Illinois Press.

Toulmin, S. (1958). *The uses of argument.* Cambridge, UK: Cambridge University Press.

Tufte, E. R. (1997). *Visual explanations: Images and quantities, evidence and narrative.* Cheshire, CT: Graphics Press.

Ulmer, G. (1995). Grammatology (in the stacks) *of* hypermedia: A simulation. In M. C. Tuman (Ed.), *Literacy online: The promise (and peril) of reading and writing with computers.* Pittsburgh: Pittsburgh University Press.

Virilio, P. (1989). *War and cinema: The logistics of perception* (P. Camiller, Trans.). London: Verso.

7

From Paper-and-Pencil to Screen-and-Keyboard

Toward a Methodology for Survey Research on the Internet

DIANE F. WITMER
ROBERT W. COLMAN
SANDRA LEE KATZMAN

EVERY DAY, MORE PEOPLE DISCOVER the Internet and World Wide Web, creating an international and amorphous interaction of human agents through the digital transmission of information. The exponential growth of electronic communication and its potential for democracy, culture, and workplace productivity are drawing keen interest from researchers in both industry and academia. Topics of inquiry include how the technology is adopted (e.g., Rice, Grant, Schmitz, & Torobin, 1990; Schmitz & Fulk, 1991), its role in

AUTHORS' NOTE: An earlier version of this chapter was presented to the Communication and Technology Division of the International Communication Association at the 46th Annual Conference, May 23-27, 1996, Chicago, Illinois.

creating culture and community (e.g., Baym, 1995; Beniger, 1987; Jones, 1995; Reid, 1991, 1995), on-line work and play (e.g., Danet, Ruedenberg, & Rosenbaum-Tamari, 1998; Eisenberg, Monge, & Miller, 1983; Sproull & Kiesler, 1991; Wambach, 1991; Witmer, 1998; Witmer & Katzman, 1998), group dynamics in the computer-mediated environment (e.g., Adrianson & Hjelmquist, 1991; Dubrovsky, Kiesler, & Sethna, 1991; Hiltz, Johnson, & Turoff, 1986; Kiesler & Sproull, 1992; Lea & Spears, 1991; McGuire, Kiesler, & Siegel, 1987; Smilowitz, Compton, & Flint, 1988; Sudweeks & Rafaeli, 1996), and interpersonal relationships (e.g., Matheson, 1991; Rice & Love, 1987; Walther & Burgoon, 1992). More and more, scholars are conducting research of and through computer-mediated communication (CMC) via local area networks (LANs), group decision support systems (GDSSs), and the Internet. As a result, some researchers are raising questions concerning the nature of the research itself (e.g., Rice, 1992). Investigators are discovering that on-line research demands methods for data collection and analysis that are specific to the medium (e.g., Huff & Rosenberg, 1988; Kaplan, 1992; Kiesler & Sproull, 1986; Mitchell, Paprzycki, & Duckett, 1994; Rafaeli & Tractinsky, 1991; Smith, 1997).

The purpose of this chapter is to address some basic issues concerning on-line survey methodology. The chapter examines whether traditional paper-and-pencil methods are readily adaptable to on-line studies, and reports a study on conducting survey research via the Internet. The following sections provide background on the topic, describe how the methodology was developed, and discuss implications for future on-line survey research.

Background and Research Questions

The three authors of this paper met on-line for the first time in 1993 as members of an international research project known as "ProjectH" (Rafaeli, Sudweeks, Konstan, & Mabry, 1994; Sudweeks & Rafaeli, 1996), and were drawn together through a shared interest in the use of graphic accents (GAs)[1] in CMC. During 2 years of collaboration, we conducted all work entirely via e-mail.[2]

To answer our specific research questions on the use of GAs, we developed a three-condition survey study that we planned to conduct via the Internet. To that end, we drew on traditional methods of questionnaire design (e.g., Babbie, 1990, 1992; Dillman, 1978). Our survey instrument contained extensive formatting to maximize clarity in the electronic environment. Each questionnaire element included (a) response scales with each item so that it would not be necessary for end users to scroll up and down if they wished to refer to the scales, (b) response boxes aligned on the left margin to minimize keystrokes, and (c) graphic rules and white space for maximum readability. We then set about pretesting the questionnaire with friends and acquaintances. To our surprise, even though these particular respondents knew us and supported our project, they were either unwilling or unable to complete the questionnaire and return it. It was clear that data collection through e-mail potentially could stall our project. Thus, our focus turned to methodology.

Internet-based survey research often results in inadequate levels of participation (Pitkow & Recker, 1994), although there is little extant literature on Internet-based survey methodology, per se. Kiesler and Sproull (1986) examined the self-administered electronic questionnaire as a research tool and proposed that the electronic medium could combine some of the advantages of interviews with the advantages of traditional mail-out questionnaires, in that on-line surveys facilitated both complex branching and standardization. Their focus, however, was on the nature of the responses rather than on the fundamental concern of achieving adequate response rates. More recently, Kaplan (1992) proposed a way of describing multiple-choice questionnaires for on-line presentation but did not address methods for increasing response rates in self-administered questionnaires. Smith (1997), in a comparison of e-mail and Web-based survey techniques, addressed the wide variances of response rates to on-line questionnaires versus traditional paper-and-pencil "snail mail" instruments (e.g., Kittleson, 1995; Parker, 1992; Schuldt & Totten, 1994; Tse et al., 1995). Similarly, our chapter focuses on the problematic nature of response rates to e-mail questionnaires by specifically exploring the extent to which snail mail survey techniques might be translated to the electronic environment.

The lack of solid research on response rates in electronic surveys is no surprise, given the inconclusive and inconsistent studies that define acceptable response rates or report methods to increase them in traditional paper-and-pencil methods (Babbie, 1990, 1992). However, although a 50% response rate is typically considered minimally adequate for much traditional survey research (Babbie, 1990, 1992), response rates around 20% are not uncommon for unsolicited surveys (Fink, 1995), and response rates to on-line surveys may be 10% or lower (e.g., Patrick, Black, & Whalen, 1995).

At the time of our questionnaire pretesting, one of us was using an old, text-based e-mail system that moved from screen to screen in jumps rather than line-by-line scrolling. He had worked out a rule of thumb: "Don't look

at more than three screens of a message of questionable import." We therefore suspected that the low response to our preliminary questionnaire might
be, at least in part, the result of its length. Our instrument consisted of 42
stimulus items, which were constituted of 12,860 characters and formatted
to 384 lines. This translated to 19 screens on a desktop computer (assuming
that a computer screen displays 21 lines of text). We believed this might seem
too long and require more time and effort than end users would invest. In the
nearest analog to our research, the snail mail survey (Babbie, 1992), high
expenditure of user energy tends to suppress response rates. Although
Dillman (1978) proposes that the length of mail surveys does not necessarily
have a major impact on response rate, it can decrease responses (Dillman,
Sinclair, & Clark, 1993). We therefore hypothesized the following in regard
to a self-administered e-mail survey:

> H1: A short e-mail questionnaire will yield a significantly higher response rate
> than a long questionnaire.

The question then became one of whether mere length suppressed the
response rate or if the way in which a questionnaire was shortened might
affect respondents' willingness or ability to respond. Our ultimate goal was
to maximize our data collection, if possible, by shortening the questionnaire
through formatting changes rather than by reducing the number of stimulus
items. We reasoned that respondents might be reluctant to complete the
questionnaires either because they found scrolling through repeated screens
onerous or because they tired of completing many stimulus items. In other
words, we hoped to determine if the number of items or the sheer length
affected response rate. Thus, our research questions were as follows:

> RQ1: Is response rate increased by reducing the number of screens through which
> the respondent must scroll?
>
> RQ2: Is response rate further increased by decreasing the number of stimulus items?

Method

INSTRUMENTATION

To answer our questions and test our hypothesis, we designed three
questionnaires that varied in length and format. All three questionnaires were

shaped by our shared interest in graphic accents. Because we ultimately intended to carry out a systematic study of GA impact on reader perception, our questionnaires for this study were all modifications of one condition from the three-condition communication study on GAs that we ultimately planned to complete. Our questionnaires asked respondents to rate the perceived intensity, the likability, and the emotion conveyed (positive, negative, or none) of single-line statements that might be found in e-mail messages, both with and without GAs. The instruments were based on 12 response items, each of which was associated with a graphic accent and presented repeatedly in separate questionnaire sections that asked for user ratings of perceived intensity, likability, and perceived emotion.

All three questionnaires shared certain common elements:

- Informed consent information, including a statement that the study's purpose was to explore respondents' "thoughts on sample e-mail messages" and that explained both how to respond and how to return completed questionnaires
- The sample messages themselves, arrayed in sections that asked respondents to give ratings on a perceived intensity scale running from *least intense* (1) to *most intense* (7); for example,

    I hate ice cream with a vengeance! :-(

- Ratings on a liking scale running from *strongest disliking* (1) to *strongest liking* (7)
- Ratings on a nominal scale of the "emotion conveyed by each message": *positive emotion* (P), *negative emotion* (N), or *no emotion* (X)
- A set of six demographic items that asked for respondents' gender, age, education, native language, and length of time using CMC and computers in general

EXPERIMENTAL VARIATIONS

The length of the questionnaires was our independent variable, and there were three lengths: long, short format, and abbreviated. The first condition (long) used the original questionnaire format from which we had received such low response rates from acquaintances. It consisted of 12 messages, repeated three times, once in each of the "intensity," "liking," and "emotion conveyed" sections mentioned above. Every response item included a response scale and response box.

The second condition, the short-format questionnaire, condensed the physical length of the survey instrument by giving the response scales solely in the introduction to each section. Thus, the short-format version included the response scales solely in the introduction to each section.

The third condition, the abbreviated questionnaire, used the same format as the short-format condition but further abridged the instrument by cutting the number of repeated messages from 12 to 6 (plus the six demographic items). Thus, in the abbreviated version, the overall number of items dropped from 42 to 24.

In terms of physical length, the final short-format and abbreviated questionnaires were similar, totaling 251 lines (approximately 12 screens) and 222 lines (approximately 11 screens), respectively. The long questionnaire consisted of 384 lines (approximately 19 screens). The short-format questionnaire was 65% of the length of the long one, and the abbreviated was 59% of the long one (and only 6% less than the version with double the number of stimulus messages).

Sampling

We collected data in two phases. For the first phase, we used Usenet newsgroups as a sampling frame for two reasons: First, they represented a broad demographic range of end users. Second, they were easily accessible and allowed us to draw publicly posted e-mail addresses for our sample. To that end, we obtained a current list of Usenet newsgroups via a "gopher" search on the Internet.[3] The first step was to eliminate all newsgroup hierarchies that were inappropriate for inclusion because of narrowly focused topics or those in which we believed our survey might be viewed as disruptive and counter to the spirit of the groups.[4] The remaining hierarchies, alt.*, misc.*, rec.*, soc.*, and talk.*, yielded a total of 1,835 newsgroups from which we could draw a sample of e-mail addresses.[5]

To compensate for anticipated low response rates and still have adequate responses for statistical analysis, we attempted to reach at least 100 respondents for each of the three questionnaire conditions. To that end, we drew a stratified random sample from the appropriate newsgroup hierarchies. We based the strata on the relative percentages of the total number of newsgroups represented by each hierarchy as shown in Table 7.1.

The procedure described above yielded 31 groups. Our criterion for minimal traffic volume was based on postings during a specified period. If at least 12 users with different e-mail addresses had not posted to the group

TABLE 7.1 Stratified Sample of Newsgroups

Hierarchy	Number of Groups in List	Percentage of Groups in List	Number of Groups in Sample	Percentage of Groups in Sample
alt.*	1259	69	21	68
misc.*	59	3	1	3
rec.*	367	20	6	19
soc.*	129	7	2	6
talk.*	21	1	1	3
Totals	1835	100[a]	31	99[a]

a. Difference due to rounding.

during the 72-hour collection period, we discarded the group as a collection site and randomly selected a replacement group from within the same hierarchy. Additional newsgroups from appropriate hierarchies were added to replace those that yielded obsolete or invalid addresses.

Although we could stratify the sample according to numbers of groups in each hierarchy, we were unable to stratify the sample by percentages of individual users[6] because we lacked accurate projections for how many people would frequent each of the groups during the proposed sampling period. We chose, therefore, to select the stratified sample of the 31 newsgroups, randomly select from each group 12 addresses of people who posted there, and then randomly assign 4 of the 12 collected e-mail addresses to each of the three survey conditions. We eliminated any duplicate addresses from the resulting mailing lists before sending out the questionnaires.

For the second phase of data collection, our sample frame consisted of subscribers to two large e-mail subscription services. In the interest of good "netiquette," we chose subscription lists that had some relationship to the nature of our research, specifically, the Communication and Information Technology listserv, and the American Communication Association listserv. We randomly selected 294 nonduplicative e-mail addresses from the lists.

PROCEDURE

During the first phase of data collection, we each distributed one third (100 copies) of the questionnaires. We opted to send out the questionnaires over a single weekend to minimize possible systematic differences in response rates due to the time of week or season. The first attempt to mail the questionnaires drew hostile responses to several of 145 questionnaires sent by two of the researchers. The speed and vehemence of the responses (which argued, with varying degrees of obscenity, that we should not have sent a long, unsolicited questionnaire) convinced us that we should abort the mailing. We immediately halted the project to reformulate our plan.

Drawing again on traditional snail mail survey techniques, we decided to send short introductory messages in advance of the questionnaires, which would allow respondents to decline participation after receiving only a brief note. Thus, we replenished our stratified sample, drafted an introductory e-mail message to be sent out 2 weeks in advance of the questionnaires, and wrote a new introductory paragraph for the questionnaires. The new procedure, we hoped, would minimize inconvenience to recipients who might be using e-mail systems through which they paid for their messages by volume. Reasoning that some recipients might be more inclined to respond to the questionnaire after seeing it, we also decided to ask only those who did not wish to participate in the study to reply to our message. They could decline participation and be removed from our lists simply by using their reply features and typing "NO." We used a similar method with a slightly modified message of introduction for the second phase of data collection.

Results

During the first phase of data collection, our second mailing, as expected, went far more smoothly than the first, aborted mailing. Our first attempt to send an introduction along with the questionnaire evoked some comments of a hostile nature that generally is described on the Internet as "flaming." Some of these responses came from individuals with access providers whose fee structures included charging for e-mail by volume. Others expressed a general objection to receiving "junk mail." In contrast, the introductory message that we subsequently sent in advance of the questionnaire elicited little negativity, a number of respectful responses, and some complimentary comments on our approach from individuals who chose not to participate in the study.

Of 509 total addresses collected, 145 were sent in the aborted mailing and another 33 were invalid addresses. Of the remaining 331 individuals to whom we sent introductory messages, 47 (14.2%) of the individuals responded that they did not wish to participate in the study. Thus, we sent questionnaires to the remaining 284 individuals. Of those questionnaire recipients, 66 (23.2%)

returned completed questionnaires, 5 (1.8%) responded that they did not wish to participate, and 213 (75.0%) did not respond. One aberrant response is worth mentioning here, because it affected both our database and our inferences concerning on-line survey research methodology.

One respondent returned a fully completed questionnaire through an anonymous server, which stripped all identifying information from the message header. In addition, the respondent removed the introductory paragraphs, which made it impossible to determine the correct subject number or newsgroup. It appeared that the participant had returned a valid response but in a desire to remain anonymous, had used technology to alter the survey instrument. We were reasonably certain that the data were valid, that the questionnaire had been returned to the team member who sent it, and that it was from the second, rather than the first, mailing. This meant that although we had sent out a total of 284 questionnaires, the final data set would represent 285 questionnaires. To compensate for this inaccuracy, we substituted the data for the extra response for the missing data of one nonresponding subject number, taking care that the substitution corresponded to the correct researcher and questionnaire version. Although this meant that the respondent might be assigned to a different newsgroup than that from which the address was drawn, newsgroup information was not an integral element of the study. Thus, to maintain the integrity of the study in terms of our hypothesis, we favored accuracy of the response rate over accuracy of newsgroup assignment.

The second phase of data collection yielded a total of 50 responses from a total of 277 questionnaires successfully sent (and presumed received) for a response rate of 18.1%. In this second phase, a total of 3 people (1.1%) responded that they did not wish to participate in the study.

We used a chi-square statistic to determine if response rates differed between the two sets of data. The response rates of 23.2% and 18.1% for the first and second phases of data collection were not statistically different (chi-square [1, $N = 561$] = 2.00, $p = .16$; see Table 7.2). As a result, we combined the two sets of data for further analysis.

Of the total 561 questionnaires we sent, 187 were the long version, which produced 33 responses, for a 17.6% response rate. We sent a total of 177 short-format questionnaires and received 43 answers or a 24.3% response rate. The abbreviated version from which items were deleted yielded 40 responses out of 197 sent, or a 20.3% response rate. The overall response rate across questionnaires was 20.7%.

TABLE 7.2 Chi-Square for Response Rates, by Phase of Data Collection

| | Phase of Data Collection | | |
| | Phase I | Phase II | |
Response			*Total*
Response with answer	66	50	116
No response or decline	218	227	445
Total	284	277	561
	50.6%	49.4%	100.0%

NOTE: Chi-square value = 1.99644; *df* = 1; significance = .15767.

We used chi-square statistics to test the hypothesis that the short-format and abbreviated versions of the questionnaire would produce a significantly higher response rate than the long version. First, we used a chi-square to determine if there was a significant difference in response rates between the two shortened versions of the questionnaire (see Table 7.3). The results indicated that there was no significant difference between short-format and abbreviated (chi-square [1, $N = 374$] = 0.64, $p = .42$). We then combined the two shortened versions of the questionnaire for a comparison between the response rates of the long version (17.6%) compared with the combined short-format and abbreviated versions (22.2%). The chi-square (see Table 7.4) indicated that the difference between combined short versions and the original, long version was not significant (chi-square [1, $N = 561$] = 1.31, $p = .25$).

TABLE 7.3 Chi-Square for Response Rates, by Short-Format and Abbreviated Questionnaires

| | Questionnaire Version | | |
| | Short Format | Abbreviated | |
Response			*Total*
Response with answer	43	40	83
No response or decline	134	157	291
Total	177	197	374
	47.3%	52.7%	100.0%

NOTE: Chi-square value = 0.64375; *df* = 1; significance = .42236.

TABLE 7.4 Chi-Square for Response Rates, by Long Questionnaire Compared With Combined Short-Format and Abbreviated Questionnaires

	Questionnaire Version		
	Long	*Short & Abbreviated*	
Response		*Combined*	*Total*
Response with answer	33	83	116
No response or decline	154	291	445
Total	187	374	561
	33.3%	66.7%	100.0%

NOTE: Chi-square value = 1.30550; $df = 1$; significance = .25321.

Discussion

Although the study did not yield the expected results, a number of valuable lessons can be learned from these data. The information concerning both response rates and questionnaire design indicate that on-line research should reflect sensitivity to the peculiarities of the electronic environment.

RESPONSE RATES

The data do not support the hypothesis that the short versions of the questionnaire would produce significantly higher response rates than the long version. The answers to the research questions also remain equivocal. Although there was a slight difference in the raw results, the chi-square test did not reveal a significant difference in response rates between the short-format or abbreviated versions of the questionnaire. This may be due to the nature of the end user respondent making a decision to complete or not complete the questionnaire after looking only at the introductory paragraph rather than looking at the questionnaire in its entirety.

Another possible explanation for the lack of difference between response rates across the three versions of the questionnaire is the learning process of the respondents. In on-line examinations, Rafaeli and Tractinsky (1991) found that reduced resting time and participants' learning curves during the course of the exams resulted in time saved during longer tests. Similarly, respondents to our long questionnaire may have become more adept at answering the items than those responding to the short instruments. This may have resulted in similar expenditures of end user time and energy across the three versions and, thus, similar response rates.

The results of this study indicate that like response rates for other self-administered questionnaires, response rates for on-line surveys may not be particularly sensitive to questionnaire length, per se. Our response rate was low across all three versions of the instrument. We believe the low response rates were due to three critical factors. First, the questionnaires appeared fragmented because there was no internal coherence between stimulus items. Because we were interested in user perceptions of GAs on e-mail messages, we varied the content of the single-line messages in the survey instruments. Second, the end users probably had low interest in the survey topic, which was unrelated to their newsgroup themes. In a similar on-line survey, one of the authors attained a markedly higher response rate (26%) than we attained in this study, despite the technical challenges of conducting the survey through an anonymous server (Witmer, 1998). In that research, however, all the respondents presumably had keen interest in the newsgroup topics, and the questionnaire asked about their personal senses of safety in posting to the alt.sex.* newsgroup hierarchy. Because the sample was drawn from the alt.sex.* hierarchy, which traditionally is one of the most popular on the Internet, respondents may have had a higher personal investment in the subject or a higher interest level in the general study. Third, our relatively bland subject matter, coupled with the repetitious pattern of unrelated statements, may have appeared trivial or boring to many of our questionnaire recipients.

INSTRUMENT DESIGN AND IMPLEMENTATION

This study indicates that provision of an incentive to participate appears even more critical in on-line research than in snail mail surveys. In the latter, if an individual doesn't care to participate, he or she must still deal with the physical instrument. Disposal of a paper questionnaire requires folding, scrunching, or some other manipulation, which may, to some small measure, delay the decision to dismiss the study. In an e-mail survey, touching a key is all a respondent needs to do to cancel or delete an instrument, whether it has been answered in whole or in part. Such ease of document removal makes advanced, introductory contact with respondents particularly important in on-line research.

Our results indicate that attaching an introductory paragraph with no forewarning to a full, on-line survey instrument is inadequate and inappropriate to the electronic environment. Although enclosing a cover letter may be acceptable for snail mail surveys, the computer-mediated medium mandates consideration of the systems in which respondents receive their e-mail, the costs involved for users, their keyboard skills, and their technical expertise. Unsolicited e-mail, particularly when it is of substantial length (and thus uses excessive "bandwidth") is widely seen as, at best, a breach of "netiquette" and, at worst, as a violation of personal privacy. Thus, e-mail surveys require a two-step process of introduction and instrument.

Our second mailing of a brief introductory message gave potential respondents an easy way to avoid receiving the full instrument, which for some users, could create a technical hassle and a personal expense. By giving the recipients of our mailing some control over the matter, our second mailing drew far less ire than did the first one and even evoked positive comment. The unanticipated positive responses by nonparticipants are especially significant, because they represent an extra (and unsolicited) allocation of time and effort to formulate, write, and send the electronic message.

Another methodological consideration of computer-mediated survey research is that, unlike those who receive other forms of self-administered questionnaires, respondents have the capability of altering the instrument itself. In our study, the case of the response sent via anonymous server illustrates the potential difficulty associated with this capability. Our outgoing questionnaires were altered when some respondents deleted the introductory paragraph, and this proved problematic when one altered instrument was returned through an anonymous server. Although the integrity of our study was not compromised, the clear inference is that on-line survey methodology should include (a) technological safeguards against alterations of the instrument (such as those offered by Web-based forms) and (b) contingency plans for handling altered or untraceable instruments during analysis.

Conclusions

This study indicates that both as a mode and a locus of study, CMC has enormous potential. We see, however, that survey methodology does not translate across the board to computers from older, "lower-tech" forms of communication, although some points of reference may be useful. Our results suggest that on-line survey research requires incentives for participation, introductory messages separate from the instruments, and safeguards against alteration of the questionnaires. The study also raises the question of how questionnaire length affects response rate and at what level of instrument brevity a researcher reaches the point of diminishing returns.

Clearly, computer-mediated research needs specific and carefully designed instruments that not only accommodate but exploit the features of the electronic environment to attract respondents who otherwise may have their fingers on a delete key. Researchers cannot merely import paper-and-pencil methodologies to on-line studies, but must adapt them to the electronic environment and create new methods to expand our knowledge in and of computer-mediated communication.

Notes

1. The term was coined by a Stanford doctoral candidate in communication, Dennis Kinsey, in a personal communication with one of the authors.

2. Only once did two of the three authors meet face-to-face, for a brief lunch meeting.

3. The Usenet Newsgroup list that served as our sampling frame was dated October 3, 1994.

4. Posting e-mail messages that do not conform to a specific newsgroup topic or user expectations is widely considered poor *netiquette,* the popular term for good manners on the Internet, and can result in hostile responses (see, e.g., Virginia Shea's 1994 *Netiquette,* available on-line at http://www.albion.com/netiquette/book/index.html).

5. Newsgroup hierarchies are distinguished by the first string of characters preceding a period in the newsgroup name. For this study, we eliminated from our sampling frame scientific hierarchies, those that seemed to be primarily constituted of business or technical announcements, or those that had any sort of fee structure. We tried to focus on hierarchies that were widely known throughout the Internet and where our survey might be least likely to be perceived by users as a breach of netiquette. Among those we eliminated were bionet.*, bit.*, biz.*, clari.* comp.*, gnu.*, hepnet.*, ieee.*, sci.*, info.*, k12.*, relcom.*, u3b.*, vmsnet.*, and news.*.

6. Although we recognize that more than one person may access an e-mail account, we use the term *individual user* or *end user* to refer to e-mail recipients. Typically, only one person responds to a single e-mail message, but the reader should keep in mind that responses to questionnaires administered through e-mail may be individual or collaborative efforts. This, in fact, is not altogether different from a mail-out survey, in which recipients may collaborate on a single instrument.

References

Adrianson, L., & Hjelmquist, E. (1991). Group process in face-to-face and computer-mediated communication. *Behaviour & Information Technology, 10,* 281-296.

Babbie, E. (1990). *Survey research methods* (2nd ed.). Belmont, CA: Wadsworth.

Babbie, E. (1992). *The practice of social research* (6th ed.). Belmont, CA: Wadsworth.

Baym, N. K. (1995). The emergence of community in computer-mediated communication. In S. G. Jones (Ed.), *CyberSociety: Computer-mediated communication and community* (pp. 138-163). Thousand Oaks, CA: Sage.

Beniger, J. (1987). Personalization of mass media and the growth of pseudo-community. *Communication Research, 14,* 352-371.

Danet, B., Ruedenberg, L., & Rosenbaum-Tamari, Y. (1998). "Hmmm . . . where's that smoke coming from?" Writing, play and performance on Internet relay chat. In F. Sudweeks, S. Rafaeli, & M. McLaughlin (Eds.), *Network and Netplay: Virtual groups on the Internet.* Menlo Park, CA: AAAI/MIT Press.

Dillman, D. A. (1978). *Mail and telephone surveys: The total design method.* New York: Wiley.

Dillman, D. A., Sinclair, M. D., & Clark, J. R. (1993). Effects of questionnaire length, respondent-friendly design, and a difficult question on response rates for occupant-addressed census mail surveys. *Public Opinion Quarterly, 57,* 289-304.

Dubrovsky, V. J., Kiesler, S., & Sethna, B. N. (1991). The equalization phenomenon: Status effects in computer-mediated and face-to-face decision making groups. *Human-Computer Interaction, 6,* 119-146.

Eisenberg, E. M., Monge, P. R., & Miller, K. I. (1983). Involvement in communication networks as a predictor of organizational commitment. *Human Communication Research, 10,* 179-201.

Fink, A. (1995). *How to sample in surveys.* Thousand Oaks, CA: Sage.

Hiltz, S., Johnson, K., & Turoff, M. (1986). Experiments in group decision making: Communication process and outcome in face-to-face versus computerized conferences. *Human Communication Research, 13,* 225-252.

Huff, C. W., & Rosenberg, J. (1988, October). *The on-line voyeur: Promises and pitfalls of observing electronic interaction.* Paper presented at the 18th Annual Meeting of the Society for Computers in Psychology, Chicago.

Jones, S. G. (1995). Understanding community in the information age. In S. G. Jones (Ed.), *CyberSociety: Computer-mediated communication and community* (pp. 10-35). Thousand Oaks, CA: Sage.

Kaplan, H. L. (1992). Representation of on-line questionnaires in an editable, auditable database. *Behavior Research Methods, Instruments & Computers, 24,* 373-384.

Kiesler, S., & Sproull, L. (1986). Response effects in the electronic survey. *Public Relations Quarterly, 50,* 402-413.

Kiesler, S., & Sproull, L. (1992). Group decision making and communication technology. *Organizational Behavior and Human Decision Processes, 52,* 96-123.

Kittleson, M. J. (1995). An assessment of the response rate via the postal service and e-mail. *Health Values, 18*(2), 27-29.

Lea, M., & Spears, R. (1991). Computer-mediated communication, de-individuation and group decision-making. Special Issue: Computer supported to operative work and groupware: I. *International Journal of Man-Machine Studies, 34,* 283-301.

Matheson, K. (1991). Social cues in computer-mediated negotiations: Gender makes a difference. *Computers in Human Behavior, 7,* 137-147.

McGuire, T. W., Kiesler, S., & Siegel, J. (1987). Group and computer-mediated discussion effects in risking decision making. *Journal of Personality and Social Psychology, 52,* 917-930.

Mitchell, T., Paprzycki, M., & Duckett, G. (1994). Research methods using computer networks. *Arachnet Electronic Journal on Virtual Culture* [On-line], 2(4). Available: Send the command GET EJVCV2N4 MITCHELL to LISTSERV@KENVM.KENT.EDU, leaving the subject line empty.

Parker, L. (1992, July). Collecting data the e-mail way. *Training and Development,* 52-54.

Patrick, A. S., Black, A., & Whalen, T. E. (1995). Rich, young, male, dissatisfied computer geeks? Demographics and satisfaction from the National Capital FreeNet. In D. Godfrey & M. Levy

(Eds.), *Proceedings of Telecommunities 95: The International Community Networking Conference* (pp. 83-107). Victoria, British Columbia, Canada: Telecommunities Canada. Available: http://debra.dgbt.doc.ca:80/services-research/survey/demographics/vic.html

Pitkow, J. E., & Recker, M. M. (1994). *Results from the first World-Wide Web user survey* [On-line]. Available: http://www.gvu.gatech.edu/user_surveys/survey-01-1994/survey-paper.html

Rafaeli, S., Sudweeks, F., Konstan, J., & Mabry, E. (1994). *ProjectH overview: A quantitative study of computer-mediated communication* [On-line]. Available: http://www.arch.usyd.edu.au/~fay/projecth.html

Rafaeli, S., & Tractinsky, N. (1991). Time in computerized tests: A multitrait, multimethod investigation of general-knowledge and mathematical-reasoning on-line examinations. *Computers in Human Behavior, 7,* 215-225.

Reid, E. (1991). *Electropolis: Communication and community on the Internet relay chat.* BA honors thesis, Department of History, University of Melbourne, Melbourne, Australia [On-line]. Available: http://www.uni-frankfurt.de/gnomic/electropolis.html

Reid, E. (1995). Virtual worlds: Culture and imagination. In S. G. Jones (Ed.), *CyberSociety: Computer-mediated communication and community* (pp. 164-183). Thousand Oaks, CA: Sage.

Rice, R. E. (1992). Contexts of research on organizational computer-mediated communication: A recursive review. In M. Lea (Ed.), *Contexts of computer-mediated communication* (pp. 113-144). Herts, England: Harvester Wheatsheaf.

Rice, R. E., Grant, A. E., Schmitz, J., & Torobin, J. (1990). Individual and network influences on the adoption and perceived outcomes of electronic messaging. *Social Networks, 12,* 27-55.

Rice, R. E., & Love, G. (1987). Electronic emotion: Socioemotional content in a computer-mediated communication network. *Communication Research, 14,* 87-108.

Schmitz, J., & Fulk, J. (1991). Organizational colleagues, media richness, and electronic mail: A test of the social influence model of technology use. *Communication Research, 18,* 487-523.

Schuldt, B., & Totten, J. (1994). Electronic mail vs. mail survey response rates. *Marketing Research, 6,* 36-39.

Shea, V. (1994). *Netiquette* [on-line]. San Francisco: Albion. Available: http://www.albion.com/netiquette/book/index.html

Smilowitz, M., Compton, D. C., & Flint, L. (1988). The effects of computer mediated communication on an individual's judgment: A study based on the methods of Asch's social influence experiment. *Computers in Human Behavior, 4,* 311-321.

Smith, C. B. (1997). Casting the Net: Surveying an Internet population. *Journal of Computer-Mediated Communication* [On-line], *3*(1). Available: http://www.ascusc.org/jcmc/vol3/issue1/smith.html

Sproull, L., & Kiesler, S. (1991). *Connections: New ways of working in the networked organization.* Cambridge: MIT Press.

Sudweeks, F., & Rafaeli, S. (1996). How do you get a hundred strangers to agree: Computer mediated communication and collaboration. In T. M. Harrison & T. D. Stephen (Eds.), *Computer networking and scholarship in the 21st century* [On-line] (pp. 115-136). New York: SUNY Press. Available: http://www.arch.usyd.edu.au/fay/papers/strangers.html

Tse, A. C. B., Tse, K. C., Yin, C. H., Ting, C. B., Yi, K. W., Yee, K. P., & Hong, W. C. (1995). Comparing two methods of sending out questionnaires: E-mail versus mail. *Journal of the Market Research Society, 37*(4), 441-446.

Walther, J. B., & Burgoon, J. K. (1992). Relational communication in computer-mediated interaction. *Human Communication Research, 19,* 50-88.

Wambach, J. A. (1991, February). *Building electronic mail coalitions: Network politics in an educational organization.* Paper presented to the Western States Communication Association, Phoenix, AZ.

Witmer, D. F. (1998). Practicing safe computing: Why people engage in risky computer-mediated communication. In F. Sudweeks, S. Rafaeli, & M. McLaughlin (Eds.), *Network and Netplay: Virtual groups on the Internet* (pp. 127-146). Menlo Park, CA: AAAI/MIT Press.

Witmer, D. F., & Katzman, S. L. (1998). Smile when you say that: Graphic accents as gender markers in computer-mediated communication. In F. Sudweeks, S. Rafaeli, & M. McLaughlin (Eds.), *Network and Netplay: Virtual groups on the Internet* (pp. 3-12). Menlo Park, CA: AAAI/MIT Press.

8

Measuring Internet Audiences
Patrons of an On-Line Art Museum[1]

MARGARET McLAUGHLIN
STEVEN B. GOLDBERG
NICOLE ELLISON
JASON LUCAS

THE WORLD WIDE WEB (WWW or the Web) is especially well suited to the display of art. Although there are numerous galleries and museums on the Web, most suffer from limitations owing in part to the novelty of the medium and the relative infancy of on-line exhibition culture (McLaughlin, 1996). For example, much of the work available on-line bypasses the traditional curatorial filter. Our objective in creating the University of Southern California (USC) Interactive Art Museum has been to develop a structure in which the assembling and display of objects takes place within contextualized exhibitions and is informed by a sense of curatorial presence, selectivity, and mission (Schertz, Jaskowiak, & McLaughlin, 1998). On-line galleries wishing to exhibit three-dimensional art (sculptures, assemblages, and installations) have had to be content largely with displaying digitized slides of the works, and the viewer's vantage point with respect to such objects has ordinarily been confined to a single, frontal, two-dimensional view. We have developed new technologies for exhibiting three-dimensional works and avant-garde performances and events on-line that allow the viewer to enjoy multiple and varying perspectives on objects and people in the museum and to feel a sense of "presence" (Lombard & Ditton, 1997) in the remote environment.

A fundamental challenge has been to develop coherent virtual spaces that take advantage of the interactive nature of the WWW to enable dialogue and information sharing among artists, curators, and viewers. With respect to the facilitation of dialogue, we have developed an interactive museum where visitors can communicate, asynchronously or in real time, with museum staff and other museum goers; participate in the design of installation art (e.g., add new elements or rearrange existing ones); and monitor the evolution of the collaborative work over time. Furthermore, we have created a number of mechanisms to permit us to learn who our visitors are, why they've come, and what they can contribute to our understanding of the patron base for on-line museums. In this chapter, we report on some of our methods for coming to know our audience.

The USC Interactive Art Museum

The virtual museum project, known as the USC Interactive Art Museum at the Fisher Gallery (http://digimuse.usc.edu/museum.html) currently features three exhibitions. Presently on view are "Romance With Nature," an exhibition of 19th-century American landscapes; "Light in Darkness: Women in Japanese Prints of Early Shôwa (1926-1945)"; and *"Trinkendes Mädchen"* (Drinking Maiden), a telerobotic stereo display of an early 20th-century sculpture by Ernst Wenck. Also available on the museum site is archived video from the live Webcast of the opening of an exhibition of the works of Spanish artists Miguel Navarro and Carmen Calvo. The site is fully searchable by means of the Excite search engine, which provides summaries and confidence estimates for documents containing the user's keyword or concept.[2]

THE EXHIBITIONS

*"Romance With Nature:
American Landscapes in the USC Collections"*

This exhibition features works by 19th-century landscape artists, including American masters Albert Bierstadt, Thomas Cole, Asher B. Durand,

Thomas Doughty, Henry Inman, George Inness, David Johnson, and Thomas Moran. The landscapes represent a nationalistic and romantic tradition in American art history characterized by worship of the unspoiled American wilderness and an effort to capture a developing sense of national identity. The pictures reflect the conflicting themes of pride in the progress represented by westward expansion and concerns that the inevitable consequence of that progress would be the irretrievable loss of the frontier (Casamassima & Lineker, 1996).

A highlight of the exhibition is a set of commentaries on Cole's "The Woodchopper: Lake Featherstonehaugh," by scholars from several areas of the humanities, including art history, feminist studies, religion, and American studies. The exhibition is accompanied by RealAudio voice annotations by Fisher Gallery Director Selma Holo. Each image is provided with an accompanying didactic panel that provides a historical context for the work.

"Light in Darkness:
Women in Japanese Prints of Early Shôwa (1926-1945)"

This on-line exhibition of Japanese *shin hanga* woodblock prints, many of which were loaned by the Los Angeles County Museum of Art, takes as its subtext the depiction of women in art produced between the two world wars. The works in the exhibition exemplify the conflict between the cultural yearnings and backlash against modernity represented by the *bijin,* or traditional beauties, and the impulses favoring modernization and Western practices, of which the *moga,* or modern girl, was emblematic (Brown et al., 1996). The prints in the exhibition were aimed primarily at the export market and are notable for their traditional themes and idealized notions of womanly beauty. Selected pages from the exhibition have been translated into Japanese.

"Trinkendes Mädchen (The Drinking Maiden)"

Central to the mission of the USC Interactive Art Museum are (a) the development of new telerobotic technologies for exhibiting three-dimensional works of art over the Internet and (b) the discovery of techniques for facilitating remote collaboration in the creation of nonplanar art objects (McLaughlin, Osborne, & Ellison, 1997). The museum's first telerobotic art installation, the Tele-Garden, permitted visitors to seed and water a remote garden over the Internet (Goldberg, Bekey, Akatsuka, & Bressanelli, 1995).

The Tele-Garden is now on display at Ars Electonica in Austria (see McLaughlin et al., 1997, for an account of the formation of an on-line community in this virtual environment). For our most recent exhibition, *Trinkendes Mädchen,* a statue by German sculptor Ernst Wenck, was placed on a rotating platform at USC's Fisher Gallery. The system has been designed so those who have a Web connection can manipulate remote, robotically controlled CCD (charge coupled device) cameras to view images of the statue. Stereo viewing is available for users with head-mounted displays. To complement the interface to the Drinking Maiden exhibition, text materials and curator's voice annotations to the exhibition have been made available, the latter via a RealAudio server. In addition to viewing the exhibition over the Web, visitors to the Fisher Gallery on the USC campus can view the telerobotic installation and watch as the robotic arm moves the cameras and rotating platform in response to commands from remote users around the world.

The system consists of a 6 degrees-of-freedom arm and a rotating platform with separate workspaces. The workspaces were intentionally separated to make it impossible for the robot to come into contact with any part of the statue. On the end of the robot, there is a vengeance head that provides for the correct viewing angles required for comfortable viewing of stereo images. This is linked in software to a sonar panel that determines the range to target for the vengeance head. The two CCD cameras are mounted under the vengeance head. Each CCD camera has autofocus and a powered zoom that will allow the user to get closer to the statue than the robot's workspace will allow. Our user interface provides a four-image, four-click control over the manipulator. The first image is a side view of the statue. In this view, the user chooses where on the statue the cameras will point in respect to the x and z axes. The second image is a side representation of the robot and its workspace. This will allow the user to choose any permissible location within the workspace as presented in the x and z axes. The third image is a top view of the statue that will allow the user to control the pan of the cameras. The fourth image is a top projection of the robot and workspace as defined in the second image. This allows the user to turn the robot about its y axis and still extend the arm in the x axis. In both representations of the robot, the links are presented as flat rendered polygons so that the user can manipulate the end effector with visual feedback as to how that will effect the joint positions. There is a preview window that suggests what the user will see if he or she requests a picture from a particular vantage point. This image is intentionally locked into 15-degree perspectives to inspire the user to use the robot to obtain a particular image. The preview window also acts as an interface for rotating the statue. Two arrows are to be used to rotate the statue either clockwise or counterclockwise. When users request pictures to be taken, they execute a local program on the Web server that will either put them in a queue or begin decoding the position data sent by the user's applet. When all motion is completed, images are taken from both cameras and returned to the user for viewing.

Analysis of Server Logs

The data described below are taken from the cumulative log file record, a 61-megabyte corpus, for a 7-month period from February 4, 1997, when the museum project was officially "launched," through September 8, 1997. The project was given a considerable publicity push by USC's news service, resulting in our being featured on CNN and MSNBC broadcasts, as well as being written up or picked as a worthy site by the *Chronicle of Higher Education, USA Today,* the *Los Angeles Times,* and other print and on-line sources. Each new episode of publicity resulted in a flurry of activity on the site, which was duly reflected in our server logs. These logs, in the extended log file format, keep track of who was visiting the site (unique Internet addresses), when they came, what they requested, how long they looked at each page, where they were before they came to the site, what browser they were using, what country they were from, and more. Log files were analyzed using WebTrends.[3] Table 8.1 presents the overall access statistics for the 7-month period.

TABLE 8.1 Access Statistics for the Digimuse Server, February 4, 1997, to September 9, 1997

Total number of successful hits	269,967
Total number of user sessions	14,078
User sessions from the United States	57.13%
International user sessions	15.79%
Origin unknown user sessions	27.06%
Average hits per day	1,244
Average user sessions per day	64
Average user session length	04:23

SITE TRAFFIC

Traffic to the site peaked following the initial publicity blitz, then tapered off considerably during the late spring and early summer, probably in correspondence with the academic calendar, and then picked up and resumed a steady state of about 64 user sessions per day. (User sessions are defined as a sequence of HTTP requests from a unique user, as determined by Internet protocol address. Sessions are considered to have terminated if there are no requests for a 30-minute period.)[4] During the 7-month period, there were an estimated 14,078 user sessions, lasting an average of 4.23 minutes. The majority (57.13%) of users was of U.S. origin. Sessions were split roughly equally between daytime (8:00 a.m.-5:00 p.m., user's local time) and evenings (5:00 p.m.-8:00 a.m., user's local time). There were 6,973 sessions in the daytime and 7,105 sessions in the evening hours. Most users connected to the site during the week (77.28%) as opposed to the weekend (22.71%).

REQUESTS FOR SITE FEATURES

With respect to features of the site that were accessed, 58.08% of the users requested the page introducing the telerobotics exhibition, whereas the less high-tech print and landscape exhibitions attracted comparatively less attention. However, the number of users actually accessing the telerobotic interface itself dropped off to less than 25%, which may reflect in part the presence of a substantial number of users whose Web browsers did not support Java, the programming language in which the applets for rotating and viewing the Drinking Maiden were written. The search engine provided was used in less than 1.5% of the sessions.

MOST ACTIVE ORGANIZATIONS

Analysis of the log server data indicated that the top organizations visiting the museum site were Internet access providers, suggesting that the most common ways in which the museum pages were retrieved was over a modem and dial-up connection to a commercial service provider or from a computer at the user's place of business. With respect to domain, 44.81% of the accesses were from the .com domain, 33.86% from .net, 15.89% from .edu, 3.39% from .org, 1.49% from .gov, .54% from .mil, and .02% from Arpanet. The top 10 organizations accessing the site are presented in Table 8.2. They

TABLE 8.2 Top Ten Organizations Accessing the Museum Web Site

	Organizations	Hits	Percentage of Total	User Sessions
1	America Online aol.com	9,481	3.51	538
2	Uunet Technologies Inc. uu.net	6,393	2.36	276
3	Netcom on-line Services netcom.com	5,555	2.05	257
4	EarthLink Network Inc. earthlink.net	3,588	1.32	135
5	Compuserve Incorporated compuserve.com	2,874	1.06	127
6	Pacific Bell Internet Services pacbell.net	2,496	0.92	120
7	Mindspring Enterprises Inc. mindspring.com	1,761	0.65	68
8	Performance Systems International Inc. psi.net	1,645	0.60	61
9	netvision.net.il	1,477	0.54	97
10	ARTEMIS webtv.net	1,371	0.50	73

included America Online (AOL), Compuserve, Pacific Bell, Netcom, WebTV, and other well-known and highly marketed access providers.

ANALYSIS OF REFERRER LOG ENTRIES

Analysis of the referrer log data suggests that most of the traffic that did not come as a direct result of one of the publicity blitzes (for example, 786 of the sessions were referred from the *USA Today* "Hot Site" page, another 487 from the "Cool Site of the Day" pages, 97 from the *Chronicle of Higher Education* Web site, and 84 from the CNN site) arrived at the museum pages from a net guide or search engine. For instance, 3,489 of the sessions were referred from Yahoo, 310 from Excite, 186 from AOL Netfind, and so on. The keywords that most frequently brought visitors to the site were "art" and "museum." Many visitors came to the site as a result of searches for information on specific artists featured in the landscapes exhibition, particularly

Bierstadt, Cole, and Moran, although there were no occurrences in the log file of keyword searches on the names of Japanese artists featured in the prints exhibition. Presumably, these names are less well-known among a largely Western visitor base. A few arrived at the site by accident; that is, it is unlikely that visitors searching on keywords and phrases such as "angel fish" or "Selma Hayek nude" expected to be pointed to an on-line art museum. Such errors occur when users of search engines fail to constrain their keyword searches to exact phrases or adjacent word pairs.

INTERACTIVE SITE FEATURES AND THE ON-LINE MUSEUM PATRON

A real-time chat server was installed on the museum site to elicit user feedback, monitor response to the site, and permit visitors to chat with each other or query any staff who happened to be on-line. A chat window is also available on the robot interface page. Two on-line feedback forms are used, one of which solicits general reaction to the site, the other of which seeks feedback from visitors on information they might possess relative to one of the exhibitions. An e-mail alias, virtual_museum@usc.edu, is used to receive e-mailed feedback and circulate it quickly among members of the project team.

MUSEUM CHAT ROOM

A Web chat system was installed that permits real-time chat for visitors to the museum. The system also allows HTML formatting of messages and inclusion of on-line images. All messages and images posted are logged, along with the visitor's name, Internet address, and the time of the posting. Certain actions can be performed in the chat room (privately whispers to, winks, informs, shows picture to) by selecting from a drop-down menu, and users may direct their comments to all or to specific others. These choices are also reflected in the log file when selected. Our data indicate that fewer than 5% of the user sessions involved a visit to the chat room. Typically, during the 7-month period, a user entered, found the chat room deserted, and left, although the rare conversation occurred. Only a few took advantage of the forum to post images or the URL of their own art-related sites or to pose questions in hopes of catching the attention of a staff member or an art historian passing through. Below is a sample group of adjacent entries from the chat room log file. The first entry is the time of posting, followed by the user name assumed on entry into the chat room (for which we have substituted the generic ChatUser#), and the visitor's message.

> (22:39:40) (ChatUser1) of (Porcelain Company Name): Hello I am new to your chat room.
>
> (22:40:41) (ChatUser1) of (Porcelain Company Name): Is anyone here now?
>
> (17:02:08) (ChatUser2): Enters the lobby . . .
>
> (17:02:25) (ChatUser2): Leaves . . .
>
> (13:08:42) (ChatUser3): Enters the lobby . . .
>
> (13:14:46) (ChatUser3): well, it's difficult to say any reasonable thing in a line of text; cisono molte distanze tra me e questa chat room, da o ostalih problemih niti negovorimo; wie sagt man? omedetou gozaimasu? . . . pa drugic kaj vec!
>
> (13:17:51) (ChatUser3): and don't forget to visit my museom-on-line (home made) at http://xxxxxxxxx.UNIV.TRIESTE.IT/ arigatou ! spasiba !
>
> (13:18:13) (ChatUser3): Leaves . . .
>
> (15:54:41) (ChatUser4): Enters the lobby . . .
>
> (15:55:49) (ChatUser4): not receiving at 38,800 xxxxxxx@aol.com
>
> (15:56:00) (ChatUser4): Leaves . . .
>
> (08:07:58) (ChatUser5): Enters the lobby . . .
>
> (08:08:40) (ChatUser5): any one here i could use some help to write a report
>
> (15:10:39) (ChatUser6): Enters the lobby . . .

Curator on Call

A unique feature of the USC Interactive Art Museum is "Curator on Call." During the 7-month period covered by this report, the curator of the Drinking Maiden exhibition made himself available in the chat room each Thursday at 11 a.m. PST to answer questions. For example,

> (10:22:17) Curator on Call: Welcome to the weekly Curator on Call feature at the USC Interactive Museum
>
> (10:30:34) (ChatUser7): Enters the lobby . . .
>
> (10:31:13) Curator on Call: The curator on call will be available to answer questions from 10:30-11:30 a.m. Pacific Standard Time every Thursday
>
> (10:31:39) Curator on Call: Greetings and Welcome (ChatUser7)
>
> (10:32:08) (ChatUser7): What are the highlights of the collection at the museum?
>
> (10:32:56) Curator on Call: On the interactive museum, we have an exhibit of American Landscapes of the 19th century and the Drinking Maiden

(10:34:29) (ChatUser7): I am particularly interested in 19th century American Landscapes where Machines are depicted.

(10:35:46) (ChatUser7): Are there any of Sheeler's works on the interactive museum?

(10:36:09) Curator on Call: Our landscapes usually depict nature—mountains and streams, farmlands. The landscapists were interested in the notion of America as an "untouched" land (unlike the urbanized nations of Europe)

(10:37:10) Curator on Call: As far as I know, we don't have any Sheelers in our collection, although I will happily look in our records and e-mail you

(10:39:47) (ChatUser7): I understand that the notion of the untouched land is only part of the picture. Towards the end of the 19th century, some American artists showed an interest in the transformed America as well. Any, If you come across any such works please contact me at xxxxx@xxxx.egnet.net

(10:41:30) Curator on Call: (ChatUser7), your last message was lost; could you please send it again

(10:43:31) Curator on Call: (ChatUser7), Your message about the end of the 19th c. came through, finally. No, we do not have any paintings by Sheeler in the collection. We do, though, have a painting by a man named Arthur Dodge, called "the Dredger." It is not very exciting visually

(10:45:08) (ChatUser7) says to Curator on Call: Your message was only partly transmitted. Can you please send it again?

(10:46:39) (ChatUser7) says to Curator on Call: How about the Drinking Maiden? Can you tell me about it?

(10:47:29) Curator on Call: We seem to be having a few technical difficulties. The last of the message was [lost] unfortunately, and I have not had the opportunity to research the artist or painting to date. Dodge was not as precise in his rendering as Sheeler; the clean, machine-like

(10:49:33) Curator on Call: The Drinking Maiden was created in 1901 by the German Sculptor Ernst Wenck. It reflects the academic training Wenck received at the Royal Academy of Art, Berlin and the neo-classical aesthetics that the Academy sought to instill in both artists and the public

(10:50:57) (ChatUser7) says to Curator on Call: You are right about the technical problems. I am connecting from a long way though, Egypt, which may explain it. Your last message was also interrupted halfway through. Anyway, it was nice talking to you. Maybe I'll call in again next week. Thank you.

Although the curator faithfully reported for duty, only five visitors to the museum site took advantage of the feature during the 7-month period. Some visitors to the chat room left inquiries behind, presumably on the theory that the person with the answers would log in before the screen refresh removed the item from view. Few if any left an e-mail address to which an answer might be sent:

(03:37:41) (ChatUser8): Hi. I am looking for a source of Inness prints of his painting "Home of the Heron." Any help in this area would be greatly apreciated. Thanks much.

(12:02:03) (ChatUser9): Does anyone know aything about William Hogarth's painting's "Gin Lane" and "Beer Street"?

Although there were exceptions:

(14:59:05) (ChatUser10): I am looking for the George Inness painting "Summer Pastoral, SarcoValley, Leeds, NY 1008-85. Need to buy reproduction rights. Contact xxxxxxxxx@aol.com

An additional feature of the chat room was the availability of guided tours of the museum site conducted by the curator of the Drinking Maiden exhibition or other museum staff. Using Itinerary™ software developed by Contigo, Inc., virtual museum docents can set up on-the-fly tours for museum visitors. The software effectively captures the visitors' browsers so that as the docent moves about the site, the visitors are automatically led to the same pages. Pop-up chat windows permit the docent to converse with members of the tour and answer questions regardless of the group's location on the site. One or more members of the tour may be appointed as coleaders if desired. Unfortunately, the log files of the chat room record no instances in which visitors requested a guided tour.

Survey and Feedback Forms

Forms to solicit feedback from museum visitors were designed by the Fisher Gallery staff in collaboration with the first author.[5] One of the uses of feedback forms on the museum site was to gather information about our visitors and their "real-world" museum-going habits. A preliminary examination of survey responses seems to indicate that most of them were not habitual museum goers; to date, only one respondent has indicated being a museum member or subscriber. Interestingly, the majority of those responding to the survey so far were from the local (Los Angeles) area, and most indicated that they were interested in receiving further information about the Fisher Gallery and being added to its mailing list. Such forms may serve as an unobtrusive means to increase a museum's patron base by providing entrée to the visitor's in box.

A second feedback form was designed to fill in the gaps in the museum staff's knowledge about the history of the Drinking Maiden:

> The Fisher Gallery was eager to participate in this project partly because it gives us the opportunity to communicate more directly with visitors to the exhibition. Aside from creating a closer bond between the Gallery and our audience, we hope that our visitors will be able to contribute to our investigation of Ernst Wenck and the Drinking Maiden. When the Gallery received the statue in 1970, there were no records of when and from whose hands the *Trinkendes Mädchen* entered USC's collections. As managers and caretakers of an art collection, we were disturbed by other gaps in our knowledge of the history of the statue; what happened to the statue between 1919, when Wenck removed it from the National Gallery, Berlin, and 1936 when the statue was reportedly in the hands of the New York collector Axel Beskow? We solicit any information you have that might further our research.

In fact, the form did serve to flush out several promising sources of information, including the husband of a woman who had done her master's thesis research on the life and work of Ernst Wenck. Another visitor offered the following suggestion:

> I'm reading the 1966 edition of E.BENEZIT "Dictionnaire critique et documentaire des Peintres, Sculpteurs. . . ." In the 8th Volume, page 708, I read : "Le Musée de Berlin conserve de lui Fillette buvant et Linos." This "Fillette buvant" is -no doubt-the "Trinkendes Mädchen." Why, then, you don't quote (and verify, perhaps) the existence of such a copy in the Berlin Museum?

As a final device for communicating with our visitors, a clickable e-mail alias, virtual_museum@usc.edu, appears on every page of the virtual museum site, so that anyone who wishes can provide unstructured feedback or ask questions of the museum staff. In the early days of the project, this often took the form of pointing out technical problems or letting us know that certain museum features were not supported by thus-and-such a platform or browser. More recently, we have received requests for reciprocal links to other art-related web sites, offers of artwork to display in the virtual museum, requests for appraisals of American landscape paintings in the letter writer's possession, and notes from people who own reproductions of the Drinking Maiden from the Rosenthal porcelain factory.

Our family has a porcelain reproduction of "Drinking Maiden" which my grandfather brought from Europe after World War II. First, can you tell us approximately how many were made and if copies like the one we have are rare now? Second, we are curious about the market value of a reproduction like ours. Thank you for your time. The on-line museum is great!

And the occasional word of praise:

In the process of writing a business article on digital interactive TV, I stumbled upon your Web site—what a delight! What a surprise! What a joy! In the middle of some very dull, dry research, I felt I'd suddenly slipped through a door into a cool, luscious, beautiful place and though I haven't memory or time enough to linger now, I leave refreshed, sated, quenched, as if I've just partaken of a sumptuous meal.

Conclusion

Similar to the way in which discussions of "virtual community" have forced us to reconsider definitions of community (Jones, 1995; Sudweeks, Mc-Laughlin, & Rafaeli, 1998), researchers of the Internet community have been forced to create new methodologies for studying computer-mediated spaces. Even self-reported characteristics such as gender, age, and race as claimed by on-line participants must be subject to scrutiny, because many embrace cyberspace as an arena for experimentation with identity, communication, and sexuality (Curtis, 1997; Stone, 1996; Zaleski, 1997).

On the USC Interactive Art Museum site, we implemented a combination of features that allowed us to triangulate, giving us more accurate and richer information about our audience. We encouraged our audience to give us immediate feedback through interactive features such as "Curator on Call" and the e-mail alias. We also encouraged interactivity among our audience by creating and maintaining the chat room. (See Rafaeli & Sudweeks, 1998, for a discussion of definitions and applications of "interactivity" on the Net.) Through analysis of the logs and e-mail we received, we were able to capture a more nuanced and sophisticated portrait of our audience, as opposed to more traditional procedures in which hits to each page are counted, resulting in little information about who is visiting the site and why.

Those who wish to study traditional museums have accurate information about their audience from ticket sales, subscription information, head counts, interviews, and surveys. Curators and creators of on-line museums have digital counterparts to these measures: We count hits, not heads, and provide a way to communicate with us through an on-line feedback form as opposed to a "comments" box. We also use unobtrusive measures. Webb, Campbell, Schwarz, and Sechrest (1966) suggest examining the tiles in front of various exhibits to see which are more worn, indicating greater popularity. Although curators of virtual museums cannot examine tiles or glass cases to see which show wear and tear, we can peruse log files and use software such as WebTrends to assess traffic to the site, without the sorts of errors inherent in self-reported information such as surveys. In this chapter, we attempt to outline some methods we used to construct a richer conception of the audience of the USC Interactive Art Museum. It is hoped that other researchers will be able to adapt some of our methodologies to suit their purposes.

Notes

1. Acknowledgments: USC Interactive Art Museum Project Team

Project Directors

(P. I.) Margaret McLaughlin, Professor, Annenberg School for Communication, USC Faculty, Integrated Media Systems Center, USC

(Co-P. I.) Selma Holo, Director, Fisher Gallery, USC Faculty, Integrated Media Systems Center, USC

(Co-P. I.) George Bekey, Gordon Marshall Professor of Engineering, USC Director, Robotics Research Laboratory, USC

(Co-P. I.) Ken Goldberg, Assistant Professor, Industrial Engineering and Operations Research University of California, Berkeley

(Co-P. I.) Ellen Strain, Department of Cinema-TV, Georgia Tech University

Interactive Museum Project Team

Yuichiro Akatsuka, Olympus Optical Company
Mirco Bresanelli, Robotics Research Laboratory, USC
Alan Case, School of Business Administration, USC
Nicole Ellison, Annenberg School for Communication, USC
Steve Goldberg, School of Engineering, USC
Jennifer Jaskowiak, Fisher Gallery, USC
Jason Lucas, Annenberg School for Communication, USC
Toyone Mayeda, School of Engineering, USC
Lana Norton, Fisher Gallery, USC
Peter Schertz, Fisher Gallery, USC
Sachiyo Sekiguchi, Annenberg School for Communication, USC
Kasey Sirody, Annenberg School for Communication, USC
Howard Smith, Art and Architecture Library, USC

This project has been funded by research grants from the Annenberg Center for Communication at the University of Southern California, with additional support from the Integrated Media Systems Center, a National Science Foundation Engineering Research Center, Hitachi America, Ltd., and the California Trade and Commerce Agency. The robot used in the Drinking Maiden exhibition is on loan from the Jet Propulsion Laboratory, Pasadena. Photographs of terra-cotta and marble statues on loan from the J. Paul Getty Museum, Malibu, California. Itinerary™ donated by Contigo Software. Search engine from Excite, Inc.

2. We are currently working with colleagues to develop a fuzzy logic-based intelligent agent for searching our database of images. The agent will be able to learn a user's preferences for images (colors, shapes, etc.) after a few trials and find like items in the database that would fit the user's needs or wants.

3. WebTrends is one of a number of commercially available software products for extracting data from server logs. We selected it for the main analysis of our log files because it offers certain speed advantages over competing products in dealing with large files and can process logs directly from the web server in .gz (zipped) format. We have also used Hit List Pro (http://www.marketwave.com), which uses a cumulative log file database as opposed to raw logs, and has some special features, such as the ability to generate reports of keywords used to bring visitors to the site, parsed by search engine of origin.

4. Efforts to identify visitors and count page requests are fraught with difficulty. Dreze and Zufryden (1997) sum up the two major impediments to precise measurement as (a) the problem of unique identification of visitors and (b) the issue of caching. With respect to the former, the use of proxy servers and dynamic Internet protocol address allocation by some Internet service providers requires us to regard our computations of "sessions" and "visitors" with a certain degree of skepticism. With respect to the issue of caching, web clients such as Netscape may pull previously viewed pages from the cache rather than request the page again from the web server, depending on how this parameter is adjusted when the client options are set. And large Internet access providers such as AOL may cache popular pages on their proxy servers. The net result of both is that the number of page accesses may be seriously underestimated. The use of cookies or user authorization procedures helps to address the first problem, although these techniques introduce ethical and methodological complications of their own.

5. Items for the feedback forms were written by Lana Norton and Peter Schertz of the Fisher Gallery at the University of Southern California.

References

Brown, K. H., Dartnall, C., Goodman, S., Hong, S., Marmion, A. J., Schertz, P. J. M., Jaskowiak, J., & Lenihan, M. (1996). *Light in darkness: Women in Japanese prints of early Showa (1926-1945)*. Exhibition Catalogue, Fisher Gallery, University of Southern California.

Casamassima, T. A., & Lineker, B. (1996). *Introduction to the American Landscapes* [On-line]. Available: http://digimuse.usc.edu/landscapes/America.html

Curtis, P. (1997). Mudding: Social phenomena in text-based virtual realities. In S. Kiesler (Ed.), *Culture of the Internet*. Hillsdale, NJ: Lawrence Erlbaum.

Dreze, X., & Zufryden, F. (1997). *Is Internet advertising ready for prime time?* Unpublished manuscript, Marshall School of Business, University of Southern California, Los Angeles.

Goldberg, K., Mascha, M., Gentner, S., Rothenberg, N., Sutter, C., & Wiegley, J. (1995, October). *Desktop teleoperation via the World Wide Web.* Paper presented at the IEEE International Conference on Robotics and Automation, Nagoya, Japan.

Goldberg, S. B., Bekey, G. A., Akatsuka, Y., & Bressanelli, M. (1997). *DIGIMUSE: Interactive remote viewing of three-dimensional art objects.* Internal report, USC Robotics Research Lab. [Available from Steve Goldberg, Robotics Research Laboratory, University of Southern California, Los Angeles, CA 90089]

Jones, S. G. (1995). *CyberSociety: Computer-mediated communication and community.* Thousand Oaks, CA: Sage.

Lombard, M., & Ditton, T. (1997). At the heart of it all: The concept of presence. *Journal of Computer-Mediated Communication* [On-line], *3*(2). Available: http://www.ascusc.org/jcmc/vol3/issue2/lombard.html

McLaughlin, M. L. (1996). The art site on the World Wide Web. *Journal of Communication, 46,* 51-79. See also McLaughlin, M. L. (1996). The art site on the World Wide Web. *Journal of Computer-Mediated Communication* [On-line], *1*(4). Available: http://www.usc.edu/dept/annenberg/vol1/issue4/mclaugh.html

McLaughlin, M. L., Osborne, K. K., & Ellison, N. B. (1997). Virtual community in a telepresence environment. In S. Jones (Ed.), *Virtual culture* (pp. 146-167). London: Sage.

Rafaeli, S., & Sudweeks, F. (1998). Interactivity on the nets. In F. Sudweeks, M. L. McLaughlin, & S. Rafaeli (Eds.), *Network and net-play: The virtual group on the Internet.* Menlo Park, CA: AAAI/MIT Press.

Schertz, P. M., Jaskowiak, J., & McLaughlin, M. L. (1998). Evaluation of an interactive art museum. *SPECTRA, 25*(1), 33-37.

Stone, A. R. (1996). *The war of desire and technology at the close of the mechanical age.* Cambridge: MIT Press.

Sudweeks, F., McLaughlin, M. L., & Rafaeli, S. (1998). *Network and net-play: The virtual group on the Internet.* Menlo Park, CA: AAAI/MIT Press.

Webb, E., Campbell, D. T., Schwarz, R. D., & Sechrest, L. (1966). *Unobtrusive measures: Nonreactive research in the social sciences.* Chicago: Rand McNally.

Zaleski, J. (1997). *The soul of cyberspace: How new technology is changing our spiritual lives.* New York: HarperCollins.

9

Analyzing the Web
Directions and Challenges

ANANDA MITRA
ELISIA COHEN

THE LATE 20TH CENTURY HAS WITNESSED the development and growth of the Internet much like the post-World War II era saw the growth of television. Use of the Internet, and applications such as the World Wide Web (WWW), is no longer a novelty but is becoming as commonplace as the use of the telephone and the television. To be sure, this increasing transparency of the Internet leads to questions about the impact of this technology on the lives of its users as well as nonusers. This chapter is a move toward developing a critical framework to begin to understand this phenomenon in a systematic way.

The use of the Internet is becoming increasingly ingrained as a global popular cultural activity, and before long, the networked computer could become as ubiquitous as the television. Billboards to television advertisements encourage the use of the "WWW" word, which is getting to be as common as phrases such as "toll free" (December & Randall, 1994). The WWW provides a public forum where everyone who has access to the

Internet is able to maintain a virtual presence in cyberspace while simultaneously consuming images placed on the WWW by its multitude of users. To provide a systematic way to understand the Internet and the WWW, this chapter first addresses some of the unique characteristics of the WWW and the analytical challenges posed by it. Eventually, we offer a few preliminary guidelines that address its uniqueness and provide directions for a thorough examination of the WWW phenomenon.

Past Research

The increasing popularity of the Internet and WWW has naturally attracted the attention of a vast body of researchers, ranging from philosophers to technocrats. In general, WWW research has progressed in two directions. First, there has been an attempt to examine the people who use the WWW. These "rating" studies have been empirical analyses of the extent of WWW use and the assessment of the behavior and opinions of the WWW users. Many of the major American polling companies such as Gallup and Nielson have entered into WWW ratings research. Given the dynamics of WWW use, with its rapid changes and the ongoing addition of innumerable users, any analysis of WWW usage yields conflicting results. Sometimes, however, such conflicting results are also the product of inadequate and untested (thus unreliable) methods of counting WWW users and obtaining data about their opinions and behaviors. Thus, researchers are often quick to point out that their results could be "dated" or slanted, depending on their methodology. One such example is the CommerceNet and Nielsen study that is updated frequently (see the information available at the address http://www.commerce.net/nielsen/press_97.html and at sites such as http://www.interlog.comEbxi/size.htm). In this case, there is an attempt to provide frequently updated counts of Internet users while recognizing that even the most carefully planned research can miss sections of users as they constantly move in and out of cyberspace.

The second kind of analysis has focused on the text exchanged by the users of the WWW. There is a presumption in this analysis that the WWW and the Internet can be considered a mass medium (Newhagen & Rafaeli, 1996). This perspective on the Internet, which legitimizes the analysis of the Internet's content, is supported by Morris and Ogan (1996), who contend that "the Internet is a multifaceted mass medium, that is, it contains many different configurations of communication" (p. 42). Clearly, the analysis of the message/text/discourse content has been more popular with exchanges observed in newsgroups.[1] However, popular recognition of the "mass media" appeal of the WWW turns attention to the WWW text. This interest leads researchers to examine questions about the content of the WWW.[2] In fact, debates around the censoring of the WWW text begin with the presumption that textual content can have specific effects on its audiences. However, how the effect might manifest and how the text can be analyzed has not been explored in great detail.

Both the user-based and the content-based approaches to the analysis of the Internet, however, recognize that the glue that holds the Internet together is the text exchanged between the different users of the Internet (Mitra, 1996, 1997a, 1997b). Here, *text* is used in a relatively broad sense without necessarily concentrating on the written word but also bringing into the analysis the associated multimedia images that are becoming common on the WWW. Users of the WWW simultaneously produce and consume these texts. Consequently, we argue that if this text can be analyzed systematically, it could shed some light not only on the content and implications of the text but also on the users who have produced the text.

By making the text central, questions about the content of the text can be supplemented with questions about "how" the text presents information. However, such an analytical move also calls for the mobilization of strategies of textual analysis that go beyond the more "reductionist" content analysis. In this chapter, we suggest the exploration of critical/cultural textual analysis to understand the WWW text. Using this approach, the focus is not only on the content of the WWW texts but also on the way in which the content is presented and on its significance. Furthermore, it is important to recognize that the image is the result of specific conditions of production that can determine the way the text becomes meaningful in the public sphere. The objective of critical textual analysis is to move beyond an analysis of the volume of text and its content to the level of understanding the effectivity of the text and what it says of the community of people who produce and consume the texts.[3] Critical textual analysis offers interpretations of how a text can become polysemous and effective when placed in the public domain of cyberspace. Critical textual analysis can thus focus on the central aspect of the WWW—its textuality—and begin to answer questions about the WWW by considering the unique characteristics of the text.

In most cases, the process of critical textual analysis considers three aspects of the text (see Berger, 1995; Fiske, 1987). First, it is necessary to look at the formal aspects of the text and its signifying strategies. This examination can be conducted in a variety of ways, such as semiotic analysis and structural analysis, to uncover the way in which one particular text is constructed. Second, critical textual analysis considers the way in which a single text is connected with other similar texts. This is the realm of inter-textuality in which the effectivity of a single text depends on the larger discourse it is a part of (e.g., Barthes, 1979; Beach & Anson, 1992; Chi, 1995; Fairclough, 1992; Fiske, 1987; Kristeva, 1980; Leitch, 1983; Moulthrop, 1989; Porter, 1986). It is presupposed that texts do not operate in a vacuum and that any text gains meaning from its own formal and aesthetic qualities, but meaning is refracted by the primary text's connection with other texts.[4] Finally, critical textual analysis considers the role of the various readers of the text who, through their reading, make the text meaningful. From this critical perspective, in the absence of the reading, the text has no meaning, and its very existence can be called into question.

Independent of the exact direction of the critical textual analysis, in the case of the WWW, the textual analyst is faced with a set of unique challenges based on the specific characteristics of the text. These characteristics are the products of the technology used to produce the texts. Thus, even before applying the critical tools to the WWW text, it is necessary to develop a set of strategies that can address the unique characteristics of the WWW text. Consequently, it is important to categorize some of the aspects of the WWW text that make it unique and to raise a set of methodological issues that need to be resolved before the analysis can be performed. This chapter is primarily an attempt to understand and explore these characteristics of the WWW text. We would argue that only after addressing the uniqueness of the WWW is it possible to move on to any specific kind of critical textual analysis.

Characteristics of the WWW

INTERTEXTUALITY

One WWW characteristic that sets it apart from traditional text is the overt intertextuality of the WWW texts. Unlike printed analog text, the virtual digital text offers the opportunity to connect various virtual texts with specific "links" that allow the reader to move from one text to another in an effortless manner. The WWW text has made these links appear natural and has made moving from one text to another very simple. Indeed, the ability to use the links and to move from one point in a particular text to another text is the strongest attribute of the WWW text. The analyst has to confront this phenomenon.

The uniqueness of the WWW is that it is placed in the public domain and is being used by a large number of people. In principle, this form of intertextuality is not necessarily new. Soon after World War II, Vannevar Bush suggested the potential usefulness of developing a system of interconnected texts that could be used in a related fashion to gather the greatest amount of information (see Barbacci's speech at http://vislab-www.nps.navy.mil/ ieee_stu/looking_forward/CompSoc_PresMsg.html). This also marked the beginning of the notion of *hyper* text, now a common term, often used and abused in the popular and academic literature. It is useful to digress for a moment to consider the notion of "hyper"ness with relation to texts. In essence, any phenomenon that has a sense of impermanence and unpredictability can be called "hyper." Being hyper constitutes the characteristic of being impatient and multiply extended. When applied to texts, this suggests that hypertext is a distant relation of traditional text, because by being hyper, the text can be expected to be multiply connected, impermanent, and infinitely stretched. Although Bush did not necessarily envision such a complex text, it did come to pass several years after Bush conceptualized such an interconnected textual system. Leapfrogging to the 1980s, this concept was actualized in the form of the HyperCard system—a development pioneered by Apple Computers. In this system, an author could create a stack of information contained on virtual "cards." The reader would be able to move seamlessly from one card to another as the reader followed an inquiry pattern linking the different cards (see http://www.pcwebopedia.com/ HyperCard.htm; http://www.glasscat.com/hypercard.cgi).[5]

This form of hypertext was limited by two primary constraints. First, the author needed to have collected all the information and connected it together in a fashion that all the cards were adequately networked and users did not reach "dead ends" in their explorations. Second, the information was limited to what the author would have collated on a single machine working by itself, disconnected from all other machines. Both of these constraints place limits on the scope of intertextuality.

These constraints, however, disappear in the case of the WWW. The WWW text is truly hyper because every WWW text can be in some way connected to another. This is what makes the WWW particularly attractive to analysts because the WWW text is far larger in scope than any past hypertext. There is a certain "infinite" aspect to the WWW text, because it is always possible to move on from a page and never stop or reach the "end" of the text. In fact, there might be little logical connection between the texts, but given the hyperness of the textual form, it is perfectly possible, for instance, to move from the home page of Cable News Network (CNN) to the product specifications of a specific kind of computer manufactured by a corporation called Bravo.[6] Thus, the movement from one page to another can happen in any way the reader chooses to move. It is this seamless intertextuality that the analyst has to confront.

At the same time, the notion of intertextuality has always been a component of literary and textual production and analysis. Authors of texts do not usually work in a cultural vacuum, and thus, their work is almost always intertextual because of the way in which existing and past texts tend to impinge on new texts. For example, it is difficult to write a spy fiction without in some ways being influenced by the number of such fictions written in the past. Analysts, critics, and scholars recognize this tendency in authors, and analysts are able to point toward textual characteristics that reflect a text's connections with other preceding texts. Connections with other texts not only point toward textual characteristics but also to the conditions of the text's production and the way in which one text, along with its intertextual connections, can become a commentary on the cultural arena within which the texts are produced and consumed. The recognition of the necessary intertextuality of texts led to the development of theories of genre in literary and media studies, the use of the syntagmatic and paradigmatic structure of texts to point toward vertical and horizontal intertextuality, the development of the syntactic and semantic approach to genre, and other approaches to understanding the interconnection between texts. In all these cases, however, there is a presumption that the intertextuality of the texts needs to be "teased" out of the text and that the intertextuality is not necessarily overt but is often embedded in the style and narrative of the texts. This presumption, however, disappears in the case of hypertext.

For the WWW text, the intertextuality is not implicit or hidden. Rather, it is explicit and unambiguous, and the effectivity of hypertext often depends on its extent of intertextuality. Because hypertextuality can be synonymous with intertextuality, the raison d'être for the WWW text is its intertextuality. Landow (1992b) points this out to say that the nature of hypertext depends on its connections with other texts and not on its singular existence (also see Aarseth, 1993; Bernstein, 1990, 1991; Bolter, 1990, 1991, 1992; Bolter & Joyce, 1987; Joyce, 1991; Landow, 1992a, 1994; Moulthrop, 1994). The analyst is thus no longer attempting to ferret out the nature of the intertextuality but often has to be more interested in the extent of the intertextuality and the way in which the intertextual quality of the text serves as the source of its meaning. In some cases, a WWW text might be no more than a well-organized index of "links" to other pages, but in the case of WWW texts, such an "index" becomes meaningful vis-à-vis the particular links it offers and what it does not offer. For example, the setup of the CNN site provides a visitor an option to scan through the top news stories of a particular day and then click on the "index" to access the complete story, which in turn can lead to other stories about the same issue. Sometimes, the additional links will provide access to information beyond the domain of CNN and then provide the reader with an option to be intertextual in an elaborate way, exploring information that would be unavailable from traditional linear text. In other words, the notion of intertextuality becomes far more central in the analysis of WWW texts than it has been in the analysis of other texts. Indeed, this focus on intertextuality leads to the examination of a set of other unique characteristics of hypertext that are often products of the explicit and necessary intertextuality of hypertext—its resultant nonlinearity.

NONLINEARITY

Traditionally, texts have been characterized by having a specific beginning and a recognizable end (Aarseth, 1994; Levi-Strauss, 1955; Propp, 1975; Todorov, 1977). Narrative analysis has paid attention to this element of the text. Narrative theorists have made the argument that stories are arranged around a specific structure in which the flow from the beginning to the end of the story is geared by a logic that eventually makes the end appear natural and obvious. Furthermore, in the case of most printed texts, there is a progression in the reading of the text in which the sections of the text appear in a specific order, and lacking that order, the text would become meaningless. This is the logic of grammar and the codes of language that connect the discrete elements of the text together. All these are the characteristics of the linear text.

Hypertext, however, presents the reader with a different set of assumptions. With its overt intertextuality, hypertext challenges the presumption of linearity in two ways. First, the fundamental presumption that there needs to be a well-recognized beginning and end is problematized.[7] In the case of the WWW hypertext, it is impossible to determine what can be the authentic beginning of the text. Although every site on the WWW presents a top and bottom of a page, that is only a microscopic part of the WWW discourse. When considered as a part of the larger WWW text, any page provides only a point of entry into the mammoth labyrinth of texts where the beginning and end become particularly difficult to identify.

The second way in which the WWW text challenges linearity is through the overt intertextuality of the text. Unlike other texts, the WWW text is self-consciously intertextual, constantly inviting the reader to move to another textual node. The presumption of reading to the end is replaced by the expectation that the reader will "explore" and "surf" to follow the links that appear in the text. Here the notion of surfing is similar to the description provided in the *PC Webopaedia,* which describes surfing as what occurs when "the user jumps from page to page rather whimsically, as opposed to specifically searching for specific information" (http://www.pcwebopedia. com/surf.htm). In the case of more primitive hypertext, the possibilities of exploration were limited because the texts were contained within one computer. However, in the networked version of hypertext, the limits are far less visible.

This hyperness also changes the role of the reader. The text no longer presumes that all readers will gain the same meaning from the text. This polysemic potential of the text was already recognized in the case of traditional texts. Witness how Eco (1972) pointed toward the readerly texts open for multiple interpretations. However, even within Eco's perspective, the reader has little control on the textual flow, and the reader remains imprisoned within the finite beginning and end of the text. In the case of hypertext, however, the reader is liberated to produce whatever text the reader pleases, given the overt nonlinear connections the text provides. Thus, it is important to reconsider the role of the reader in the understanding of hypertext.

THE READER AS WRITER

The role of the reader/audience of traditional texts has typically been one of "receiver" who reads the text in a relatively passive manner. Any introductory text on communication makes the argument that the audience or the receiver of a message is relatively passive and, particularly for mass-mediated message, has few options for "feedback." The only sense of agency counterbalancing the passivity is that readers bring to the text a series of ideologies that can inform the way in which meaning is produced from the text. For example, Hall (1980) suggests that the decoding process in the reading of text is implicated by the position a reader takes with respect to the dominant ideology. From these arguments, there has been the recognition that the audience of media is empowered to the extent that readers may not accept the preferred meaning of the text but gain only the meaning that fits with their everyday experiences. Nevertheless, the reader is not empowered to alter the original text but only to use it in the fashion that he or she chooses. De Certeau (1984) also presents this argument by claiming that the passive reader is only partly empowered by using the text to produce a very socially and politically contextualized meaning. However, this process is not truly an active process and is constrained because linear texts are typically static and written with well-defined and preferred meanings built around specific beginnings and endings.

The nonlinear text, with its overt intertextuality, however, invites the reader to take up a much more active role in the reading process. The links from the text call for exploration, and the meaning produced by selecting a set of links could be very different from the meaning produced by selecting an alternative set of links. Even though an author of hypertext might control the specific links provided from the text, there is little control on the links that one of the other pages might provide. The author can thus only "contain" the potential of meaning to a limited degree, and the reader can "explode" the potential meanings extensively by selecting a set of links preferred by the reader. This, we argue, is a unique characteristic of the WWW text, in which the reader needs to recognize the potential offered by the text and explore it in a way to construct a hypertext that he or she chooses. In this context, the reader becomes the author because the reader is the agent who actively selects the links to follow.

This changing role of the reader calls into question the responsibilities of the author. The author is expected to give the reader the potential to transcend the role of a passive reader to an active reauthor of the text as he or she follows and explores the links offered by the primary author. The struggle over meaning thus shifts from the centrality of the linear text to the decentered potential offered by the nonlinear text. The author is no longer bound to producing a preferred meaning but only offers a large set of potential meanings, and the reader now has the responsibility of collaborating with the author, or undermining the author, to reauthor the text to produce the customized meaning.

Thus, in the context of the WWW, the responsibilities of authoring and the responsibilities of conscientious reading change. An author has the responsibility of providing the maximum potential for the production of meaning, and the reader has the responsibility of exploring those potentials. This enlarged potential for meaning is actualized with the use of the technological possibilities of "multimedianess" that the WWW text offers.

THE MULTIMEDIA WWW

The meaning produced from the text depends largely on the polysemous potential of the text. If the text is relatively "open," it is likely that many meanings can be produced from the text. Indeed, this openness is the notion of polysemy that critical scholars claim to be an essential element of any text (see Fiske, 1987). In the case of traditional printed text, meaning was constrained because the text was composed primarily of words and sentences that presented narratives with occasional use of pictures. In many ways, the printed text was made up of the symbolic sign as suggested by Pierce (1985) and occasionally used the iconic sign to supplement the symbols. On the other hand, in the case of audiovisual texts, such as television and film, the text did not offer the possibility of using the printed word but was principally iconic in nature. Thus, both these texts were constrained in their potential for polysemy.

The WWW text, however, offers a convergence of different kinds of representational strategies. Given the technological tools available to the author of the WWW text, it is possible to combine the written word with audiovisual images. Consequently, the WWW is a medium in which the characteristics of the book and television are combined to produce a non-linear text whose meaning is the product of the synergy between the two different kinds of texts.[8]

The multimedianess of the WWW text is a significant element of the text. The continuing changes in technology are making the WWW text look like television. Improved technologies of video compression, developments in better data transmission technology, and speedier processors in computers are making it possible to supplement the written text of the WWW with streaming video and audio.[9] Thus, the written word is not only hyperactive in the WWW text, but its meaning is constantly implicated by the multimedia images that accompany the text. Furthermore, given the hyperlinked nature of the WWW text, it is not necessary for the author of the written word to be the originator of the video and audio components. It is quite simple for the author to provide links to other WWW texts that provide the images and sounds, and to the reader, such "borrowing" might not be immediately evident because of the seamless connection between hypertext links. The role of the author is thus further altered because the author is not only the creator of new texts (and meanings) but also the facilitator of meanings by providing an index of specific WWW texts and images available in cyberspace.

The author does not produce these images but simply provides access to them, thus altering the meaning of the text that the author offers and the reader uses.

Furthermore, given the way in which the Internet backbone of the WWW delivery system has become increasingly global, the author can choose from images and texts that could reside thousands of miles apart, but those distances can disappear when the author weaves them together into one page. Given the global reach of the multimedianess of the WWW text, it is important to consider the ways in which the author has the global depository of texts to work with.

THE GLOBAL WWW

Hypertext has advanced from HyperCard to an interconnected multimedia system that spans the entire globe. This explosion of the connectivity offered by the Internet has not only reshaped the way humans can communicate over long distances but also expanded the access to texts that can be used to produce a site on the WWW. An author now has the option of using texts from nationally diverse sources and linking the sources and sites together to produce the author's own text. However, this global reach also resulted in the emergence of a set of characteristics of the WWW text that can affect the polysemic potential of the WWW text.

The first significance of the global reach of the WWW text is that it is constrained by language. Increasingly, the *lingua franca* of the WWW is English. This has, however, been contested, and there continue to be arguments about the implications of English becoming the unofficial global language of the WWW. Resistance to this tendency appears in the form of WWW sites written in different languages, some of which might use the English script, but many of which use a different script altogether. Witness, for instance, a site written in the Bengali language using the Devanagari script (http://www.parabaas.com). The page is produced by creating the documents as image files and then providing the image files as the primary content of the site. Similarly, numerous sites are written in the Japanese and Chinese scripts. Such sites remain inaccessible to readers unfamiliar with the language. Thus, the reader of the global WWW text could be lost in a sector of cyberspace where the language is unintelligible. For the segment of the global population who can, however, read, write, and understand English, much of the WWW space remains accessible.

In the context of the WWW text, because of its nonlinear hypertextuality, it is quite possible for a text that begins in English to lead to a text that is not in English. The reader then faces an artifact quite different from a text in which the language remains linear and static and is expected to remain the same across the entire text.

A second significance of the global reach of the WWW lies in the fact that authors have access to material that was previously unavailable due to barriers of distance and time. Given that WWW texts are available instantaneously to anyone on the WWW, it is far simpler now to access any material on the WWW and link it to an author's page. It matters little if the destinations of two links are separated by thousands of miles; in the technologically seamless cyberspace, such distances are inconsequential, and the reader can "transparently" hover between texts that might have been produced in different corners of the globe under different conditions of production. Using the presumption that the meaning of a text is influenced by its conditions of production, a text produced within the "free speech" environment of America could be quite different in meaning from a text produced under a more oppressive system of government. However, to the reader, these WWW texts can appear next to each other and in their juxtaposition can produce meanings that neither of the texts could have created individually. The global linkages offered by the WWW produce the possibility of combining texts from different national sources and create different potentials of meaning.

The matter is further complicated because this global WWW text is virtual; its only tangible existence lies in hard copy paper printouts that might be produced by the reader. In the case of a hyperconnected text, there is no tangible trace of a text that links together files in different continents. It is meant for this text to be read on the monitor of a multimedia computer. This virtuality also lends it an element of impermanence.

THE DISAPPEARING HYPERTEXT

The hyperconnected WWW text does not reside in any particular tangible medium. As Negroponte (1995) has pointed out, in entering the digital era, many artifacts have a "byte"-based existence, where the atoms are replaced by binary bits. Although the traditional artifact would be something that one can touch, the contemporary text of the WWW is a set of images that can be viewed on the computer screen. It is futile to want to create a printed version of the WWW because it would not only be extremely voluminous, but it would also be completely purposeless without its hyperlinkage. WWW texts thus reside as computer files on innumerable computers across the globe, and these files are most often authored and maintained by individual owners of files. Some are owned and controlled by large corporations and conglomerates, but by and large, the files belong to individuals or small groups.

These file owners also often exercise their ability to remove the files from the public domain, change the content of the files, remove links from the files, and add multimedia information to the textual files. Such changes can have a "ripple" effect in cyberspace because if a single file changes, hundreds of other files linked to it would also change because those links now point to a new and different text. When a file disappears, numerous links can deliver the reader to a dead end where the reader is greeted with an error message. Given the ease with which it is possible to manipulate bits and digital objects, it is often the case that the WWW text tends to change with no warning. In some cases, the text is expected to change. A group that might provide WWW-based news is expected to change its information frequently so that the reader has access to the most recent news. However, as the files change, there is no guarantee that the previous version of the file is retained. Unless the reader is printing out the digital images, it is quite likely that earlier versions of files will disappear.

Unlike the traditional text, with its central focus on a linear "stand-alone" text, the digital text of the WWW might not leave any traces of its existence. As a file disappears and other authors feel the ripple effect, they may simply remove the link to the nonexistent file, and soon, all traces of that file would vanish from cyberspace. It could be impossible to reconstruct that text unless the author was willing to resurrect the file from a personal archive. This phenomenon makes the WWW text far too ephemeral and impermanent. This is, however, significant because it points toward a specific characteristic of the text that sets it apart from other types of text.

The consequence of impermanence calls into question the criteria that can be used to judge the "value" of a text. The traditional text, the printed word or the images created by an artist or a musician, lends itself to some presumptions of permanence. In such cases, if texts disappeared from the public domain because of a lack of public interest, that disappearance could be a telling commentary on the text. In the case of the WWW, the disappearance is not a function of the reader's interest in the text but of the author's intention to remove the text from the public domain. The author can erase a text from cyberspace even if the text was getting multiple visits. In the case of the traditional text, the author has little control over that.

In summary, the WWW text has a set of specific characteristics predicated by its hypertextuality. These characteristics include the nonlinear nature of the text, its global reach, and its use of the multiple images borrowing from different media. Eventually, this special text is also far more ephemeral than its predecessors. The analyst of WWW hypertext needs to consider these unique characteristics carefully before being able to analyze the text. In the next section, we present some of the key questions the analyst needs to address in the process of crystallizing the analytical approach.

Analytical Questions

WHERE TO BEGIN THE ANALYSIS?

Given the large volume of WWW texts and that these texts are intertextually connected to each other, a critical question concerning textual analysis is deciding on what could be considered a starting point. In the case of traditional linear texts, which were not hypertextual, it was far simpler to consider a central text around which the analysis could be performed. Thus, textual studies of media typically focused on a single text and then analyzed that text, perhaps in relation to other, related texts.[10] The nonlinear and hyperconnected text of the WWW, however, problematizes this fundamental centrality of the text. If an analyst wanted to understand the representation of a particular concept on the WWW, there could be numerous texts that address the topic. From this abundance, the critic has to choose what might appear to be the best starting point of the analysis and then be able to defend that choice.

Two criteria appear to be critical in making this choice. First, because of the hypertextuality of the WWW text, those texts best connected could serve as legitimate starting points for the analysis. This claim is made on the basis of the various characteristics of the WWW text, all of which point to the uniqueness of the WWW text stemming from its being interconnected with other texts. The second assumption that underlies the claim is that the goal is to select a text that represents, or speaks to, a particular issue, compared with starting with a predefined text. Usually, the researcher has to make a choice between various sites, and in such cases, the two deciding factors could be the number of hyperlinks the site offers and the number of times the site has been cited by other pages.

The first factor addresses the way in which a text is able to use the unique characteristics of hypertext to produce an Internet presence that provides the opportunity of surfing and hovering beyond the text. Based on the earlier discussion of the characteristics of hypertext, it is clear that the greater the opportunities of surfing provided by the text, the greater the likelihood that readers are empowered to "write" their own texts. WWW sites that remain "closed-ended" do not provide empowerment to readers and could thus be far less suitable as the starting point of the analysis. These pages often address localized and special interests, and the pages can be self-contained. Consider, for instance, the page related to a private business, an Internet toy "store," or even a sporting event such as the Kentucky Derby horse race (see, http://www.reds.com; http://www.toys.com; http://www.kdf.org). These texts are limited in scope and fail to use the full potential of the WWW.

The second factor, based on the number of citations to the page, is a measure of the extent to which a page is recognized among other pages that deal with the same issue. A page that is better cited is likely to be more hypertextually connected than pages that exist in isolation. There are two primary ways of determining the "popularity" of a site. The thorough way is to use Web-mapping tools that can work as intelligent agents and provide a visual and numeric map of the connections between the texts. Such tools are available on the WWW itself and can be used to map Web sites, indicating the different links available from the site. A second, somewhat imprecise method is to use a "surrogate" measure of citation—the number of "hits" or visits to the page. Most pages offer a "hit counter" that records the number of times a page has been visited in a given span of time. This number can be an indicator of the popularity of the page. The disadvantage with this method is that hit counters can be manipulated, and the number of visits might not really indicate the number of visits by different readers but visits by a small group of readers. In the latter situation, the hit counter might not be the best measure. Nevertheless, two key factors should be considered: (a) the number of links *from* the page and (b) the number of links *to* the page. This focus on links is a direct result the fact that WWW pages gain their meaning and purpose from the interconnectedness designated by the links.

It is also important, however, to note that the starting point of the analysis must not be given too much importance. In the interconnected world of the WWW, a starting point serves only as a gateway and could end up being the most inconsequential part of the analysis. Because the WWW produces interconnected texts that have a constant decentering tendency, to concentrate on a starting point is to deny the WWW text its greatest strength.

Furthermore, the starting point itself is a provisional locus because the WWW texts are notoriously impermanent. There have been instances in which the starting point simply ceases to exist after a while, and if the focus had been primarily on the starting point, the research is doomed.[11] Thus, the decision about the starting point is immediately followed by the question about the stopping point, or how deep into hypertext one needs to go in the process of analyzing the interconnected text. In other words, the question is, How many texts to analyze?

HOW MANY TEXTS TO ANALYZE?

Given their abundance, innumerable texts can address a specific issue. For instance, a search for the word *Calcutta,* the city where Mother Theresa worked, yielded about a thousand "hits" when a search was conducted the day after her funeral in Calcutta. It is clear, when considering the WWW, that the text analyst is faced with a plethora of texts. Because of the interconnected nature of the WWW, there is an expectation that the researcher will go beyond the starting point of the analysis. In doing so, the research process prompts the question, How many links to follow and where to stop and turn back?

The answer, in our estimation, lies in the research question that motivates the textual analysis. If the question is primarily topical—that is, with the goal of investigating the extent to which a particular issue is addressed by WWW texts—the textual analysis needs to include all the different ways in which the issue is approached on the WWW. Thus, the analyst has to explore most of the links that the primary page offers, and then begin to categorize similar links and concepts. In many ways, this is a process similar to genre analysis as suggested by Altman (1987), who maintained that to understand a genre it is necessary to develop a syntactic/semantic map of the content of representative texts and then use that typology to delve into other texts that fall into the genre. Similarly, in the case of the large number of WWW texts, it is likely that the analyst would find several texts that fall into the same genre, and selecting representations from the different genres could provide the data for making claims about the collection of text. This process is facilitated by the use of standard Web mappers that create a visual representation indicating what texts are related to each other and how the specific categories can be developed. Often, the title of the WWW site provides ample directions for judgment. Consider, for instance, the way in which pages present information on broad interest areas. The AT&T "India Horizons" page (http://

www.att.com/indiahorizons/) is an example of a site that provides a list of sites that deal with various aspects of the country. This page can thus work as a starting point to develop categories that can inform the analytical process. The presumption in this process is that the quantity of texts analyzed is less critical than careful examination of a selection of texts that address various components of the issue being examined.

On the other hand, if the research is driven by the need to analyze a particular site on the WWW and then explore other texts from the starting point, a slightly different approach can be considered. In such cases, the Web mapper provides a good starting point, because it shows the different levels of connections provided from a seed text. It is important here to consider the notion of "levels" in the analysis of the WWW. Pages on the WWW are connected with each other by varying degrees of separation. Any text on the WWW can potentially lead to any other text on the WWW independent of any topical logic. This phenomenon can, for instance, be witnessed with the appearance of banner advertising on WWW pages. For example, a user wanting to seek information on any particular issue could use the "Net Search" option provided by a popular WWW browser and access one of several search engines. However, the search engine sites often have advertisements that could be completely unrelated to what the surfer wants but that could entice the surfer to move in a direction totally unrelated to the user's original purpose.

However, even the logical connections between texts begin to disintegrate with greater degrees of separation between the texts. We define degrees of separation as the number of links that a user has to follow to move from one site to another. Degrees of separation can be measured by the number of "clicks" necessary to go from one WWW page to another. This can be mapped with the use of a Web mapper, and a researcher can designate the degrees of separation desired. Thus, if the interest is in the CNN Home Page (http://www.cnn.com), it is possible to begin with the CNN page and decide that three degrees of separation is what the researcher is interested in and then consider the texts that fall within that distance of the seed text. Larger degrees of separation will result in the inclusion of greater numbers of texts. It is likely, therefore, that the more the degrees of separation, the greater would be the need to classify and categorize the texts so that a representation of the texts could be examined more closely. Thus, the decision about the degrees of separation could be made on the basis of the purpose of the analysis. In the case of the example of the search engine page, the connection would be lost within one level of separation.

It is, however, important to provide a word of caution at this point. It is often tempting to settle on an arbitrary degree of separation. This needs to be avoided. Instead, it is necessary to do some exploratory work that can provide indications about the number of degrees of separation that retain a logical connection. For instance, if the issue under examination is particularly narrow, it is possible that as the degrees of separation increase, there is an increasing reciprocity among the texts. Thus, text "A" might lead to "B," which leads to "C," and after the second degree of separation, "C" might lead back to "A" because a loop has been completed. In such cases, the second degree of separation could be enough, but this needs to be explored in detail before settling on a definitive answer.

A third criterion in deciding on the number of pages has to do with the authorship of pages. A researcher has to confront a plethora of authors who produce texts and make them available for circulation. However, unlike for traditional texts, these authors did not use any mass production system or mass distribution system to bring the texts to the public domain. Indeed, the strength of the WWW stems from the authors' being empowered to produce texts and "publish" them without the need for any mediation of a centralized publication and circulation system. In this individualized authoring and publication scenario, anyone with the right computing tools now has the world as an audience. This produces a Babel of texts whose authenticity and reliability are constantly called into question because they do not represent the traditional "authentic," but centralized, sources of information. Thus, a common question asked among undergraduate students using the WWW for research is precisely about what would be considered reliable. Yet in raising this question, the very rationale of the WWW is compromised. The technology of the WWW has, for the first time, provided a space where everyone can have a voice, and in questioning the authenticity of the voice, by couching the question in the language of empirical reliability, the very purpose of the WWW is undermined.

The dilemma faced by the researcher of the WWW text is not unlike the confusion a college sophomore faces when the WWW search engine spews out thousands of hits when he or she is looking for the occurrence of a key word in the WWW space. The researcher too needs to consider which authors to include and who to exclude from close scrutiny. One of the best ways of making that decision is to use the strategy outlined earlier—develop typologies, categorize, and select from the groups of texts. This might not lead to a focus on all the authors, but this strategy could ensure that the authors who would be considered authentic and reliable by the traditional yardsticks are not privileged in cyberspace. After all, that an author has placed a work in cyberspace makes it likely that the text will be read and that the text will have an impact. Often, it is the impact and effectivity that might be more critical to the researcher than focusing on known authors. Pages of special interest groups with specific political agendas and points of view are illustrative. Notable among these are radical political groups that have now found a "voice" on the WWW, as Barlow (1997) suggested by saying, "Suddenly, overnight, the odious have their podium" (p. 73). In such cases, the author remains far less important than the point of view being presented by a set of WWW sites (see Zickmund, 1997). By not considering the texts of the unknown authors, the altered role of the individual author in cyberspace is ignored.

The issue of recognition and finding "authentic" sources is further problematized by the global nature of the nonlinear text and the way in which the text is recombinant—a virtual pastiche of a variety of textual elements, including visual and aural images. The author is no longer stabilized within a particular geographic space but is indeed a global and nomadic author and may combine elements of original text with recycled material "borrowed" and digitally appropriated from other authors or simply co-opted by a hypertextual link. These tendencies call into question the specificity of the author as well as the need to address the different authors residing in cyberspace.

Thus, the number of texts to analyze can often be determined by a careful process of exploration and categorization. Once the groups have been developed, it would be possible to select a few of the texts to be considered for more careful analysis. However, one final challenge remains for the analyst. Even the selected texts might not remain available for analysis too long. The analyst has to confront the impermanence of the WWW text.

THE IMPERMANENT TEXT

As discussed earlier, the WWW texts do not often have a specific tangible mooring. The researcher thus has to be acutely aware that the text under scrutiny is subject to disappear from the public domain with little warning. This is exemplified by users' often being confronted with the well-known "404" error that says that the location was not found. Indeed, this phenomenon has become so well-known among WWW users that the word has entered the popular cultural language of users, as illustrated below:

404—Someone who's clueless. From the World Wide Web message "404, URL
Not Found," meaning that the document you've tried to access can't be located.
"Don't bother asking him . . . he's 404, man." (Anonymous, 1997)[12]

This disappearance is taken for granted, and authors of the texts do not
provide any assurance that the texts are permanent. This textual characteristic
requires the researcher to retain records of the texts being examined. More
important, the researcher has to make it clear that the results of the analysis
are always provisional because the subject of analysis is impermanent.

Because texts become meaningful through reading, the role of a text or a
series of texts is called into question when the text disappears from the public
sphere. Even though there might be traces left as saved files and occasional
hard copies, the text is meaningless if it cannot be accessed by anyone on the
WWW. The researcher has little control of this process, other than making it
clear in the analysis that the result of the analysis is a snapshot of cyberspace.
The role of the analyst is thus not only to understand the process of transformation by synchronically examining the traces of the text but also to speculate on the implications of the disappearance of the text. In some cases, the
disappearance of the text can be a telling phenomenon, and in its absence,
the text can take on posthumous meaning.[13] Thus, if a text is deliberately
removed from the public cybersphere, it is necessary to explore why that
might have happened and what it implies. Sometimes, such disappearance is
also contestable because even if the author might have removed the text from
the public domain, a mirror image of the text might remain somewhere, and
the audience can find such a presence of the text.

It is thus important for the researcher to acknowledge this impermanence
of the text and recognize two principal implications of the impermanence.
First, the researcher needs to be able to demonstrate that a trace of the text
was maintained. Keeping a "copy" of the text could accomplish this. Second,
the researcher needs to be able to demonstrate that the implications of the
text's disappearance were considered. Questions about the reasons for the
disappearance need to be deliberated and an analytical approach needs to be
taken to understand the implications of the disappearance.

Summary

The WWW text poses a unique analytical challenge because of its characteristics. An analyst is confronted with a textual form that has many elements

of the traditional text and is thus open to analysis with time-tested tools. Thus, it is possible to consider a critical textual analysis, a narrative analysis, a semiotic analysis, or a combination of these approaches when tackling the WWW text. Similarly, the concepts of "discourse community," methods of discourse analysis as suggested by Bakhtin (1981) and Foucault (1979), can be used to understand the relation between the WWW text and society, just as the structural analysis of the text in the tradition of Barthes (1975) and Eco (1972) can be conducted to uncover the ways in which the WWW texts take on specific meanings. However, independent of the critical approach used, there is a set of fundamental concerns about the uniqueness of the text that needs to addressed. These are the issues related to the specificity of the text—its inherent intertextuality, its lack of center, its volume, its multimediainess, its international scope, its impermanence, and the resulting altered sense of authorship. If these elements are not taken into consideration, the critical analysis will be incomplete and unreliable. Consequently, this chapter provides some guidelines that can be used to address the uniqueness of the WWW text.

Furthermore, because of the differences between traditional texts and the WWW text, the traditional methods of analysis can be called into question as well. What has worked well for traditional texts might not be smoothly transferable to the new text. Thus, the theoretical underpinnings of the traditional analytical methods need to be rethought. Such challenges offer the opportunity to reexamine the methods that have worked well with the traditional texts and consider how the methods themselves can be modified to address the emerging textual form. It would be a mistake to force the methods on a textual form that offers the opportunity to improve on our existing methods. It is far more useful to ensure that the traditional methods have been rethought to "fit" the specificity of the new text. In such negotiations between the text and the critical approach, it is possible not only to improve methodologies but also to develop fresh theoretical understanding of the hypertext phenomenon on the WWW.

Notes

1. Significant attention has been paid to the textual strategies used in computer-mediated communication. Witness for example, the elaboration on the phenomenon of "flaming" and "spamming" on one hand, and the development of netiquette and emoticons on the other hand. This body of research acknowledged the textuality of the Internet exchanges and then probed the specific aspects of the textuality, such as flaming and spamming (Dubrovsky, Kiesler, &

Sethna, 1991; Hiltz, Turoff, & Johnson, 1989; McLaughlin, Osborne, & Smith, 1995; Thompsen & Ahn, 1992; Siegel, Dubrovsky, Kiesler, & McGuire, 1986; Smolensky, Carmody, & Halcomb, 1990; Weisband, 1992). This text-based research is now being extended to explore the representational strategies used in the production of the WWW texts.

2. For instance, with reference to the sexually explicit textual content of the Internet, a great deal of controversy surrounds the issue of indecency, obscenity, and pornography on the WWW. The focus of this debate has been on the proposal of the Communications Decency Act and the eventual rounds of discussion that followed about the means that can be used to control the presence and availability of indecent material on the Web.

3. Here, a specific critical approach to textual analysis is being adopted. Such an approach is informed by the work of textual analysts such as Fiske, Barthes, Eco, and others who have used the tools of semiotics and structuralism to begin to uncover the various "layers" of texts and the role of the text in popular culture.

4. This is the area of research that addresses the question of textual similarities and conventions. Witness for instance, the vast amount of research in the analysis of genres of literary texts and film (Altman, 1987; Neale, 1981, 1990). These bodies of scholarship point toward the inherent similarities of texts and how texts can be arranged and categorized around specific representational conventions.

5. For instance, if the cards address Shakespearean literature, a user could look at Shakespeare's work, move to cards about Victorian England, and then move to information about contemporary production of the Bard's work.

6. The trail was created by five clicks as follows:

CNN Home Page of September 5, 1997
CNN Miami Voter's Story (first click)
AST—Bravo advertisement (second click)
New Bravo MS-LC page (third click)
AST Bravo LC 6233 (fourth click)
Bravo LC 6233 Specs (fifth and last click)

7. Aarseth (1994) provides an elaborate analysis of the constitutive elements of nonlinear texts and argues that nonlinear text is made up of units that are unpredictable in their construction and are thus not adaptable to the location of a beginning or end.

8. McLuhan (1964) drew a distinction between the "hot" and "cool" medium, attempting to find a difference between media that excited different senses in different ways. Using that model, it was possible to distinguish between media such as the book and television. However, in the case of WWW text, that distinction begins to disappear.

9. The innovation of "streaming" video and audio allows authors of the WWW text to send video and audio messages rapidly. This technology does not require time-consuming downloading of the video and audio files, but the images come to the screen in a continuous fashion, making the process more efficient.

10. There are numerous examples of such studies from scholars such as Barthes (1973, 1975, 1977), Eco (1972), Fiske (1987, 1989), and Fiske and Hartley (1978). These authors demonstrate how to analyze texts in association with other texts that might surround the primary texts.

11. There is evidence of this phenomenon in researching the Web. This is related to Web sites becoming obsolete and disappearing, and in other cases, the pages are changed without notice, thus posing challenges to the researcher.

12. From an anonymous e-mail spam received by one of the authors.

13. The process of disappearance is often the result of a site's becoming particularly popular or important. Disappearance in such cases could be because the site merges with a bigger site and thus takes on a far more important role in cyberspace. Such disappearance can suggest that a WWW site was so important that it needed to "grow out" of its original modest shell.

References

Aarseth, E. J. (1994). Non-linearity and literary theory. In G. P. Landow (Ed.), *Hypertext theory* (pp. 87-120). Baltimore, MD: Johns Hopkins University Press.

Altman, R. (1987). *The American film musical.* Bloomington: Indiana University Press.

Bakhtin, M. M. (1981). *The dialogic imagination* (M. Holmquist, ed.; C. Emersam & M. Holmquist, trans.). Austin: University of Texas Press.

Barlow, J. P. (1997). The best of all possible worlds. *Communications of the ACM, 40*(2), 69-74.

Barthes, R. (1973). *Mythologies.* London: Paladin.

Barthes, R. (1975). *The pleasure of the text.* New York: Hill & Wang.

Barthes, R. (1977). *Image-music-text.* London: Fontana.

Barthes, R. (1979). From work to text. In J. Harrari (Ed.), *Textual strategies: Perspectives in poststructuralist criticism.* Ithaca, NY: Cornell University Press.

Beach, R., & Anson, C. M. (1992). Stance and intertextuality in written discourse. *Linguistics and Education, 4,* 335-357.

Berger, A. A. (1995). *Cultural criticism: A primer of key concepts.* Thousand Oaks, CA: Sage.

Bernstein, M. (1990). An apprentice that discovers hypertext links. In A. Rizk et al. (Eds.), *Hypertexts: Concepts, systems and applications* (pp. 212-223). Cambridge, UK: Cambridge University Press.

Bernstein, M. (1991). The navigation problem reconsidered. In E. Berk & J. Devlin (Eds.), *Hypertext/hypermedia handbook.* New York: McGraw-Hill.

Bolter, J. D. (1990). Topographic writing: Hypertext and the electronic writing space. In G. P. Landow & P. Delany (Eds.), *Hypermedia and literary studies.* Cambridge: MIT Press.

Bolter, J. D. (1991). *Writing space: The computer, hypertext, and the history of writing.* Hillsdale, NJ: Lawrence Erlbaum.

Bolter, J. D. (1992). Literature and electronic learning space. In M. C. Tuman (Ed.), *Literacy online* (pp. 19-42). Pittsburgh: University of Pittsburgh Press.

Bolter, J. D., & Joyce, M. (1987). Hypertext and creative writing. *Hypertext '87 Proceedings* (pp. 41-50). Chapel Hill, NC: Association for Computing Machinery.

Chi, F. (1995). ESL readers and the focus on intertextuality. *Journal of Reading, 38,* 638-644.

De Certeau, M. (1984). *The practice of everyday life.* Berkeley: University of California Press.

December, J., & Randall, N. (1994). *The World Wide Web unleashed.* New York: SAMS.

Dubrovsky, V. J., Kiesler, S., & Sethna, B. N. (1991). The equalization phenomenon: Status effects in computer-mediated or face-to-face decision-making groups. *Human-Computer Interaction, 6,* 119-146.

Eco, U. (1972). Towards a semiotic inquiry into the TV message. In J. Corner & J. Hawthorn (Eds.), *Communication studies: An introductory reader.* London: Arnold.

Fairclough, N. (1992). Intertextuality and critical discourse analysis. *Linguistics and Education, 4,* 269-293.

Fiske, J. (1987). *Television culture.* New York: Methuen.

Fiske, J. (1989). *Understanding popular culture.* Boston, MA: Unwin Hyman.

Fiske, J., & Hartley, J. (1978). *Reading television.* London: Methuen.

Foucault, M. (1979). What is an author? In J. V. Harari (Ed.), Textual strategies: Perspectives in post-structuralist criticism (pp. 141-160). Ithaca, NY: Cornell University Press.

Hall, S. (1980). Encoding/decoding. In S. Hall, D. Hobson, A. Lowe, & P. Willis (Eds.), *Culture, media, language* (pp. 128-139). London: Hutchinson.

Hiltz, S. R., Turoff, M., & Johnson, K. (1989). Experiments in group decision making, 3: Disinhibition, deindividuation, and group process in pen name and real name computer conferences. *Computer Support Systems, 5,* 217-252.

Joyce, M. (1991). Selfish interaction: Subversive texts and the multiple novel. In E. Berk & J. Devlin (Eds.), *The hypertext/hypermedia handbook.* New York: McGraw-Hill.

Kristeva, J. (1980). *Desire in language: A semiotic approach to literature and art.* New York: Columbia University Press.

Landow, G. P. (1992a). Hypertext, metatext and the electronic canon. In M. C. Tuman (Ed.), *Literacy online* (pp. 67-94). Pittsburgh: University of Pittsburgh Press.

Landow, G. P. (1992b). *Hypertext: The convergence of contemporary critical theory and technology.* Baltimore, MD: Johns Hopkins University Press.

Landow, G. P. (1994). What critics do: Critical theory in the age of hypertext. In G. P. Landow (Ed.), *Hypertext theory* (pp. 1-50). Baltimore, MD: Johns Hopkins University Press.

Leitch, V. B. (1983). *Deconstructive criticism.* Ithaca, NY: Cornell University Press.

Levi-Strauss, C. (1955). The structural study of myth. *Journal of American Folklore, 68,* 270.

McLaughlin, M. L., Osborne, K. K., & Smith, C. B. (1995). Standards of conduct on Usenet. In S. G. Jones (Ed.), *CyberSociety: Computer-mediated communication and community* (pp. 90-111). Thousand Oaks, CA: Sage.

McLuhan, M. (1964). *Understanding media: The extensions of man.* New York: McGraw-Hill.

Mitra, A. (1996). Nations on the Internet: The case of a national newsgroup, "soc.cult.indian." *Convergence: The Journal of Research in New Media Technologies, 2,* 44-75.

Mitra, A. (1997a). Diasporic web sites: Ingroup and outgroup discourse. *Critical Studies in Mass Communication, 14,* 158-181.

Mitra, A. (1997b). Virtual commonality: Looking for India on the Internet. In S. Jones (Ed.), *Virtual culture: Identity and communication in cybersociety* (pp. 55-80). London, UK: Sage.

Morris, M., & Ogan, C. (1996). The Internet as a mass medium. *Journal of Communication, 46*(1), 39-51.

Moulthrop, S. (1989). Polymers, paranoia, and the rhetoric of hypertext. *Writing on the Edge, 2,* 150-159.

Moulthrop, S. (1994). Rhizome and resistance: Hypertext and the dreams of a new culture. In G. P. Landow (Ed.), *Hypertext and literary theory.* Baltimore, MD: Johns Hopkins University Press.

Neale, S. (1981). Genre and cinema. In T. Bennett, S. Boyd-Bowman, C. Mercer, & J. Woollacott (Eds.), *Popular television and film* (pp. 6-15). London: British Film Institute.

Neale, S. (1990). Questions of genre. *Screen, 31*(1), 45-66.

Negroponte, N. (1995). *Being digital.* Boston: MIT Press.

Newhagen, J. E., & Rafaeli, S. (1996). Symposium: The Net. *Journal of Communication, 46*(1), 4-12.

Pierce, C. H. (1985). Logic as semiotics: The theory of signs. In R. E. Innis (Ed.), *Semiotics: An introductory anthology* (pp. 4-23). Bloomington: Indiana University Press.

Porter, J. E. (1986). Intertextuality and discourse community. *Rhetoric Review, 5,* 34-47.

Propp, V. (1975). *The morphology of the folk tale.* Austin: University of Texas Press.

Siegel, J., Dubrovsky, V., Kiesler, S., & McGuire, T. W. (1986). Group processes in computer-mediated communication. *Organizational Behavior and Human Decision Processes, 37,* 157-187.

Smolensky, M. W., Carmody, M. A., & Halcomb, C. G. (1990). The influence of task type, group structure and extraversion on uninhibited speech in computer-mediated communication. *Computers in Human Behavior, 6,* 261-272.

Thompsen, P. A., & Ahn, D. (1992). To be or not to be: An exploration of E-prime, copula deletion, and flaming in electronic mail. *ETC: A review of general semantics, 49,* 146-164.

Todorov, T. (1977). *The poetics of prose.* Oxford, UK: Blackwell.

Weisband, S. P. (1992). Group discussion and first advocacy effects in computer-mediated and face-to-face decision making groups. *Organizational Behavior and Human Decision Processes, 53,* 352-380.

Zickmund, S. (1997). Approaching the radical other: The discursive culture of cyberhate. In S. Jones (Ed.), *Virtual culture: Identity and communication in cybersociety* (pp. 185-206). London: Sage.

10

There Is a There There
Notes Toward a Definition of Cybercommunity

JAN FERNBACK

FOR THOSE SCHOLARS RESEARCHING THE RICH TERRAIN of social relations in cyberspace, there are methodological concerns that alert our sensibilities as researchers. How can we apply traditional sociological terms to the patterns of human interaction that develop in the "bodiless" province of cyberspace? How should we approach computer-mediated communication (CMC) research with an eye toward the accepted wisdom of the tenets of ethnomethodology, observation, interpretation, and empirical verification? So much has been written, both in popular and scholarly venues, about one such form of virtual human interaction—cybercommunity. Virtual interaction transforms the ways people relate to each other, and admittedly, not all of these ways involve community building per se. That process of transformation is a dialectic one, and virtual social relations encompass many behaviors: individual bonding (e.g., friendship, romance, professional interests), public address in virtual fora for debate, calls to political action, underground networking for illegal activities, and virtual stalking, rape, and anarchy. At present, however, the spatial metaphor we have adopted for discourse surrounding CMC lends itself to thinking of virtual social relations in terms of community. Cyberspace has been positioned as the town hall, the public sphere, the virtual agora, or just a fun "place" to gather and chat. Thus, *community*, and the various meanings the word evokes (such as *fellowship* and *conviviality*) has become an efficacious symbolic term for characterizing virtual social relations. This chapter examines the methodological difficulties of conceptualizing such social phenomena within cyberspace and seeks to offer grounds for further scholarly exploration into cybercommunity and other cultural constructs within cyberspace.

Problems of Definition

Like the terms *religion* or *culture,* the term *community* has proven difficult to define. These terms have mutable definitions that can vary widely in different disciplines and among different individuals. Like religion and culture, community has both symbolic and functional definitions. We group ourselves into aggregated physical villages that we call communities— urban, rural, suburban, or even walled; we similarly group ourselves into symbolic subdivisions based on lifestyle, identity, or character that we call communities—religious, leisurely, philosophical, or even virtual. The problem with mutable definitions is that they can often seem arbitrary. As Melford Spiro argues in "Religion: Problems of Definition and Explanation," scholars try to seek essentialist definitions that are "true statements about entities or things," but they must do so without being abstruse and without ignoring that which can be observed empirically (see Kilbourne & Langness, 1987). The essence of community is *commonality* (e.g., of interests or physical location), but community is difficult to observe empirically because its boundaries are continually renegotiated. Raymond Williams (1983) has, in an attempt to discover the "essence" of community, observed that community is not just a bounded locale but also "the quality of holding something in common, as in community of interests, community of goods . . . a sense of common identity and characteristics." These senses indicate a "particular quality of relationship (as in *communitas*)" (p. 75). Thus noting the evolution of the word *community* to encompass not only spatial relations but also quality/social relationships, Williams has identified an empirical element to the concept of community which has been popularized with the rise of social theory.

Scholars have indeed risen to Williams's exhortation; hundreds of case studies on various types of communities have been published over the decades. But most of these studies pursue that universal, essentialist definition without regard for the *process* of community; it exists as an entity, but community has an elastic character as it expands and contracts to accommodate fringe elements, to incorporate new symbolic meanings into its lexicon, and to withstand threats from outside its boundaries. Because definitions of the phenomena in question are necessary for scholarly inquiry, this chapter explores the difficulties in seeking a definition of community that encapsulates the real, observable practices that result from what cybercommunity participants claim is their authentic community *as well as* a more essential definition.

The problems of definition are not unique to scholars of CMC. But whether scientists or humanists, scholars across disciplines have rightly argued for the preeminence of defining cultural phenomena to articulate something meaningful about their connection to the human condition. Indeed, definitions of social phenomena are the grist for both the scientific mill of explanation and of the humanistic mill of interpretation. And with the methodological move described by some within the social sciences from "certainty to uncertainty"—that is, from positivism toward interpretivism—we have more cause to reexamine our methodological priorities. For scholars concerned with human action in the domain of cyberspace, defining social patterns of behavior in a virtual realm can seem almost absurd, if not intangible. Do the same normative roles and modes of behavior that govern our physical social world also apply to the virtual world? Can we seek empirical verification of hypotheses regarding social activity that involves bodilessness? Is there a sociology of the "placeless"? Is there cybercommunity? These questions require a reexamination of the adequacies of applying social theory about *community* to computer-mediated communicative relationships. The ability to communicate in a one-to-many form via technology is a novelty of the late 20th-century cultural landscape; we know already that many of the assumptions we hold about the negotiation and formation of social relationships, and particularly about community, do not seem to apply in the complex realm of CMC. Community is both an object of study (an entity, a manifestation) *and* the communicative process of negotiation and production of a commonality of meaning, structure, and culture. The terrain of community is mapped through a process of reconciling interpersonal dynamics, collective dynamics, and ideologies. These processes take on new significance when they are executed in cyberspace among people whose connectedness to one another is enabled only by a medium of mass communication.

I begin the exploration of these definitional problems in relation to CMC scholarship by sifting through the discourse on cybercommunity and how it resonates with both the popular and intellectual imagination in contemporary Western culture. This resonance is exemplified in political scientist Robert Booth Fowler's (1991) statement, "The intellectual engagement with community bursts across boundaries with abandon. . . . Community, its nature, and its desirability are now a part of the conversation of many political intellectuals in the United States; it has become a watchword of the age" (pp. 2-3).

Community as Place

The cultural metaphors we have adopted to refer to CMC are *place centered;* we have conceived of cyberspace as a place where community can develop and be sustained, new social and economic relationships can be created, and new horizons can be reached. Although the ability to transcend space and time through electronic means is not unprecedented (see Meyrowitz, 1985), we have not placed the same hopes for a revitalized sense of community into the unifying power of, for example, television, as we have in the unifying power of CMC. The idea of community resonates deeply within the human psyche, and traditionally, we have identified community with place.

This section will explore the notions of place-community as articulated in particular by Ferdinand Tönnies and Georg Simmel during the height of modernity in European society. For these social theorists, forms of 19th-century social existence reflected these changing notions of the value of collective social experience. Communities became more centralized and urban, peasant societies declined, and city life was seen as exemplifying the decay of oral culture, traditional morality, and familial ties.

Tönnies's well-known 1887 work *Gemeinschaft und Gesellschaft* (translated in the United States as "Community and Society") explores the historical changes in the organization of social life that emerged with the ascendancy of modernity. *Gemeinschaft* and *Gesellschaft* are ideal types conceived by Tönnies to correspond to natural will (Wesenwille) and rational will (Kurwille). *Gemeinschaft,* which is characterized by natural will, is distinguished by a guiding sense of the totality of the cultural past; conversely, *Gesellschaft,* which is characterized by rational will, is distinguished by a driving sense of progress and individualism. Hence, late 19th-century Europe had undergone an evolution from *Gemeinschaft* to *Gesellschaft* in the wake of the culture of modernity.

Gemeinschaft is indicated by an organic sense of community, fellowship, family, and custom, as well as a bounding together by understanding, consensus, and language. *Gemeinschaft* collectives are natural groupings that connote a social organization based on common property and fellowship (such as the Amish communities of the Pennsylvania Dutch) or professional groups oriented around a livelihood of some sort (such as mining communities or even communities of thieves).

Gesellschaft, then, corresponded to the *zeitgeist* of the modern era. When communal spirit is charged with individualism and people's interests, needs, and desires become more individually rather than collectively driven, relations among people become more mechanical, transitory, and contractually oriented—this is *Gesellschaft.* Tönnies claimed that a negative attitude permeates the notion of *Gesellschaft* and that individuals interact with one another only as a means of exchange of equally valued commodities (Tönnies, 1887/1957). It is a polite form of society in which people regard each other as equals, but the pleasantness and services are weighed to produce the desired result.

Tönnies demonstrates a true nostalgia for *Gemeinschaft,* arguing that *Gemeinschaft* was a "state of health," whereas *Gesellschaft* was a "state of pathology" (Liebersohn, 1988, p. 31). His critique of *Gesellschaft* as a form of social organization that has forsaken instinct, habit, and collective memory in favor of hyperindividualism, progress, and market economics echoes the lament of social historians and philosophers of the late 19th and early 20th centuries (e.g., Benjamin, Nietzsche, Proust). Of course, Tönnies was not the only social philosopher to speculate about the nature of the contemporary social order. Durkheim's notions of organic and mechanical solidarity reflect a similar ideal-typical construction: Mechanical solidarity is based on the similarity of individuals and was prevalent in preindustrial societies, whereas organic solidarity is based on heterogeneity of individuals that arises with a well-articulated division of labor in industrial nations.

In contrast to Tönnies, Simmel, although still a utopian, attempted to illuminate the gains of modernity rather than simply lamenting the loss of *Gemeinschaft.* Simmel (1950) argued that modern society did indeed possess unity and was thus not completely fragmented into *Gesellschaft.* He asserted that modernity contributed to a more sociologically grounded personal identity that was formed in part by social relationships; thus, individuals were never completely isolated or completely absorbed into a community. These social relationships and positions constituted boundaries that were both limiting and freeing for the individual. Like Tönnies, Simmel believed in organic society and also lamented the growing absence of *Gemeinschaft,* but he recognized that the individual's link to the social whole worked against this organic, natural will (Liebersohn, 1988).

Aside from the 19th-century social theorists, anthropologists, urban planners, and sociologists have dismantled and reconceived the ideal-typical definitions of community of Tönnies and Simmel. Sociologist George Hillery (1955) compiled more than 90 definitions of community, and similarly, other social scientists have struggled to ascribe a fundamentally communal nature to humankind in the face of early 20th-century fears about alienation and hyperindividuality. In fact, Hillery's definitions have only one common dimension—they all deal with people. Scherer (1972) notes that the term community consistently elicits discussion about commitment, identity, conflict resolution, tensions between the collective and the individual, and negotiation of community boundaries. It is part of the social nature of human beings to cohere around communal ideals, yet to maintain a sense of self, of individual desires. But many of the conceptualizations of community that have been popularly accepted have been derived from the dichotomous, structural definitions of Tönnies, Durkheim, and Simmel. For example, Redfield (1955), in his classic anthropological study *The Little Community,* claims that community can be typified on a folk-urban continuum, where folk communities exhibit characteristics reminiscent of Tönnies's *Gemeinschaft*—homogeneity, solidarity, and fellowship—and communities toward the urban end of the spectrum exhibit a loss of these elements. Clearly, however, definitions of the term from all manner of scholars have relaxed enough to incorporate less dichotomous notions of boundaries to the typically spatially oriented definitions of community.

Nonetheless, these approaches to community studies presuppose *physical place* to be an inherent component in communities. Historically, an inextricable affiliation between place and community has existed, despite vast societal changes brought about by the cultural upheaval created by the Industrial Revolution. Elias and Scotson (1974) claim that the essence of community is making a home: "Communities are essentially organizations of home-makers, residential units such as urban neighbourhoods, villages, hamlets, compounds, or groups of tents" (p. 27). The Chicago School sociologists demonstrated that sprawling cities could comprise a mosaic of smaller neighborhoods, each with distinct boundaries and organic *Gemeinschaft* values (Park, Burgess, & McKenzie, 1925). Anthropologist Mercer (1956), like many other social scientists studying community prior to the 1980s, defines community as "a functionally related aggregate of people who live in a particular geographic locality at a particular time, share a common culture, are arranged in a social structure, and exhibit an awareness of their uniqueness and separate identity as a group" (p. 27).

All of these perspectives on community, in addition to focusing on locale as a central concept in its definition, also encompass the notion of interdependency in community life. These approaches to the study of community suggest a functionality arising from this interdependency, whether based on commonality of location, interest, values, economic livelihood, behaviors, or roles. What these perspectives fail to address, however, is the antinomy to functionality—dysfunctionality. Certainly, there is room for conflict in functional community relationships, but true dysfunction is rarely, if ever, addressed in community studies. Because functionalism posits itself as an examination of the social usage of a particular institutional phenomenon as it contributes to the maintenance of the larger social whole, it never moves deductively from theory to explanation, has no explanatory power, and is thus inevitably a tautology. It can obscure the reality that true dysfunctionality can lead to ultimate destruction.

Community as Symbol

Themes of self-interest balanced against the common good have pervaded literature about community, public life, and democracy for decades. Recognition of these tensions by scholars of community led, in part, to the expansion of community studies to encompass more than just functional or formalist concepts of community as physical locale. Like any other social construct, community has a symbolic dimension to it as well (e.g., Cohen, 1985; Geertz, 1973). For purposes of describing cybercommunity, this distinction is of paramount importance. Through interpretive practices, Western culture has embraced a symbolic dimension of community that exceeds its social functional or formalist nature. Certain material, geographical, or ecological characteristics may frame the creation of community in the natural world, but humans symbolically infuse their communities with meaning. This symbolic scope of community emphasizes *substance* over *form;* it is a constructivist approach that illuminates the process of creating and embodying the meaning of community.

Anthropologist Anthony Cohen (1985) addresses community as it is symbolically constructed, as a conglomeration of normative codes and values that provide community members with a sense of identity. By emphasizing *meaning* rather than structure, Cohen rightly demonstrates that community is substance over form. He argues that the traditional sociological preoccupation with the "structure" of community has resulted in the assertion of community as normative formula over community as it can be empirically observed. Thus, the illuminating issue in the study of community, as Cohen sees it, is "not whether its structural limits have withstood the onslaught of social change, but whether its members are able to infuse its culture with vitality, and to construct a symbolic community which provides meaning and identity" (Cohen, 1985, p. 9). Therefore, based on Cohen's arguments, I assert that community should be studied as an entity of meaning. This avenue of inquiry allows us to conceive of community as existing in cyberspace, beyond the limits of physical locale. And scholars of community must remember to emphasize local meaning over universal meanings—community is not an anachronism; it very much exists on the local level in concerns over ethnicity, sexual orientation, even political orientation, rather than on the level of McLuhan's global village.

Here, it is important to note that Cohen's thesis about symbolically constructed community does not preclude the existence of a physically shared community. Although community can indeed be symbolically constructed, it is also a materially determined, preexisting physical reality, as discussed in the previous section. Etzioni (1995) reminds us that the scope of community is so encompassing that people are members of a multiplicity of communities simultaneously. This multiplicity includes both symbolic and material community; humans are participants in communities of their own creation, and they are recipients of physically constituted community. Cohen simply assigns more scholarly weight, in sociological and anthropological terms, to explorations of symbolically constructed community.

Virtual communities are such communities of meaning. Regardless of our ability (or lack thereof) to grapple with notions of global communities, transcended space, and computer-mediated reality, the very concept of cybercommunity addresses what Calhoun (1980) refers to as "community as a complex of ideas and sentiments" (p. 107). In this sense, participants in virtual communities may derive a range of experiences and meanings from the same cybercommunities, from a romanticized *Gemeinschaft* (see Rheingold, 1993) to a destructive *Gesellschaft* (see Slouka, 1995).

Community as Virtual

Benedict Anderson, in his treatise on nationalism, *Imagined Communities,* posits that all communities are imagined because, "in the minds of each [community member] lives the image of their communion" (Anderson, 1983, p. 15). Anderson's notion of communion strikes at the heart of most definitions of virtual community. Howard Rheingold (1993) has defined cybercommunity as "social aggregations that emerge from the [Internet] when enough people carry on those public discussions long enough, with sufficient human feeling, to form webs of personal relationships in cyberspace" (p. 5). Echoing Rheingold, Nancy Baym (1995b) argues in her work on the Usenet group rec.arts.tv.soaps,

> r.a.t.s. is only one electronic community on one computer network. There are thousands more Usenet groups, many with richly developed cultures, and countless groups on other burgeoning networks. Computer-mediated communities show users transforming a new medium into something unforeseen by its creators. (p. 51)

Rheingold and Baym are arguing that virtual community is a *real* entity that is given meaning by its participants.

But cybercommunities are characterized by common value systems, norms, rules, and the sense of identity, commitment, and association that also characterize various physical communities or other communities of interest. It is human nature to characterize new social phenomena in already recognized terms, whether through cultural memory or mythmaking. Baym (1995a), for example, argues that the distinctive cultures that develop around CMC groups are rooted in traditional theories of communicative practice. Thus, cybercommunity is generated by the participants' appropriation of accepted structures of communication as well as by the rules for interaction within those structures (Baym, 1995a). Similarly, Jones (1995) notes that issues of *space* are not to be ignored in conceiving of cybercommunity but, rather, that definitions of virtual community must engage both space and the social. Here, Jones is advocating an exploration of the links between social relations, values, beliefs, and spatial practices that encompass currently held conceptions of community. But in grappling with various ideals that have marked community studies of the past, Jones argues that issues of virtual community are inherently unique because the computer is a new element in the definitional mix. Because computers are regarded as "linking" machines, Jones states, "They inherently affect the ways we think of linking up to each other, and thus they fit squarely into our concerns about community" (p. 32). It is precisely this notion that arouses polemical theorizing about the relative worth of virtual community. Virtual community's many detractors adhere to the same nostalgic view of community as Tönnies does—that community is a local phenomenon, unmediated by technology, and bound by place.

Concepts of the "Real" Versus Concepts of the "Virtual"

If we accept the notion that CMC is socially constructed space, is it appropriate, then, to impose the community metaphor onto the social relations emanating from this space? Clearly, the place-bound notions of community advanced by Tönnies, Simmel, Durkheim, and others don't seem readily or entirely applicable in cyberspace. It becomes difficult to conceive of cyberspace as a site for community when the creation and control of space itself is dictated by concerns such as power, rebellion, authority, and dominance. But Michael Benedikt (1991) argues that certain material dimensions of physical space (including some laws of physics) can be reinvented in cyberspace. Virtual space is parallel to physical space in that

> cyberspace has a geography, a physics, a nature, and a rule of human law. In cyberspace the common man and the information worker—cowboy or infocrat—can search, manipulate, create or control information directly; he can be entertained or trained, seek solitude or company, win or lose power . . . indeed, can "live" or "die" as he will. (Benedikt, 1991, p. 123)

Thus, just because we can't see "it" doesn't mean "it" doesn't exist. Hillis (1997) suggests that virtual worlds are "being positioned as the ideal public sphere for imaginative subjectivities believing themselves virtually freed of bodily constraints" (p. 20). Despite these sentiments, some theorists of the virtual argue that cyberspace is not "real" because it has no physical manifestation and that resulting human contact in cyberspace is artificial or, at least, fleeting (see Talbott, 1995). But is it necessary to be able to conceive of cyberspace in spatial terms in order for it to be real? Indeed, certain dimensions of our social existence are difficult to conceive of in their present form in cyberspace. For example, how do we conceptualize the material aspects of community, such as the control of resources and the resulting hierarchies of power in cyberspace? This is not to say that power is not a force within cybercommunities (e.g., frequent flamers may be cast out of a cybercommunity or newbies may undergo sanctions from long-term group members when they fail to observe the proper rules of netiquette) but that power relations, like all social relations, take on a different character in cyberspace. The commodities of power in cyberspace may be wit, tenacity, and intelligence rather than brawn, money, or political clout. So while we may need to reconceive the elements of power in cyberspace, we may also need to reconceive the character of other social relations in the virtual realm.

But if we embrace the *symbolic* form of community (that is, not the *physical* manifestation of the term community but, rather, a community of substance and meaning), concerns of the "real" juxtaposed against the "virtual" are of less importance. Cyberspace encompasses this symbolic dimension; so, too, does cybercommunity. Reality is socially constructed, and as Cohen (1985) and Anderson (1983) assert, community exists in the minds of participants; it exists because its participants define it and give it meaning. This doesn't mean that the community exists *solely* in the minds of the participants but in the connection between what social constructs the user imagines (such as community) and the CMC-generated representations of these constructs. Thus, if we log on, form relationships in cyberspace, and believe we have found community, it is real for us. In fact, Watson (1997) claims that there is no true distinction between "virtual" community and "real" community:

> The term "virtual" means something akin to "unreal" and so the entailments of calling online communities "virtual" include spreading and reinforcing a belief that what happens online is *like* a community, but isn't *really* a community. My experience has been that people in the offline world tend to see online communities as virtual, but that participants in the online communities see them as quite real. (p. 129)

So if, as Dewey (1927) claims, communication is the core of community, then community is real whether it exists within the same physical locality or half a world away via the telephone wires. We must then express a willingness to treat these manifestations of what we imagine as real.

Further, in accordance with Williams's (1983) appeal that we not neglect the empirical dimension of community, many researchers (e.g., Baym, 1995b) have observed the substance of community relations in cyberspace. Tönnies argued that *Gemeinschaft* is constituted through language, creed, land, buildings, treasures, and monuments, which serve to maintain and perpetuate a commonality through heredity and education, and that art and ritual also serve to retain cultural memories, promote a unity of spirit, and to cultivate a sense of the legacy of a group within itself (Tönnies, 1887/ 1957). Some of these same devices for sustaining community can be empirically observed in cybercommunities, albeit without the physical manifestations mentioned by Tönnies. On-line communities are nourished through language (Howard, 1997), through ritual (Fernback, 1996; O'Leary, 1996), by cultivating the group's legacy (Rheingold, 1993), and even through a community-generated system of punishment (Ross, 1994). Simmel (1950) also warned that nostalgia for organic, rural community can be misguided because the progression of rural community to metropolis is practically inevitable. Thus, a community forms as a cohesive, closed circle perpetuated through custom, history, and knowledge of the group's legacy. Ultimately, however, the community expands and teems at its boundaries, threatening the unity and rigidity of the group. The community's borders are then permeated by outside connections, and individual members of the group gain more autonomy. The community becomes larger and its sphere of influence widens (Simmel, 1950). Indeed, some cybercommunities have splintered in this fashion as they've grown too large. One such on-line community, LambdaMoo, a real-time chat group, was forced to enact a "zero population growth" edict to stem the growth of the community. Many of the longtime users claimed that the group's homey atmosphere had been violated by hostile, disrespectful newbies (Ross, 1994). The statute stated, "Lambda-Moo's population has grown beyond the point where the technical and social systems can effectively cope. At the current rate of growth, 'environmental' stresses will continue to degrade the quality of life on the MOO" (Ross, 1994, p. 22). The language in this edict could very well apply to any physical community.

Just as the exploration of the American western frontier provided an opportunity for humanity to conquer new space, so does the exploration of cyberspace. We seek to pioneer new spaces, to create in them, to live in them. And in those new spaces, we seek to relate to one another. It represents our humanity, our freedom. Kellogg, Carroll, and Richards (1991) argued the point well when they said, "People live in the world, and their practices have evolved in the world. Virtual worlds do not exist solely in some enclosed cyberspace: they exist in human culture, knowledge, and values as well" (p. 430).

New Directions in
Conceiving of the "There" There

Returning to the observations raised at the beginning of this chapter, how do we conceptualize virtual community? What methodological approaches are best suited to study cybercommunity? Since, as this chapter has asserted, cybercommunity is symbolic in nature—that is, it is substance rather than form, meaning rather than structure—a grounded theoretical approach is the most efficacious way to address issues of social phenomena as they occur in cyberspace. Because grounded theory emphasizes the relationship between the concept (in this case, community) and the human actor (participants in virtual communities) as a means of connecting the various perspectives of cybercommunity members with patterns of action and their context, this method of theorizing seems particularly suited to application within the domain of the virtual. Methodologically, grounded theory considers social practices to be part of the researcher's theoretical construct. According to Strauss and Corbin (1994), this strategy of inquiry means that "theory may be *generated* initially from the data or, if existing (grounded) theories seem appropriate to the area of investigation, then these may be *elaborated* and modified as incoming data are meticulously played against them" (p. 273). The researcher then asks conceptual and generative questions as a means to develop more *conceptual density,* a term used by Strauss and Corbin to refer to a richness in theoretical development. This method moves beyond Geertz's (1973) "thick description" toward interpretive conceptualization. Moreover, a grounded theoretical approach is concerned with discovering *process,* an important dimension in the conceptualization of community (as noted earlier in this chapter).

Why does this approach seem to make more conceptual sense than other methodological approaches? If, as observers of social relations in cyberspace, we simply impose the term community onto all social aggregations in the virtual realm, we may miss the nuances of the virtual social experience. We may find communities where there are none, we may assume that any virtual social aggregation that does not conform to our definition of cybercommunity is indeed a dysfunctional community rather than a noncommunity. The imposition of a forced, nontheoretically informed definition of community onto all virtual social relations, then, does not promote the endeavor of interpretive inquiry. Interpretivists argue that the world is a construction of ideas and that meanings and symbols determine human behavior; they assert that truth is subjective and that meaning can be interpreted. The interpretive approach offers a depth of analysis based on experience and understanding; it offers a snapshot of life as it is lived, asserting that human life cannot be understood solely by speculations based on empirical observation or on the quantification of those observations. Interpretivists believe that assigning meaning to human thought and action is perhaps a more "correct," if not interesting, means of deepening the knowledge about the human condition. Interpretive methodological strategies seek to illuminate meaning in subjects' lives—in their practices, beliefs, actions.

Not all virtual social gatherings are communities. Without the personal investment, intimacy, and commitment that characterizes our ideal sense of community, some on-line discussion groups and chat rooms are nothing more than a means of communication among people with common interests (see Bromberg, 1996). Similarly, participants within these virtual groups can argue among themselves as to whether their group constitutes a community (e.g., Watson's 1997 study of the Phish.Net fan community). But the observation and theorizing about this "placeless" realm does not differ substantively from those same methods of interpretive inquiry within physical communities. Interactions in cybercommunities can be described and interpreted just as interactions in physical communities can. Issues of ideology, agency, power, ontology, roles, and boundaries affect virtual communities just as they do physical communities. The same concerns about validity in the interpretive approach that have plagued ethnographers all along are applicable to research in the virtual realm as well. Ethnographers working in cyberspace must be careful to attempt a measure of reflexivity, to separate oneself from the subjects being studied; they must develop a sense about the truthfulness and candor of their informants, just as ethnographers of the nonvirtual must; and they must use a theoretically informed framework for their research, just as ethnographers have traditionally done.

What, then, does the "there" there look like? Aside from Rheingold's (1993) much-cited definition of virtual community, few theorists have confronted the task of elucidating a comprehensive definition of the phenomenon. Despite Hillery's (1955) caution that the enterprise of defining community is a futile one, we can begin by articulating what cybercommunity is *not*. Community in cyberspace is not a manifestation of false consciousness. Real social practices are embedded in virtual interactions; virtual community has a felt nature for its inhabitants. Bromberg (1996) has argued in her study on MUDs (multi-user domains) that virtual interaction can produce altered states of consciousness, generated particularly by intense feelings of connectivity, identity exploration, eroticism, and mastery over one's environment. Cybercommunity is not commensurate with physical community in every dimension except the spatial. Virtual communities have their own cultural composition. As I have argued elsewhere (Fernback, 1997), they have their own collective sense, their own virtual ideology. Cybercommunity is not just a *thing;* it is also a *process.* It is defined by its inhabitants, its boundaries and meanings are renegotiated, and although virtual communities do possess many of the same essential traits as physical communities, they possess the "substance" that allows for common experience and common meaning among members. Cohen (1985) saw the issue in the study of community as "not whether its structural limits have withstood the onslaught of social change, but whether its members are able to infuse its culture with vitality, and to construct a symbolic community which provides meaning and identity" (p. 9). Clearly, Cohen's perspective is also the issue in the study of virtual community.

So what *is* cybercommunity? It is an entity and a process that emerges from the wisdom of our repository of cultural knowledge about the concept of community and from our observation of its manifestation in cyberspace. It is an arena in which passions are inflamed, problems are solved, social bonds are formed, tyranny is exercised, love and death are braved, legacies are born, factions are splintered, and alliances dissolved. It is a rich arena for study by scholars, cybercommunitarians, and the curious.

Regardless of perspective, however, the concept of community strikes at the heart of our humanity. It will thus remain a topic of emotional debate in the landscape of social criticism. As historian Fowler (1991) commented:

> In discussing contemporary America, the friends of community focus on the inadequacies of American culture, philosophy, or institutions. Indeed, at times the banner of community is waved more to express a diverse and almost inexhaustible set of complaints about contemporary America than for any other purpose. Yet the negative mood, the mood of criticism, is far from the entire story. The idea of community in general . . . is pervasive. Its existence as a concept, as an ideal, and a possibility represents the standard from which criticism comes—a standard which encourages the mood of substantial dissatisfaction. (p. 23)

Western cultures wrestle with the idea of community; we find it elusive, yet we pursue the idealized notion of it. The concept of virtual community is regarded by some as such an ideal. Benedikt (1991) claims that

> the advent of cyberspace is apt to be seen in two ways, each of which can be regretted or welcomed: either as a new stage in the *etherealization* of the world we live in, the real world of people and things and places, or, conversely, as a new stage in the *concretization* of the world we dream and think in, the world of abstractions, memory and knowledge. (p. 124)

Benedikt cautions, however, that we should not look toward cyberspace to "replace" our face-to-face interactions but as a realm that "becomes another venue for consciousness itself." Our notions of not only community but other domains of social interaction are changing with the coming of cyberculture according to Escobar (1994), who claims that such changes will encompass our ideas about identity, governmental rule by information, and a postmodern questioning of the wisdom of the scientific paradigm. Watson (1997) asserts that the rise of cybercommunity has cultivated new means of understanding traditional forms of community. He continues:

> Refusal to apply "community" as a descriptor for online collectivities stems either from a desire to retain a purified notion of community in the hands of those who claim to know "true" community, or from an unwillingness to recognize CMC technologies as a medium with the potential to change traditional social arrangements. . . . [T]o apply "community" to online phenomena is to give those online denizens . . . recognition of their own strengths, which are entailed by the use of the community metaphor to describe their activities and their existence as a new form of collective entity. (p. 121)

Quite simply, there is a there there, and it has both an essential nature and a manifestation in the social practices of its proponents. But it is not identical to our preexisting social constructs of community. We can make this same assertion with regard to the study of other hard-to-define social phenomena (such as religion) within cyberspace. As scholars of cyberspace more willingly embrace the uncertain, the interpretive, the uncharted, perhaps the "place" of cybercommunity within the corpus of theories of community will become more certain.

References

Anderson, B. (1983). *Imagined communities: Reflections on the origin and spread of nationalism.* London: Verso.

Baym, N. K. (1995a). The emergence of community in computer-mediated communication. In S. G. Jones (Ed.), *CyberSociety: Computer-mediated communication and community* (pp. 138-163). London: Sage.

Baym, N. K. (1995b). From practice to culture on Usenet. In S. L. Star (Ed.), *The cultures of computing* (pp. 29-52). Oxford, UK: Blackwell.

Benedikt, M. (1991). Cyberspace: Some proposals. In M. Benedikt (Ed.), *Cyberspace: First steps* (pp. 119-224). Cambridge: MIT Press.

Bromberg, H. (1996). Are MUDs communities? Identity, belonging and consciousness in virtual worlds. In R. Shields (Ed.), *Cultures of Internet: Virtual spaces, real histories, living bodies* (pp. 143-152). London: Sage.

Calhoun, C. J. (1980). Community: Toward a variable conceptualization for comparative research. *Social History, 5,* 105-129.

Cohen, A. P. (1985). *The symbolic construction of community.* Chichester, UK: Ellis Horwood.

Dewey, J. (1927). *The public and its problems.* New York: Henry Holt.

Elias, N., & Scotson, J. L. (1974). Cohesion, conflict and community character. In C. Bell & H. Newby (Eds.), *The sociology of community* (pp. 27-38). London: Frank Cass.

Escobar, A. (1994). Welcome to cyberia: Notes on the anthropology of cyberculture. *Current Anthropology, 35*(3), 211-231.

Etzioni, A. (1995). Old chestnuts and new spurs. In A. Etzioni (Ed.), *New communitarian thinking: Persons, virtues, institutions, and communities* (pp. 16-34). Charlottesville: University Press of Virginia.

Fernback, J. (1996, January). *Internet ritual: A case study in the construction of computer-mediated neo-pagan religious meaning.* Paper presented at the Conference on Media, Religion, and Culture, Boulder, CO.

Fernback, J. (1997). The individual within the collective: Virtual ideology and the realization of collective principles. In S. G. Jones (Ed.), *Virtual culture: Identity and communication in cybersociety* (pp. 36-54). London: Sage.

Fowler, R. B. (1991). *The dance with community: The contemporary debate in American political thought.* Lawrence: University Press of Kansas.

Geertz, C. (1973). *The interpretation of cultures.* New York: Basic Books.

Hillery, G. (1955). Definitions of community: Areas of agreement. *Rural Sociology, 20,* 111-123.

Hillis, K. (1997, April 18). *Information technologies, subjectivity and space: Virtual reality and social relations.* Text of speech, Geography Lecture Series, University of Colorado, Boulder.

Howard, T. (1997). *A rhetoric of electronic communities.* Greenwich, CT: Ablex.

Jones, S. G. (1995). Understanding community in the information age. In S. G. Jones (Ed.), *CyberSociety: Computer-mediated communication and community* (pp. 10-35). London: Sage.

Kellogg, W. A., Carroll, J. M., & Richards, J. T. (1991). Making reality a cyberspace. In M. Benedikt (Ed.), *Cyberspace: First steps* (pp. 411-431). Cambridge: MIT Press.

Kilbourne, B., & Langness, L. L. (Eds.). (1987). *Culture and human nature: Theoretical papers of Melford E. Spiro.* Chicago: University of Chicago Press.

Liebersohn, H. (1988). *Fate and utopia in German sociology, 1870-1923.* Cambridge: MIT Press.

Mercer, B. (1956). *The American community.* New York: Random House.

Meyrowitz, J. (1985). *No sense of place: The impact of electronic media on social behavior.* New York: Oxford University Press.

O'Leary, S. (1996, January). *Rhetoric and ritual: The recovery of performative language in cyberspace.* Paper presented at the Conference on Media, Religion, and Culture, Boulder, CO.

Park, R. E., Burgess, E. W., & McKenzie, R. D. (1925). *The city.* Chicago: University of Chicago Press.

Redfield, R. (1955). *The little community: Viewpoints for the study of a human whole.* Chicago: University of Chicago Press.

Rheingold, H. (1993). *Virtual community: Homesteading on the electronic frontier.* New York: Addison-Wesley.

Ross, K. (1994, August). *Print-based dialogism and textual orality: Communication practices in a virtual community.* Paper presented at the National Convention of the Association for Education in Journalism and Mass Communication, Atlanta, GA.

Scherer, J. (1972). *Contemporary community: Sociological illusion or reality?* London: Tavistock.

Simmel, G. (1950). *The sociology of Georg Simmel* (K. Wolff, Trans.). New York: Free Press.

Slouka, M. (1995). *War of the worlds: Cyberspace and the high-tech assault on reality.* New York: Basic Books.

Strauss, A., & Corbin, J. (1994). Grounded theory methodology: An overview. In N. K. Denzin & Y. S. Lincoln (Eds.), *Handbook of qualitative research* (pp. 273-285). Thousand Oaks, CA: Sage.

Talbott, S. L. (1995). *The future does not compute: Transcending the machines in our midst.* Sebastopol, CA: O'Reilly.

Tönnies, F. (1957). *Community and society* (C. P. Loomis, Trans.). East Lansing: Michigan State University Press. (Original work published 1887)

Watson, N. (1997). Why we argue about virtual community: A case study of the phish.net fan community. In S. G. Jones (Ed.), *Virtual culture: Identity and communication in cybersociety* (pp. 102-132). London: Sage

Williams, R. (1983). *Keywords.* New York: Oxford University Press.

11

Researching and
Creating Community Networks

TERESA M. HARRISON
TIMOTHY STEPHEN

MOST RESEARCHERS REGARD THE Internet and the World Wide Web as technologies that are transforming the world into a "global village." Indeed, as we come increasingly to rely on computer networks to communicate at work, search for information, and chat or game with distant partners, attention seems to be focused on new opportunities for interaction in various "virtual" places and, correspondingly, diverted from the social interaction we encounter in our geographical place or community.

In contrast, a rapidly growing community networking movement has chosen to use the Internet and the World Wide Web as resources to enhance the development of geographically based communities. Although estimates vary, in 1996, for example, as many as 390 computerized community networking projects existed or were under development around the world (Schuler, 1996), a number that has steadily increased since interest in the Web exploded. Furthermore, the development of community networks has been supported by the Telecommunications and Information Infrastructure Assistance Program (TIIAP), a federal funding program created by the

Clinton administration and housed within the Department of Commerce. Although community networking doesn't generally command the media attention reserved for more dazzling uses of the World Wide Web, the community networking phenomenon is robust and promises to become more significant in the future.

Community networks are organized for a variety of purposes that range from bringing the resources of information technology to individuals who have not historically enjoyed access to the Internet to using technology to address traditional issues in community development, such as unemployment, economic stimulation, health and social welfare, environmental concerns, educational needs, and so on. In addition, an important objective for many developers has been to use community networks to stimulate interest and enhance participation in local government or in other forums for community decision making.

In this chapter, we provide a descriptive overview of community networking, with the goal of stimulating interest in conducting research in this phenomenon and addressing some of the issues that researchers in this area are likely to encounter. We present information from the scholarly literature along with data from an illustrative survey we have conducted on a sample of networking projects in an effort to shed light on some basic questions about community networks: What kinds of individuals or organizations initiate such projects? What goals have community networks been designed to achieve? Because one of the goals central to the philosophy informing community networks is that of improving democratic processes, we explore the kinds of practices that support democracy that are offered by community networks.

In the second section of the chapter, we provide a brief review of the research that has sought to assess the outcomes and effectiveness of community networks. However, because little such research has been conducted to date, our discussion highlights issues that need to be addressed in planning and executing a research design. Furthermore, we argue that academic researchers should become more involved in planning and developing community networks and that such activity may contribute to the process of theory testing.

Goals and Purposes of Community Networks

Community networking projects are basically sites or services offered through the World Wide Web or the Internet that individuals using computers and modems can consult for information, resources, and/or interaction relevant to life in their local geographically based community. Frequently, they are projects taken on by members of the community who have themselves organized community support (in the form of community organizations, such as libraries, schools, local governmental bodies, businesses, etc.) for the development of these resources and acquired funding to initiate and develop the project.

Several different categories of sites on the World Wide Web offer information about geographic locales. For example, some sites exist for the purpose of marketing a geographic area to tourists; they are frequently funded by or created by local tourism councils. Other sites exist for the purpose of providing information, essentially advertising, about entertainment and business resources; such sites are operated by organizations that derive income from making this kind of information available. Although community networks may contain information about tourist attractions and frequently provide information about entertainment and business resources, their purposes encompass much more than just promoting tourism or retail business. As we shall see below, community networks are a kind of information resource initiated by individuals who are motivated by prosocial goals and values and who believe that they can use computer networking to reinvigorate the health and well-being of local communities.

Sponsors of Community Networks

According to Bowen (1996), the community networking movement may be seen as a descendent of the grassroots "public media" movement of the 1920s, which stimulated the creation of small, low-power radio stations owned and operated by average citizens and small nonprofit organizations. Ultimately, that movement failed to endure, despite a brief period of resurrection in the 1970s with the availability of citizen-operated public access cable TV channels.

This analogy calls our attention to the general fragility of the community network movement; indeed, networking projects have often been initiated by, as Cisler (1993) reports, "computer enthusiasts" who "will start an electronic bulletin board with one or two phone lines and invite other groups to disseminate their information on a dedicated part of the system, and then grow the service into a community information system." However, as our data will show, other community networking projects have also been created

TABLE 11.1 Sponsors of Community Networks

Type	Number in Category
Owned/operated by government	9
Owned/operated by libraries	4
Owned/operated by nonprofits	3
Owned/operated by universities	5
Nonprofit 501(3)(c) corporation	22
Uncategorizable	7
Total in sample	50

or sponsored by universities, libraries, and other not-for-profit organizations. Regardless of point of origin, a community network will not survive long without people and financing; some form of social organization must lie at the foundation of a community network project.

In November 1997, we conducted a survey of community networks in the United States on the World Wide Web, which was designed to answer a number of questions about networking in an evocative rather than a definitive way. The first of these questions asked, What particular forms of social organizations sponsor community networks? As a result of this examination, we were struck by the impression that, although community networks are obviously a technological phenomenon, it is apparent that each community network is also an organizational phenomenon. That is, each "community network resource" that takes the form of information or graphics electronically on the Web, is the product of a group of individuals who have organized to make this resource available to others.

Our survey focused on 50 community networks, which we selected from various lists of existing network projects.[1] Not all the network sites were operational at the time we sampled; when a site could not be contacted, we simply went on to the next available site. Of the organizations we surveyed, 7 seemed to be so new or limited in the information presented that we were unable to categorize them, a comment in itself on the extent to which the phenomenon of community networking is in flux. The remaining projects clustered into five fairly discrete categories (see Table 11.1).

A relatively large number of community networks, nine in our sample, appeared to be sponsored by governmental bodies or organizations associated with governmental bodies. Thus, we found community networks that had been initiated by city governments (such as the cities of Eugene, Oregon;

Lancaster, California; and Cambridge, Massachusetts). Other community networks were the products of local educational systems or state governmental units that had some responsibility for information dissemination, such as the SAILOR system in Maryland, a project of the Division of Library Development and Services of the Maryland State Department of Education.

Our sample of community networks also included four developed by local public libraries, a category that we distinguished from governmentally sponsored networks even though most public libraries are branches of local government. It occurred to us that libraries might have their own approach to community networking, and we wished to determine if that orientation would be evident in other meaningful differences between the community networks in the two categories.

Of the community networks in our sample, five were presented principally as projects of universities, although it was clear in every case that leaders and representatives of community groups and/or local government were heavily involved in the project. In our sample, networks such as the Blacksburg Electronic Village, a project of Virginia Polytechnic Institute and State University, and the Boulder Community Network, a project of the University of Colorado at Boulder, are represented in this category.

A fourth category, composed of three community networks, were sponsored by nonprofit organizations other than a university, with another or larger purpose. For example, one of the projects in our sample was "InfoZone" a project of the Telluride Institute in Telluride, Colorado, a nonprofit research and education organization with programs in the arts, environment, and communication. Another community network in our sample was the Cambridge Civic Network, a project of the Center for Civic Networking, devoted to the larger issue of the quality of civic life and participation in community decision making. Although it was not easy to tell, the Cambridge Civic Network is distinct from the community network sponsored by the city of Cambridge, discussed above. The third project in this category, the "ShiaNet Community Network," was sponsored by a local Chamber of Commerce and seemed to exist primarily for the purpose of providing affordable Internet access.

Finally, our survey identified 22 community networks organized as nonprofit 501(3)(c) organizations and existing as entities independent of any other larger or governing body. Our sample included some well-known networks, such as Charlotte's Web in North Carolina, and the Twin-Cities Free-Net in Minnesota as well as many others that have not garnered national attention. Many, although not all, of these organizations called themselves

"Free-Nets," a label that signaled some degree of affiliation with the recently defunct National Public Telecomputing Network, a national organization for community networking projects modeled on the Corporation for Public Broadcasting. Because these networks were legally incorporated as nonprofit corporations with certain formal requirements, the networking projects frequently featured pages devoted to articles of incorporation, organizational by-laws, and a list of the project's board of directors.

Goals of Community Networks

A number of theorist/practitioners have guided the development of the community networking movement; their arguments in favor of community networking share three consistent themes. First, possibly the most often cited objective for theorists as well as for developers and practitioners has been to use community networks to provide free or inexpensive access to computer networking technology, the Internet, and information on the World Wide Web (Carter, 1997; Civille, 1993; Tillman, 1997), as part of an effort to "democ-ratize the Information SuperHighway," according to LaMendola and Rueda (1997). This goal has generally been accomplished by making equipment for accessing network services available to the public (e.g., by placing comput-ing equipment with modem connections in public libraries) as well as by offering free electronic mail, accounts, or direct access to the Internet.

Second, Douglas Schuler (1995, 1996, 1997b), perhaps the most prolific proselytizer of the movement, agrees that community networks have the potential to provide access to information for all, but he also argues that information technology makes it possible to create a new kind of public space and to create genuine dialogues between community members. Proponents of new communication technologies in general have been quick to point out the paucity of neutral public gathering places, or "great good places" (Oldenberg, 1989), in contemporary life. They suggest that cyberspace may present an important alternative where individuals can meet virtually to engage in the kind of discourse that is critical to the reconstitution of a vibrant public sphere (Doheny-Farina, 1996; Habermas, 1989; London, 1997; Rheingold, 1993). This argument takes on particular force in the community networking literature, in which theorists view networks as sites for a poten-tially significant reinvigoration of community life, a fulfillment of the communitarian vision of democracy (Doheny-Farina, 1996; Schuler, 1994), and an opportunity for "recapturing the lost art of democratic decision making and debate" (Civille, Fidelman, & Altobello, 1993).

Finally, representatives of the Center for Civic Networking and their colleagues (e.g., Civille, 1993; Civille et al., 1993; Fidelman, 1994; Sharp & Beaudry, 1994) present a vision of "civic networking" that, in addition to subscribing to the themes discussed above, also encompasses the "transformational power" of information technology as a tool to revitalize economic and civic institutions in ways that eliminate bureaucratic hierarchy and that conserve natural resources. These theorists and activists see community networks as a means for stimulating the development of jobs, encouraging the growth of business, and enabling municipal agencies to reduce costs. The philosophy of "civic networking" is conceptualized as a larger "process facilitated by the tools of electronic communications and information, that improves and magnifies human communication and interaction in a community" (Morino, 1994, cited in London, 1997). Not all of the entities that may call themselves "community networks" are necessarily part of or subscribe to the philosophy of the civic networking movement.

We surveyed the community network projects in our sample for indications of whether or not each network subscribed to each of these three basic goals for community networking: (a) access to information for everyone, (b) democratic or community interaction (of any kind under any circumstances), and (c) reinvigorating, in any way, existing civic and economic institutions (e.g., by providing users with information about them or links to them). To ascertain the objectives of each network, we perused Web-based information about 40 of the 50 networks,[2] including the statement of mission, its welcome page, frequently asked questions and answers, and the actual services or activities that each network provided for its users; on the basis of the latter, we sometimes inferred particular goals or objectives on the part of the network.[3]

The data presented in Table 11.2 indicate that nearly all the networks subscribed to the goal of providing access to information on the Internet or World Wide Web for everyone; all of the networks in the library, university, and 501(3)(c) categories supported this goal. The only networks that did not fell into the "government-sponsored" category.

A substantial number of networks also subscribed to the goal of using computer networking and the information it provides to reinvigorate civic and economic institutions. Nearly all of the networks in the 501(3)(c) category and the governmentally sponsored networks supported this goal,

TABLE 11.2 Goals of Community Networks

Network Goal	Government (N = 9)	Libraries (N = 4)	Universities (N = 5)	501(3)(c) (N = 22)
Free access to information	6	4	4	22
Democratic/community interaction	0	0	1	10
Reinvigorating civic/economic institutions	7	0	3	19

with networks sponsored by universities somewhat less supportive. Interestingly, none of the networks sponsored by libraries indicated their support for this goal.

Finally, there was substantial variation among the networks regarding their support for the goal of fostering democratic or community interaction. Table 11.2 shows that none of the networks sponsored by governmental organizations or those sponsored by libraries subscribed to this goal. One of the university-supported networks, and 10 of the 501(3)(c) networks indicated in some way that they attempted to stimulate interaction among community members or were oriented toward improving democratic discourse. This finding was somewhat surprising given the wide support for this goal among theorists.

Democratic Goals of Community Networks

Democracy is a complex term in the community networking literature, as in other literatures; theorists use it in many different ways, some of which have already been reflected in our discussion. Advocates of equal access to the Internet have used the term *information democracy,* defined as a socio-political system in which individuals are guaranteed the opportunity to access information resources (Doctor, 1994). Information is seen as a vital prerequisite to democratic outcomes in the same way that freedom of speech and freedom of the press are, except that the primary barrier is an economic rather than a social restraint on expression. As van Dijk (1996) points out, information is required for opinion formation in democratic deliberation.

However, others have intended their discussions of democracy and communication technologies to center on breathing new life into the governmental institutions that have formed the basis of traditional liberal conceptions of democracy. Such objectives were among those that motivated the development of the PEN (Public Electronic Network) project in Santa Monica, California, the first free-access, government-sponsored, community network in the United States, created in 1989 and probably the most extensively researched of all community networks. PEN designers were committed to providing city residents with free access, which meant that even homeless individuals were able to access PEN services. But they were further committed to increasing the sense of communication between city government and city residents, which led to the creation of on-line conferences dedicated to the discussion of pressing issues in the community (Law & Keltner, 1995; Rogers, Collins-Jarvis, & Schmitz, 1994; Schmitz, Rogers, Phillips, & Paschal, 1995).

In a third variation on the theme of democracy, Bertelsen (1992) points out that the model of "participatory democracy" animates much of the discussion about the democratic potential of new communication technologies, which seem to make feasible new ways to include individual voices in political decision making. In particular, the model of communitarian democracy stresses decision making in the service of the common good, instead of that which serves the interests of individuals or specific groups (Abrahamson, Arterton, & Orren, 1988; Ess, 1996). Deliberation and persuasion in decision making are foregrounded in this model of democracy; participation in these activities is regarded as a transformative process in understanding and creating the common good (Abrahamson et al., 1988). Communitarian democracy seeks to reinvigorate the idea of a public space in which members of a community meet to engage in the communication activities that both create and sustain community life (Doheny-Farina, 1996). London (1997) argues that community networks have the ability to nurture the development of dialogue, deliberation, and the feelings of trust, social connectedness, and cooperation that bind a community together; these social qualities are vital to the development of participatory or communitarian democratic systems.

Finally, when considering democracy, it is worth reflecting on whether the designers of a system with the goal of strengthening or improving democracy in any of the respects discussed above apply democratic values to the internal administration of the project itself. As Gygi (1996) notes,

> Project developers who are concerned with building democratic institutions will need to ensure that their decision making processes are participatory and collaborative. Community-based organizations and other key stakeholders need

to be involved in project planning and implementation. The degree of outside control and representativeness of the organizational structure will likely influence the community economic development and political participation outcomes associated with the project.

We decided to explore each of these ways of conceptualizing democracy in a third analysis of the community networks in our sample. In this analysis, we pursued the possibility that the orientation toward democracy practiced by the community network might have something to do with the kind of organization sponsoring the network. That is, we expected each network's democratic orientations to be apparent from the information or opportunities for interaction provided by the information system; but we also entertained the possibility that orientations toward democracy would vary based on the kind of organization that sponsored each network.

We again surveyed the 40 community network projects in our sample for indications of their orientations to democracy, as represented by the kinds of services or activities that networks within each category provided for their users. We examined information that each community network provided on the Web, looking for a number of very rudimentary indicators that seemed to be relevant to how each network was oriented to the issue of democracy (see Table 11.3). Initially, we looked for indications that the network was oriented toward "information democracy" by attempting to provide (a) free access to information for members of a community in the form of a direct connection to the Internet or World Wide Web or in the form of a free ongoing account or disk space offered to individuals, nonprofits, or other types of organizations. We then looked for indications of a greater commitment to information democracy by (b) providing or envisioning in the future that the project would provide facilities (computers, modems, telephone lines) for public access.

Next we looked for indications that the network was engaged in efforts to promote liberal and participatory orientations to democracy, such as (c) providing services that linked users with existing government offices or officials and (d) whether they did or envisioned themselves doing anything to foster participation in community, local, or government decision making.

The last three items we examined referenced the extent to which certain kinds of practices associated with democracy were practiced in the network itself. Here, we wondered if community networking projects conceptualized themselves as democratic in character, and thus, we looked for indications of the following: (e) whether users were enabled to become members of the

TABLE 11.3 Democratic Indicators and Types of Community Networks

Democratic Indicator	Government (N = 9)	Libraries (N = 4)	Universities (N = 5)	501(3)(c) (N = 22)
a. Free access for those who can't pay	6	4	4	22
b. Public access available or envisioned	6	4	4	19
c. Fosters contact with government or elected officials	7	3	4	20
d. Fosters participation in community decision making	4	0	1	10
e. Network has members	0	1	1	13
f. Network has meetings that users or members can attend	0	1	0	13
g. Users or members can vote on something	0	0	0	11

network, (f) whether users and/or members were invited to attend meetings conducted by the individuals administering the network, and (g) whether users or members were allowed to vote on any organizational decisions about the community network.

Several interesting pieces of information are evident from Table 11.3. First, there is considerable support across networks for providing or attempting to provide access to networked information for those who cannot pay; all the 501(3)(c) projects and most of the projects in other categories provide free access, in the form of direct Internet access and in the form of equipment, to information for users. This indicates that there is generally more than lip service support for the goal of "information democracy," widely subscribed to in the theoretical literature of community networking and strongly evident in our survey of the goals of the community networks.

Furthermore, there is a great deal of support across the community networks for bringing users into contact with government institutions and representatives, supporting a traditional conception of liberal democracy. Most of the networks in each category appeared to provide services that fostered contact with existing government offices or officials. However, there is considerably less support for using the network to engage individuals in participation in community or local decision making. Note that none of the library-sponsored projects, and only one of the university-sponsored community networking projects actually provide or envision providing services that involve citizens in discussions or interaction regarding local decision making; however, interestingly, approximately one-half of governmentally sponsored networks are actively invested in this.

The networks that appear to support democratic practices within the community network itself fall almost totally within the 501(3)(c) category. Here, approximately half are oriented toward providing their users with at least some degree of participation in the life of the network, ranging from creating the opportunity for users to become members, to scheduling opportunities for users or members to meet face-to-face, to enabling users or members to participate in project decision making.

These data support our expectations that there is considerable divergence in the networks' orientations toward democracy. Nearly all the networks subscribe to and actually provide support for the goal of information access. Furthermore, most networks use their resources to encourage contact between users and government institutions, reflecting the desire to invigorate traditional conceptions of liberal democracy. However, there is considerably less support, articulated and represented in services, oriented toward more participatory conceptions of democracy. Furthermore, comparatively few networks at this time are incorporating participatory practices in the administration of the network itself, and these are almost entirely networks in the 501(3)(c) category.

Evaluating and Creating Community Networks

To date, there has been relatively little research evaluating the effects or outcomes of community networks, a situation that reflects the more general case of inadequate information about the efficacy of computer networks affiliated with certain kinds of organizations (e.g., Lopata & McClure, 1996, on academic computer networks). Most of what we know about community networks comes from research devoted to single-case studies, such as the PEN project (e.g., Collins-Jarvis, 1993; Rogers et al., 1994; Schmitz et al., 1995). Within this category are also case studies of particular community networks aimed at identifying the types and range of users that a system has been able to attract (e.g., Patrick & Black, 1996, on the National Capital FreeNet of Ottawa; Patterson & Kavanaugh, 1996, on the Blacksburg Electronic Village; and Schalken & Tops, 1994, on the Digital City in Amsterdam, The Netherlands). The goal of these studies centers principally on understanding characteristics of the population deriving services from a particular network in an effort to determine how effective the network has been at reaching members of the community it wishes to serve. A handful of other studies have explored relationships between the social, cultural, and/or economic contexts and the nature of the community networking systems created in particular geographic locales (e.g., Bryan, 1996, on the Information City of Manchester, England; Uncapher, 1995, on Big Sky Telegraph).

Because the phenomenon is still relatively new, it is perhaps not surprising that even fewer studies have examined more than one community network at a time. Law and Keltner (1995) conducted interviews with key individuals (including one or two users) at five "civic networks" with the aim of describing the individual, group, and social benefits and disadvantages of providing access to networked communication technologies for individuals who are traditionally underserved. They were also interested in determining what can be learned about the implementation of these networks that can help us understand what is necessary to provide universal access to these technologies. Doctor and Ankem (1996), on the other hand, were interested in developing a taxonomy of information needs and services provided by computerized community information systems and using it to assess the types of services provided by these systems (e.g., education, governmental processes, and social services) and the kinds of help provided (e.g., advocacy, counseling, factual, etc.). They assessed more than 600 services provided by four systems based primarily on data provided by the system on the Internet and the World Wide Web.

It is not our purpose to review in detail this research or to attempt to draw any conclusions from it about the status of community networking. There are too few studies to draw on, and they address too wide a variety of research questions. Instead, it seems more useful at this time to draw attention to a number of issues that need to be considered when a researcher embarks on the process of investigating this phenomenon.

First, researchers need to reflect on the nature of the phenomenon under scrutiny in the research. As our survey has indicated, many different kinds of community networking systems are collected under the auspices of Web sites that offer directories to community networks. But closer examination reveals that some of the systems that call themselves community networks are the products of existing organizations and do very little that other systems that call themselves community networks do. Like Doctor and Ankem (1996), we might refer to the domain of all such systems as "computerized community networking services"; but we need to realize that a smaller proportion of these may subscribe to a particular political/social philosophy of community networking—for example, free-nets because they affiliate with the goals of the National Public Telecomputing Network or "civic networks" because they subscribe to the particular philosophy of civic networking. In other words, community networking is not a unitary or uniform phenomenon. The characteristics of computerized community networking services differ, of course, based on the community they serve; but they also differ widely on the basis of sponsorship, objectives, and motivating philosophy.

Second, along these lines, it is worth emphasizing, as our survey has made clear, that in addition to being technological artifacts, community networks are also organizational phenomena and that they might be researched as such. Most of the research conducted to date has neglected this aspect of networking. However, part of the divergence noted above is due to the kinds of organizations that sponsor community networks. It may be most appropriate to view community networking from an organizational perspective, asking, for example, (a) how individuals organize, in new or existing organizations, to produce community networks; (b) about the structure of the organizations that produce community networks; (c) about the characteristics of organizations and projects that are successful in attracting the support and patronage of the communities they serve; and (d) about the relationship between the goals of the initiators and the technological systems they create to achieve their goals.

A third issue concerns when to collect data. Community networks don't just appear overnight. Because they are the products of ongoing social processes, they need time to develop and mature before it is possible to determine what the contours of the system are and what objectives have emerged as central motivators. Thus, *when* data are collected will be an important consideration in decisions about research design.

A fourth important issue will center around how to collect data and who to collect it from. There are at least three perspectives from which to collect data about community networking systems: (a) the perspectives of the initiators, (b) the perspectives of the users, and (c) the on-line perspective, which provides a more or less "objective" indication of what services the system has to offer, regardless of the motivations giving rise to the services or whether the services are being used. As was the case in our survey and that of Doctor and Ankem (1996), research might be focused on investigating the on-line characteristics of the system. What is on-line is what the user experiences and, as such, this may be the most important indication of what actually exists. However, as Law and Keltner's (1995) study shows, qualitative data based on interviews of system administrators and users can provide a very rich picture of what the system is trying to achieve and what users are experiencing. Decisions regarding these issues will depend no doubt on the objectives of the research, but it is important to realize that the choices take the researcher in some very different directions.

Creating Community Networks

Principally a practitioner, Schuler (1997a) has invited academic researchers to participate in the creation of community networks and to conduct research aimed at identifying what factors or conditions enable networks to succeed. The extent to which academic researchers are already involved in community networking is so far quite unclear. Although our survey did not specifically address the question, our examination indicated that university-sponsored community networks (e.g., the Blacksburg Electronic Village) have incorporated research into the mission of the network. However our survey, which enumerated the number of university-*sponsored* community networks in the sample, does not address the extent to which academic researchers have become involved in the creation or development of community networks, because there may be participation by academics that has not translated into university sponsorship of the network. Anecdotally, there are some examples of this type of participation (see Schamber, 1996). Along with Schuler, we would like to urge serious and systematic involvement by academic researchers in the creation of community networks for a number of reasons.

One of the most important reasons for academics to become involved in the creation and development of community networks is to take advantage of the opportunity to incorporate research and evaluation objectives into the early design of the network. As Schamber (1996) points out, most computerized community information systems have been developed ad hoc, with no well-defined program for evaluation. She further suggests that a wide variety of research questions might be considered and data collection procedures be incorporated into technical development of the system as well as into the administration of the system—questions such as how users seek information and questions about the design of the system, hardware/software choices, interface design, and information providers.

Similarly, Gygi (1996) suggests that system designers incorporate evaluation procedures into the planning and implementation of community computer networking projects. Specifically, she urges researchers to specify the model of community development that underlies the creation of the network and to determine the particular chain of events thought to link goals and activities of the project to some particular activities and outcomes in the community.

This seems like a particularly useful suggestion if one considers that community networking systems may be regarded as experiments in social action. When individuals design an on-line community network, they are putting their naive theories of community, democracy, and civic development into action. That is, they incorporate into the technical design of the network the kinds of services and system components that they believe are required for achieving their goals. Academic researchers might consider participating in such an enterprise in a more active and reflective way. In so doing, they may be able to test particular theoretical frameworks that bear on the creation of community networking projects.

In a strong sense, this is what has already happened in creating and researching certain kinds of computer-mediated communication systems, such as the group decision support systems (GDSS) that have been the objects of serious systematic research in the last decade, where academic researchers joined with corporations in attempting to understand the kinds of technical systems that enhance organizational functioning. In the case of GDSSs, researchers attempted to improve group decision making in organizations in ways that enhanced members' participation but that also made decision making more efficient and productive of high-quality decisions. Each particular technical instance of a GDSS (e.g., GroupSystems researched by Nunamaker, Dennid, Vogel, Valacich, & George, 1991, or the SAMM system researched by Poole & DeSanctis, 1990) constitutes a material instantiation of one or more theories about the kinds of factors that enhance participation among members of a group or the factors that influence the efficiency of a decision-making process. That is, the technical design of the system reflected the researchers' expectations about the particular factors at play and the way that they would influence individuals' behavior in decision-making situations.

This reasoning applies similarly to the design and development of community networking systems. Much of the literature of computerized community networking has both a critical and a practical dimension (Fay, 1987). That is, academic researchers and practitioners alike tend to recognize that community and democracy as we currently experience these phenomena, in whatever venue and in whatever form, are not as good as they could be. And this literature implies that community networking can and should be conceptualized in ways that improve or strengthen community and/or democracy.

Those who wish to use technology for community-oriented or democratic aims need to specify the kinds of development processes and designs for community networking that should be supported. To make good on such intentions requires that we understand what we mean by community and democracy, how these concepts are enacted through interaction, how technology may be designed to facilitate particular goals, and the social context in which such technologies are deployed. Such considerations should be incorporated into the processes by which community networks are designed and, ultimately, into the technical configurations of the community networks that are designed. It is not impossible for practitioners to achieve successful community networks without academic involvement, but clearly this is an opportunity for academics to test the ability of theory to guide the development of technical systems that achieve important social objectives.

Such a strategy seems to be at the heart of the work done by Kees Schalken and Pieter Tops (1994), who have created Amsterdam's Digital City and are now conducting research about how it is used. In so doing, they pit two theories about the relationship between democracy and technology against each other: The Athenian Agora in which computing technology enables citizens to participate more extensively in political decision making that affects their lives versus Orwellian forms of monitoring and control in which electronic networks enable government to do a better job of keeping track of personal data about individuals. They suggest that

> the domination of these two big scenarios—with all their ideological baggage—has in itself been an obstruction to the carrying out of more empirical research of the relationships between democracy and the information society. The Digital City offers for the Netherlands an opportunity to try to end this "deadlock" by studying the working of information technology on democratic institutions.

Conclusion

Much has been made of the democratic and community-enhancing potential of new communication technologies. This is principally because the new medium appears to offer capabilities that make it technically possible to engage in more democratic and community-oriented communication behavior: distributing information more widely, improving access to local decision makers, and providing channels for deliberating about issues that overcome the normal constraints on face-to-face discussion due to time and space. However, now that the first wave of optimism over the new technologies has passed, most of us realize that these technical capabilities will not translate directly into improvements in our social world. The crucial issue is whether individuals will take advantage of these capabilities by creating social organizations that have the ability and the will to accomplish these goals.

Those who have been responsible for initiating this first generation of community networking systems have understood that the medium could be used to support the vigor and development of the community, and they are attempting to do just that. Researching the effects and outcomes of community networks thus represents an important way of learning more about the relationship between technology and the social goals that have that inspired its use. But just as importantly, community networks represent an opportunity for putting social theory more seriously to the test. Our theories about what constitutes "community" and what kinds of interaction and deliberation create a foundation for a strong democracy can be explored through the development of community networks. If we believe that knowledge creation and theory development have any relevance to the real world, there is reason to hope that applying theory to the design and development of community networking systems will increase the likelihood that such systems will be successful.

Notes

1. The following web sites contain information about and listings of community network projects:

> The Community Connector: University of Michigan School of Information and Library Science: http://www.si.umich.edu/Community/
> Boulder Community Network: Building Community: Online Resources: http://bcn.boulder.co.us/community/resources/center.html
> Telecommunications and Civic Networking: http://civic.net/ccn.html; http://civic.net/lgnet/telecom.html
> Organization for Community Networks: http://ofcn.org/
> Freenets and Community Networks: http://www.lights.com/freenet/ Community Networks, Inc.
> E-Democracy: http://www.e-democracy.org/
> Civic Net: The Spirit of Community Networking: http://www.tmn.com/civicnet/
> National Community Network Directories: http://macsky.bigsky.dillon.mt.us/community.html

We should emphasize that to answer all the questions in our survey, we simply consulted Web pages. We realized that there may be more or less to each community network than what represents the network on the Web. However, for this analysis, we assumed that what was offered on the Web was the best representation of what was actually available through the community network.

2. The number in the sample was reduced from 50 to 40 because we chose to eliminate those that were not classifiable in the earlier examination of sponsoring organizations as well as the three networks sponsored by a nonprofit organization other than a university (which seemed to represent extremely divergent sponsors).

3. We interpreted this data quite liberally. For example, networks that said they were oriented toward or that actually provided forums or electronic conferences for democratic or community interaction on issues or problems were counted as subscribing to the goal of democratic/community interaction. Networks that discussed or actually provided information or links to government, business, or nonprofit organizations were counted as subscribing to the goal of civic/economic invigoration. We looked for any indication that the network was oriented toward the substance of the goal, even if it used language different from the language we have used to label the goal.

References

Abrahamson, J., Arterton, C., & Orren, G. (1988). *The electronic commonwealth: The impact of new media technologies on democratic politics.* New York: Basic Books.

Bertelsen, D. (1992). Media form and government: Democracy as an archetypal image in the electronic age. *Communication Quarterly, 40,* 325-337.

Bowen, W. (1996). Community networks at the crossroads. Available: http://main.nc.us/about/cmtynet.html

Bryan, C. (1996). Manchester: Democratic implications of an economic initiative. *Javnost, 3,* 103-116. Reprinted in the *Electronic Journal of Communication/La revue electronique de communication, 6*(2). Available: http://www.cios.org/www/ejc/v6n296.htm [1998, May 22].

Carter, D. (1997). Digital democracy or information aristocracy: Economic regeneration and the information economy. In B. D. Loader (Ed.), *The government of cyberspace* (pp. 136-152). London: Routledge.

Cisler, S. (1993). Community computer networks: Building electronic greenbelts. Available: http://bcn.boulder.co.us/community/resources/greenbelts.txt

Civille, R. (1993). The Internet and the poor. Available: gopher://nic.merit.edu:7043/00/conference.proceedings/network. communities/internet-poor.txt

Civille, R., Fidelman, M., & Altobello, J. (1993). A national strategy for civic networking: A vision of change. Available: gopher://gopher.civic.net:2400/00/ssnational_strat/national_strategy.txt

Collins-Jarvis, L. (1993). Gender representation in an electronic city hall: Female adoption of Santa Monica's PEN system. *Journal of Broadcasting and Electronic Media, 37*(1), 49-65.

Doctor, R. D. (1994). Seeking equity in the National Information Infrastucure. *Internet Research, 4,*(3), 9-22.

Doctor, R. D., & Ankem, K. (1996). An information needs and services taxonomy for evaluating computerized community information system. In *Proceedings of the American Society for Information Science Mid-Year Meeting* (pp. 275-283). Medford, NJ: Information Today.

Doheny-Farina, S. (1996). *The wired neighborhood.* New Haven, CT: Yale University Press.

Ess, C. (1996). The political computer. In C. Ess (Ed.), *Philosophical perspectives on computer-mediated communication* (pp. 197-230). Albany: SUNY Press.

Fay, B. (1987). *Critical social science.* Ithaca, NY: Cornell University Press.

Fidelman, M. (1994). Life in the fast lane: A municipal roadmap for the information superhighway. Available: http://civic.net/fastlane.html [1998, May 22]

Gygi, K. (1996). Uncovering best practices: A framework for assessing outcomes in community computer networking. Available: http://www.laplaza.org/about_lap/archives/cn96/gygi.html [1998, May 22]

Habermas, J. (1989). *The structural transformation of the public sphere.* Cambridge: MIT Press.

LaMendola, W. F., & Rueda, P. (1997). An evaluation of the Colorado Access-Value-Content Project. Available: http://bcn.boulder.co.us/rueda/aclin.html [1998, May 22]

Law, S. A., & Keltner, B. (1995). Civic networks: Social benefits of on-line communities. In R. H. Anderson et al., *Universal access to e-mail: Feasibility and societal implications.* Available: http://www.rand.org/publications/MR/MR650/mr650.ch5/ch.5html

London, S. (1997). Civic networks: Building community on the net. Available: http://www.west.net/~insight/london/networks.htm

Lopata, C. L., & McClure, C. R. (1996). Measures for the academic networked environment: Strategies, guidelines, and options. In *Proceedings of the American Society for Information Science Mid-Year Meeting* (pp. 177-186). Medford, NJ: Information Today.

Nunamaker, J. F., Dennid, A. R., Valacich, J. S., Vogel, D. R., & George, J. F. (1991). Electronic meeting systems to support group work. *Communications of ACM, 34*(7), 40-61.

Oldenberg, R. (1989). *The great good place.* New York: Paragon.

Patrick, A. S., & Black, A. (1996). Rich, young, male, dissatisfied computer geeks? Demographics and satisfaction from the National Capital FreeNet. Available: http://debra.dgbt.doc.ca/services-research/survey/demographics/paper/

Patterson, S., & Kavanaugh, A. (1996). Summary of user profiles and expectations. Available: http://www.bev.net/research/Useres.2-96.html

Poole, M. S., & DeSanctis, G. (1990). Understanding the use of group decision support systems: The theory of adaptive structure. In J. Fulk & C. Steinfield (Eds.), *Organizations and communication technology* (pp. 173-193). Newbury Park, CA: Sage.

Rheingold, H. (1993). *The virtual community.* Reading, MA: Addison-Wesley.

Rogers, E., Collins-Jarvis, L., & Schmitz, J. (1994). The PEN project in Santa Monica: Interactive communication equality, and political action. *Journal of the American Society for Information Science, 45,* 401-410.

Schalken, K., & Tops, P. (1994). The digital city: A study into the backgrounds and opinions of its residents. Available: http://cwis.kub.nl/~frw/people/schalken/dceng.htm

Schamber, L. (1996). Assessing impact from the outset: Establishing a strategic research program for a new community-based information system. In *Proceedings of the American Society for Information Science Mid-Year Meeting* (pp. 207-214). Medford, NJ: Information Today.

Schmitz, J., Rogers, E., Phillips, K., & Paschal, D. (1995). The Public Electronic Network (PEN) and the homeless in Santa Monica. *Journal of Applied Communication, 23,* 26-43.

Schuler, D. (1994). Community networks: Building a new participatory medium. *Communications of the ACM, 37*(1), 39-51.

Schuler, D. (1995). Creating public space in cyberspace: The rise of the new community networks. Available: http://scn.org/ip/commnet/iwdec.html

Schuler, D. (1996). *New community networks: Wired for change.* Reading, MA: Addison-Wesley.

Schuler, D. (1997a). Community computer networks: An opportunity for collaboration among democratic technology practitioners and researchers. Available: http://www.scn.org/ip/commnet/ [1998, May 22]

Schuler, D. (1997b). Internet and politics: A platform for change. Available: http://www.scn.org/ip/commnet/munich-97.html [1998, May 22]

Sharp, M., & Beaudry, A. (1994). Communications as engagement: The Millenium reports to the Rockefeller Foundation. Available: http://www/cdinet.com/Millenium

Tillman, C. (1997). Thinking about the future: The National capital FreeNet/Liberal de la Capitale Nationale. Available: http://www.si.umich.edu/Community/pro_ncf.html

Uncapher, W. (1995). New communities, new communication: Big Sky Telegraphy and its community. Available: http://www.actlab.utexas.edu/paradox/uncphbio.html [1998, May 22]

van Dijk, J. (1996). Models of democracy—Behind the design and use of new media in politics. *Javnost, 3,* 43-56. Reprinted in the *Electronic Journal of Communication/la revue electronique de communication, 6*(2). Available: http://www.cios.org/www/ejc/v6n296.htm

12

Beyond Netiquette

The Ethics of Doing Naturalistic Discourse Research on the Internet

BARBARA F. SHARF

FOR COMMUNICATION SCHOLARS, the advent of electronic correspondence or e-mail as a common mode of interpersonal exchange presents multiple and expanding research opportunities. These exchanges constitute a unique hybrid genre somewhere between written text[1] and spoken conversation. Shank and Cunningham (1996) have dubbed the process of communicating via the Internet as "multiloguing," a quasi-discussion form in which the originator of a message sends it to an unknown body of readers/listeners who may respond immediately or in a delayed mode (or not at all), with no requirements for the turn-taking sequencing typically expected in oral discussions.

Not only does this new form of communication give rise to questions about the meaning of community (Catalfo, 1993; Jones, 1995), the definition and

AUTHOR'S NOTE: I would like to acknowledge my UIC colleague Bruce Lambert for a challenging discussion that helped me to consider more seriously contrasting viewpoints regarding the conduct of communication research on the Internet.

quality of interpersonal relationships (Parks & Floyd, 1996), and other issues fundamental to the nature of human interaction, e-mail generates immense quantities of discursive interchange on an ever-widening variety of topics. The computer-assisted discussions generated through a melange of on-line formats such as chat rooms, bulletin boards, and, particularly, listservs and conferences[2] focused on specific topics draw geographically dispersed people with like interests and, possibly, with related experiences and expertise. For these reasons, the Internet is increasingly perceived as an excellent source of data, not only for those collecting interview and survey responses but also for people who wish to analyze the discourse itself. This chapter is concerned with the ethical implications of conducting qualitative investigations of naturally occurring discourse available through the Internet.

Graduate students and senior researchers alike in communication studies are attracted to electronic communication for several reasons:

- As a focus for investigating the functions, boundaries, and resources of a relatively new technology being put to innovative and expanding uses, both in terms of informational content and relational dynamics
- As an easily accessible and economical repository of interpersonal "talk," available for analysis
- As a data source on specified topics

Unlike face-to-face conversations, which must be personally observed or mechanically recorded for research purposes—methods that are intrusive as well as labor and cost intensive—electronic messages initially appear and can be recalled later on the computer monitor and can also be preserved as printed hard copy or stored on floppy or compact diskettes. Sometimes, the output of ongoing groups is archived so that an interested newcomer can look up past discussions. All these features facilitate data collection and are of great convenience to researchers. Furthermore, viewed as a type of naturalistic interpersonal communication, Internet discourse lends itself well to a variety of analytic and ethnomethodological approaches, including network, content, conversational, and participant observation studies.

Ethical Concerns

As a relatively new form of interpersonal contact minus nonvisual cues, within Internet circles, the need has arisen to develop a "netiquette," or rules of thumb, to encourage politeness, civility, and enhanced understanding among participants. These codes have been formulated by users as communicative problems are encountered and identified in the process of employing the medium. For example, expressions of accentuation (SUCH AS THE REPEATED USE OF CAPITAL LETTERS, THE E-MAIL EQUIVALENT OF YELLING) are encouraged to be used judiciously; common symbols and acronyms provide relational cues for interpreting content (e.g., a "smiley face," :-), to paralinguistically convey "I'm only joking"[3]); and discourteous behavioral practices such as flaming (insulting language), ranting (prolonged expressions of anger and complaint), and spamming ("stuffing" electronic mailboxes with unsolicited messages) have been informally discouraged and formally condemned in several contexts.

Danielson (1996) probes the ethics of computer-mediated communication (CMC) deeper through a concept he calls "Artificial Morality." He explains, "It is important to see what is ethically significant about CMC is not the technological change but the *social* changes it enables" (p. 70). Thus, for Danielson, an ethical breach is conceived as a socially irresponsible use of the common resources available on the Internet. One example he provides is the common sending of e-mail in forms that are undifferentiated visually as to degree of formality (e.g., a friendly note versus a mass mailing versus a formal request), forcing the reader to use time to read all e-mail to make such meaning distinctions.

Although formation of such rules of conduct and ethical inquiries into the communicative use of the computer are still at an early stage of development, analogous guidelines for encouraging ethical practices in the conduct of on-line research are only now being discussed. At present, because the Internet is part of a technology in continual flux and rapid evolution, there is incomplete awareness of the issues at stake, let alone consensus on the best ways to proceed. Nonetheless, several key ethical concerns have become apparent. Perhaps chief among these are issues of *privacy, confidentiality, informed consent,* and *appropriation of others' personal stories.* Although these problematics exist in other kinds of research endeavors, they are brought into particularly broad relief by the ambiguous nature of the electronic medium.

PRIVACY AND CONFIDENTIALITY

As the terms clearly signify, electronic mail goes through the Internet, a worldwide computer-connected web, that enables linkages among far-flung people and sites. An e-mail communiqué from one person to another is analogous to a letter or phone call, ostensibly private but capable of interception. Journalistic stories abound concerning teenage hackers who break through government and corporate security codes to pilfer or vandalize information. Employees are warned that intimate messages sent through institutional computer networks are rarely, if ever, totally erased; they can and may be accessed by unintended others. Unlike phone calls and more easily than letters, e-mail can be instantaneously copied or redirected (unbeknownst to the writer) to another or many other readers. The ease of passing on messages has been demonstrated in numerous infamous instances when so-called urban myths or apocryphal rumors (e.g., the so-called Kurt Vonnegut commencement address, which Vonnegut denies having delivered) have spread rapidly via the Internet through broad sectors of the population. In short, computer-aided communication, under many circumstances, is a very public medium. Despite widely announced admonitions concerning the potential for public exposure, there exists the paradox that writing to others via e-mail often feels like a private or, in the case of an on-line group, quasi-private act. Thus, for most people when chatting about a specified topic on the net, the possibility that a researcher is gathering their commentary as data to be analyzed and published is remote, if considered at all. If the topic is the next presidential election, last Sunday's football game, or the best places to shop for bargain vacation packages, the consequences of having one's words used for investigatory purposes may be minimal or nil. On the other hand, there are many vulnerable populations—people in acute stages of grief, with sexual dysfunctions, life-threatening diseases, or addictions, just to provide a few examples—for whom interchange via computer has become a primary source of information and social support. In the spirit of therapeutic alliance and human catharsis, they may pour out their very deeply held feelings to one another. Ironically, the anonymity provided by electronic communication, such as the choice not to reveal one's name or the shelter from being evaluated visually, may encourage verbal intimacies that would be withheld in other interactive contexts.

Elgesem's (1996) discussion of privacy, respect and risk via CMC throws very helpful shades of light on the knotty problem of public versus private domain. He argues that, in lieu of a rigid dichotomy between classes of public and private situations, it is more useful to acknowledge that private situations often (as in the case of CMC) occur within the scope of larger, public situations. Thus, maintenance of privacy is recognized as occurring within degrees of limits on behavior and accessibility rather than as absolutes. The norms for protection of privacy are, in fact, publicly developed and socially defined. Regarding communication among participants via electronic channels, privacy is clearly not a definite state of being; by virtue of the medium, anyone choosing to make disclosures through an on-line discussion format is assuming some risk in who will receive that information and how it will be used. Thus, the most important sense of privacy for e-mail participants becomes the matter of personal information control. Elgesem goes on to enumerate six principles of fair information processing that have been used to undergird computer-related legislation in several countries:

1. *Openness:* Existence of data banks should be publicly known.
2. *Individual access and correction:* People should have access to the data collected about themselves.
3. *Collection limitation and relevance:* Personal data should be collected for one specific, legitimate purpose.
4. *Use limitations:* Information should be used only for purposes specified at the time of collection.
5. *Disclosure limitation:* Personal data is not to be communicated externally without the consent of the subject who supplied the data.
6. *Security:* Personal data should be reasonably guarded against risks such as loss, unauthorized access, modification, or disclosure.

In his essay, Elgesem is concerned with the example of medical data collected from and about individuals. Although he does not deal with the notion of conversation as personal data, the principles he identifies are still useful for the current discussion.

For the communication researcher who wishes to study on-line discourse, when and in what form is consent required from the people whose talk is being scrutinized? What constitutes an invasion of privacy on the Net? If data collection of other people's talk is not unlawful, does it follow that it is ethical to do so? Is there any impetus to ensure confidentiality in quoted material if people who have posted messages on-line have identified themselves by name, as opposed to a user number or pseudonym?

INFORMED CONSENT AND NARRATIVE APPROPRIATION

Some forms of research, qualitative or quantitative, do not raise a red flag in this respect. If an investigator solicits respondents to participate in an on-line survey or interview, or to contribute personal anecdotes, those who do respond have made a conscious choice to do so. They have the option to disguise their identities with user names that do not reveal actual names or exact locations.[4] Respondents can also control how much information they wish to volunteer. Presenting the greater ethical dilemma are investigations that focus on the patterns of naturally occurring discourse in which those who are being studied cannot choose to exercise the same sorts of control.

Compounding the list of issues that communication scholars examining electronic conversations need to consider are concerns inherent in the nature of qualitative research, whether mediated or face-to-face. These have to do with the interpretation of the words of others, including *the appropriation of someone else's personal narratives* and *quoting out of context* (Estroff, 1995; Harris, 1996). Anytime a researcher imposes his or her own framework of analysis on the storied accounts gleaned from other people, whether by in-depth interview, participant observation, or some other form of recorded data collection, questions arise about ownership (whose story is it now?) and validity (in what ways has that story been altered through the process of interpretation and the necessity of choosing selected samples of discourse to use as supporting evidence and illustrations?). A final ethical concern is that of potential *exploitation* in regard to how the results of the research will be used, to what purposes, in which context, and to whose benefit or expense.

A Personal Example:
Breast Cancer On-Line

Like several other users of computerized communication, I did not perceive ethical difficulties until I was well in the midst of psychological and inter-personal involvement. In June 1994, I subscribed to a newly announced listserv called the Breast Cancer List. Although I was already involved in research about the public rhetoric about breast cancer, I did not join with a specific intention to conduct research about this group. In fact, it was my first experience on a listserv, and my motivation was primarily curiosity to learn how such a thing functioned and what people with a common concern about breast cancer would "talk" about on-line. In fact, I found the conver-sations quite compelling, and it eventually dawned on me that within this body of discourse, there was something worthy of investigation, although several months into my participation, I still was not sure what that was. Because this is a very active list (initially, an average of 25 messages a day, eventually averaging over 100 messages daily), it seemed impractical to save all the correspondence that transpired. Thus, after a few weeks on-line, I began a habit of printing off postings that struck me as interesting for one reason or another (e.g., arguments, empathic responses, humor), without a specific objective as to how I would make use of my collection; in short, I ended up using a grounded-theory approach (Glaser & Strauss, 1973).

For several months, my participation consisted of "lurking"—that is, reading the messages without contributing any of my own. Although I never became a very active poster during my 9 months of nearly daily participation on the Breast Cancer List, when I occasionally decided to express thoughts or feelings or asked for or provided information, I was mindful to "contextualize" myself, explaining that I was both an individual with an abiding concern about breast cancer as well as an academic researcher. When I eventually focused on aspects of the List about which I had decided to write, using discursive examples from the postings as supportive material, I briefly explained this point as well, as part of my self-introduction. In retrospect, I believe I had a sense early on that it was prudent to let fellow list members know that I had two reasons for participating in this forum. This inclination was especially prompted by both the highly personal nature of much of the content discussed and the knowledge that a majority of people who subscribe to this on-line group are survivors struggling to cope with their disease and carry on with their lives, a network of suffering and courageous people deserving of my respect and candor. For these reasons, I repeated my self-introduction with each new post, aware that membership (and, therefore, my readership) on the List changes somewhat on a daily basis, as well as its being difficult to recall individuals who post infrequently, given a membership of several hundred people (the constituency presently is at approximately 1,000). Nonetheless, despite my efforts to the contrary, it is reasonable to assume that even people who regularly—let alone sporadically—posted were not aware that their words might become part of my research.

After 8 months of participant observation, I formulated a number of research questions regarding the composition of the membership, the content of the discussions, and the communicative functions served by the List, and proceeded to write a first-draft paper, which was presented orally in a few academic forums. Within my write-up, most quotations were not attributed to a specifically named person, and in the few instances when they were, only first names were alluded to. As luck would have it, my university public relations department did a wonderfully effective job with press releases, and a few media representatives came seeking information. Although these generally did not result in media exposure, my work did get a very brief mention in a Sunday edition of the *Chicago Tribune,* and I was interviewed for a health report spot for a local cable television news show. In neither case were specific names or quotations used. Although I had no knowledge of the newspaper blurb until after it was published, during the television interview, I insisted that the publisher include the e-mail address of the List and directions for how to subscribe.[5] In the aftermath of the oral presentations, I started to feel strongly that it was now a necessary step to contact the individuals on the List whom I had quoted, to ask for and, I hoped, receive their permission to do so. Factors that prompted this conviction were that I was receiving many requests for a copy of the manuscript, and I was definitely planning to submit a revised draft to a scholarly journal to be reviewed for publication. Also, because it was so late into the process of participant observation that I decided on a formal research plan, I had not yet submitted the study to be reviewed by the campus Institutional Review Board, which oversees the ethical conduct of human subjects research. Before doing so, I wanted to have an informed consent procedure in place.

My next step, then, was to go back through my printouts to obtain the e-mail addresses, my only means of contact, for each of the individuals whom I quoted. I wrote a separate, personalized note to each in which I, again, introduced myself, gave a brief description of the research, provided the quotation I wished to use, asked for consent to do so, and offered to share the full draft and provide whatever other information might be necessary for them to make a decision. This process turned out to be time-consuming. By the time I had heard back from all the people I had contacted, several weeks had passed, a frustrating situation when an investigator is eager to publish his or her work. During this time period, I discussed what I was doing with colleagues at work. Several were incredulous that I had undertaken this task, reiterating that listserv correspondence occurs within a public forum that eliminates the need to seek informed consent.

Of the 14 people contacted, 13 gave immediate permission for me to use their words. The remaining individual was at first somewhat hostile, assuming that I had behaved voyeuristically, taking advantage of people in distress. Although researchers, along with physicians, patients, family, and friends of patients, are explicitly invited to participate in the List within the statement of objectives sent to each new subscriber, the idea of using the conversations as data had not occurred to many members, including this woman.[6] I wrote back, taking care to explain the nature of my participation and to explain my study in more detail; after the second exchange, her concerns were addressed and she, too, replied affirmatively.

In addition to receiving consent, this process yielded other benefits I had not anticipated. Several people asked to read my manuscript, and most responded with feedback, some brief and others quite detailed. Two individuals have subsequently sent me their own writings. A few provided valuable updated information, because by now, I had been off the List for several months. One person strenuously challenged the interpretation I had made concerning her remark. I was able to work their commentary into the revised draft before it was sent off to the journal; as a result, I think I wrote an improved paper (Sharf, 1997). Not only was the content of their messages meaningful, but the tone of the notes was almost universally supportive, promoting a feeling of connectedness.

In sum, although the informed-consent procedure I chose to use required extra effort and time, it ensured that explicit permission was given; confidentiality had been satisfactorily maintained; quoting out of context had not undermined the original author's intent; and my interpretation of others' comments had not amounted to erroneous appropriation. Not surprisingly, affirmation from the Institutional Review Board was readily given, after the consents were obtained. In short, I felt assured that whatever contributions my work made to scholarly literature, those were not at the expense of the individuals whose words I used and the community about which I was writing.

Once the article was published, my final step was to share it on the Breast Cancer List. Because I knew the journal in question was not easily accessible to many members, I asked permission from the editor to obtain the final version on disk, so I could attach it to a post. Unfortunately, the editor has chosen not to reply. Instead, I sent a message to the List, giving the citation and offering to send copies to people who wanted one.

Fortuitously, just as this chapter was being written, a debate about the ethics of using the words of fellow members occurred on the Breast Cancer List, nearly 2 years after my own experience. The actions of a particular individual were brought into question, an independent author who published a book about the experience of living with a cancer recurrence, using interview data collected mainly from List participants who had volunteered to participate in her research.[7] A special term, *harvesting,* has evolved to refer to the collecting of the words of others. A strong criticism was leveled at this person for harvesting the list and then talking about the resulting book on-line for purposes of making a profit and self-aggrandizement. This commentary prompted several others to reply with their own opinions. Another participant, an artist, wrote to confess that she also had harvested from the List, starting with taking photographic portraits of selected List members, later using quotes taken from on-line postings for an installation; in both instances, she had obtained consent to take the photos and exhibit the words. However, she, like the author, hoped to sell her works, and wondered if making money constituted an unethical act. In the responses that ensued, a common theme voiced repeatedly was that neither person had done anything unethical, in that they sought consent and were not secretive about their intentions in using the material. It is important to underscore that no one within this group of replies said that her or his words are public property and, thus, available for harvesting without consent. A few pointed out that there may well be intrinsic benefits for those whose words have been harvested. For many, it is an honor to be quoted in a publication. In the words of one member, "I'm not about to write anything of a significant length to get published anywhere, but as part of a larger picture, I might have something to add."

Toward an Evolving Set of Guidelines

Of course, the discussion of ethical conduct regarding harvesting was internal to the list itself, involving interactions among its own members. Many researchers in communication and other social sciences wish to harvest on-line conversations with other support and special interest groups, without becoming personally involved as participants or feeling that consent is necessary. Such data collection is doable and ostensibly legal, yet flies in the face of what thousands, maybe millions, of Internet group members feel is permissible and ethical. Such a difference in perceptions seems bound to be on a collision course. In a heated discussion about this disagreement with yet another colleague, a solution was proposed that perhaps entry to on-line discussion groups should be preceded routinely by a written warning that all postings are public statements subject to widespread accessibility. Although I think such warnings are a good idea, I do not agree that all responsibility should be presumed to fall on the shoulders of on-line communicators. For one thing, such placement of duty might go a long way toward discouraging genuine expression of ideas and feelings, in effect undermining the function of interpersonal support and information sharing that the Internet has made possible. That would be a distressing outcome for people who have come to rely on the medium and, in the end, would destroy the very communication data that researchers had sought in the first place. Second, as a matter of principle, I argue that researchers, conscious of their scholarly objectives, should bear a larger portion of the ethical burden, in lieu of those whom they hope to study. Toward that end, I offer the following guidelines to assist scholars who conduct qualitative investigations of naturally occurring discourse on the Internet. Once again, in the conceptualization of research ethics, I find Elgesem's (1996) discussion of on-line privacy particularly helpful. He distinguishes two different kinds of privacy violations. First is the "classical" form, disseminating information of an intimate nature to an interested audience without the consent of the subject. The second type posits that if an individual has consented to disclosure of intimate information, it is a privacy violation if the information is disclosed in ways in which that person has not consented. Although individuals assume risk of privacy violations through the decision to communicate on-line, the acceptability of assuming such risk is buffered by the presence of the following conditions:

- The probability of risk is generally low and not higher than necessary.
- The use of personal information by others is absolutely necessary.
- The risks assumed in revealing personal information are balanced by the good(s) achieved in the end result.
- Acceptance of the risk of violating privacy involves fulfillment of a moral obligation.
- There remains a possibility for the subject to reject the use of personal information.

Despite the existence of such philosophical tenets, I suspect it may not always be possible to prevent encountering ethical dilemmas in the midst of doing research on and/or about the Internet. Nonetheless, the particular points that follow are offered with the intention of helping scholars give forethought to what are presently common issues of concern.

1. Before starting an investigation and throughout the duration of the study, the researcher should contemplate whether or not the purposes of the research are in conflict with or harmful to the purpose of the group. Conversely, the researcher should consider whether the research will benefit the group in some way—for example, helping to legitimize the group's function.

At the very least, the researcher needs to have thought through the ramifications of doing the study on the people whose words are being used, especially in the case of vulnerable populations. This does not mean that the research must concur with the group's objectives or agree with its norms and decisions. The results may, indeed, be critical but should not leave individual participants open to ridicule, embarrassment, or other forms of harm.

> 2. The researcher should clearly introduce himself or herself as to identity, role, purpose, and intention to the on-line group or individuals who are the desired focus of study.

In other words, Who are you? Why are you interested in this set of conversations? How do you plan to go about studying them? How do you anticipate interacting with other participants? In what ways will the study be used?

> 3. The researcher should make a concerted effort to contact directly the individual who has posted a message that he or she wishes to quote in order to seek consent.

It should be clearly explained to the writer what words will be quoted, in what manner and for what purposes the quotation is expected to be used. This may require that the person from whom consent is desired be permitted to review his or her own words in the new context in which they will appear. Implied consent should *not* be presumed if the writer does not respond to the researcher's query.

> 4. The researcher should seek ways to maintain an openness to feedback from the e-mail participants who are being studied.

Although many scholars may argue that this guideline is far beyond the usual ethical responsibilities expected of researchers, I argue that only by inviting such feedback can the researcher be assured that she or he has not grossly misinterpreted another's meaning or intention, or appropriated another's story in ways that distort or damage. Again, receiving such feedback does not mean that the investigator has to agree with it, for the whole purpose of a scholarly analysis is to perceive patterns of interaction and glean insights that may not be clear to individual participants within the communicative event under scrutiny. Nonetheless, it is important that the researcher provide an opportunity for study participants to correct unintended errors (e.g., due to the nature of the medium, the tone of a remark made via the Internet can be easily misunderstood) and lend their own insights and other valuable information to the research project.

5. The researcher should strive to maintain and demonstrate a respectful sensitivity toward the psychological boundaries, purposes, vulnerabilities, and privacy of the individual members of a self-defined virtual community, even though its discourse is publicly accessible.

I am aware that this admonition is particularly applicable to a group such as the Breast Cancer List, a virtual community defined by its mutual concern about a life-threatening disease. A directly contrasting example, such as a listserv devoted to the promulgation of child pornography or racism, pointedly makes the case against the observation of this guideline. There must be room for the researcher to exercise judgment. That's why my suggestions are labeled "guidelines," not rules. Still, such patently reprehensible entities are the exception, not the norm; thus, I argue that the guideline is generally useful and appropriate in a majority of cases.

I do not pretend to know all the answers based on my own fairly limited experience and those of others that I have heard reported. Furthermore, as computer technology continues to expand and evolve (e.g., increased availability of teleconferencing), other ethical concerns are sure to arise that cannot be fully anticipated at this time. Therefore, I conclude this chapter with the sizable caveat that the guidelines I have offered are a beginning attempt, along with an invitation to other scholars with different experiences and insights, to refine, add to, and improve upon these.

Notes

1. For a study that treats e-mail discourse from a literary rather than a communicative perspective, see McLellan (1997).

2. Listservs and electronic conferences require some form of subscription rather than relying on "drop-in" participation and, thus, may be more likely to attract people who are more seriously committed to the topic at hand.

3. Smiley faces are typically formed by the impromptu use of a colon and end-of-parenthesis, which creates a sideways smile. Conversely, a sad face is formed by a colon and start-of-parenthesis. Thus, I was amazed to discover on my new computer that typing these key combinations result in two new, formalized symbols, indicating that usage of these "terms" has now become universalized.

4. There exist directories and other mechanisms for tracking e-mail addresses. It does, however, require extra effort to make use of these.

5. Very mindful that the research was concerned with how breast cancer survivors are helping themselves through this computer medium, I contacted by e-mail a survivor on the List who had an address from my own campus to invite her participation in both the television interview and one of the on-campus presentations, which she accepted.

6. It is a certainty that many members of the List are unaware that their postings can be accessed without subscribing to the List, by going to a separate archive on the Web.

7. Interestingly, the majority of these interviews took place in off-line, face-to-face circumstances during a gathering of List members.

References

Catalfo, P. (1993). America, online. In S. Walker (Ed.), *Changing community* (pp. 1-76). St. Paul, MN: Graywolf.

Danielson, P. (1996). Psuedonyms, mailbots, and virtual letterheads: The evolution of computer-mediated ethics. In C. Ess (Ed.), *Philosophical perspectives on computer-mediated communication* (pp. 67-93). Albany: State University of New York Press.

Elgesem, D. (1996). Privacy, respect for persons, and risk. In C. Ess (Ed.), *Philosophical perspectives on computer-mediated communication* (pp. 45-66). Albany: State University of New York Press.

Estroff, S. (1995). Whose story is it anyway? Authority, voice, and responsibility in narratives of chronic illness. In S. K. Toombs, D. Barnard, & R. A. Carson (Eds.), *Chronic illness: From experience to policy* (pp. 76-102). Bloomington: Indiana University Press.

Glaser, B. G., & Strauss, A. L. (1973). *The discovery of grounded theory: Strategies for qualitative research.* Chicago: Aldine.

Harris, B. A. (1996). The researcher as narrator. In *The potential for empowerment in five nurse-patient relationships in psychiatry* (pp. 60-70). Unpublished doctoral dissertation, University of Illinois at Chicago.

Jones, S. (1995). Understanding community in the information age. In S. Jones (Ed.), *Cybersociety* (pp. 10-35). Thousand Oaks, CA: Sage.

McLellan, F. (1997). A whole other story: The electronic narrative of illness. *Literature and Medicine, 10*(1), 88-107.

Parks, M. R., & Floyd, K. (1996). Making friends in cyberspace. *Journal of Communication, 46,* 80-97.

Shank, G., & Cunningham, D. (1996). Mediated phosphor dots: Toward a post-Cartesian model of computer-mediated communication via the semiotic superhighway. In C. Ess (Ed.), *Philosophical perspectives on computer-mediated communication* (pp. 27-41). Albany: State University of New York Press.

Sharf, B. F. (1997). Communicating breast cancer on-line: Support and empowerment on the Internet. *Women & Health, 26*(1), 65-84.

13

Thinking the Internet
Cultural Studies Versus the Millennium

JONATHAN STERNE

CONSIDER THE ROLE OF THE INTERNET in the life of one of my students. She is an undergraduate at a large midwestern research university. She lives in the dormitories and walks a few blocks each morning to class. Between morning courses, she ducks into one of the many campus computing facilities and quickly checks her e-mail. She finds a note from a high school friend, several forwarded lists of jokes, and a few announcements about a club she once visited. She fires off a quick e-mail to one of her professors to see if they can meet the following day about a paper that will be due after the weekend. She quickly logs off and heads to her next class. Later in the day, while at the library, she uses the campus library network to locate some books she needs for the research paper. As she works on an assignment later that

AUTHOR'S NOTE: Many thanks to the members of the spring 1998 cultural studies reading group at the University of Illinois (and especially Greg Dimitriadis for organizing it) and to Kelly G⸻ Steve Jones, Carrie Rentschler, Geoff Sauer, and Greg Wise for their helpful advice in co⸻ this chapter.

night in the dormitory's computer lab, she procrastinates by visiting some of the Web sites for her favorite television shows and replying to her friend's e-mail. When she checks her e-mail again, the professor has left her a message to call during her office hours the next day. Other messages have arrived. Later in the semester, she will show up at the same computer lab to do her course work only to discover that it is full and there is a line out the door. Although many students depend on the school for their access to a computer, campus facilities cannot meet student demand during midterms and finals.

A few things should be immediately obvious about this banal scenario. First, the Internet is part of the fabric of my student's daily life. It is no more a break from her daily experience than getting on a crowded elevator to move up three stories in a building. Second, the relationships she maintains on-line are not strictly or necessarily separate from the relationships she maintains off-line. Her on-line activities may mark her only participation in the club or her only activity as a fan of certain television shows apart from watching them, but even in these cases, her experiences on-line are connected with her off-line experiences. Third, her computer use is very much determined by her social location. She doesn't have a computer of her own, but the university provides extensive facilities and requires her to use them. As a result, like many of her colleagues and mine, she has enough practical knowledge of computing to use her e-mail, browse the web, and do her course work, but beyond that, the workings of computer hardware and software are a mystery for her. Her experience of computing is likely analogous to the relationship most American motorists have with their cars: She knows enough to get around and no more. Finally, she is on her way to becoming a certified member of the educated classes (through her undergraduate degree) and is likely preparing for a career in which computer use will be part of her job.

Despite the Internet's relative banality for the majority of its users, its connection to other media (in my student's case, telephony and television), its institutional connections, and the relative privilege of its users, critical scholars have largely followed other academics' leads in depicting the Internet as a *millennial* cultural force. In these millennial scenarios, the ltural critic wonders at the possibilities and "impact" of the "new" me- it revolutionize our lives or be a tool of alienation? The perceived rnet may suggest to some people that the available works for thinking about communications need this transformative technology. But where do l transformation come from? Passing familiarity with the discourses of advertising and technological change yields the insight that "new" is not an empirical description of a technology but a value judgment about the technology that comes with a great deal of intellectual baggage. Images of technologies affecting our lives, solving our problems (or creating new ones), or transforming our self-understandings have populated advertising since the turn of the 20th century and are present in other kinds of technological discourse going even further back (see Carey, 1988; Czitrom, 1982; Marvin, 1988; Miller, 1991; Spigel, 1992). Millennial claims about technology can take either technophilic or technophobic turns: Either the new technologies are going to transform everything for the better or for the worse. Both positions, however, take for granted the relative autonomy and agency of technology—its transformative power—and often, they separate technologies from the contexts in which they are developed and used (Stabile, 1994, offers a critique of this dichotomy in feminist thinking).

The current predicament for cultural studies-based Internet research is how to think about its central object of study—the Internet—outside the millennial frameworks in which new communication technologies are often presented to us. Sociologist Pierre Bourdieu argues that the fundamental methodological problem for all social inquiry is the *construction of the object.* In other words, it is a question of being able to engage in very high theoretical stakes by means of "very precise and often apparently mundane, if not derisory, empirical objects" (Bourdieu & Wacquant, 1993, p. 220). Cultural studies writers have largely worked in this vein, spending considerable time and ink on defining just what it is they are studying. Following that lead, this chapter is not a "how to" concerning cultural studies and the Internet. Rather, it considers some of the problems that cultural studies scholars have run into when conceptualizing the Internet and offers some directions for future research. Specifically, I argue that cultural studies needs to continue to develop alternatives to millennial conceptions of the Internet—those that separate the Internet from other social forces or bracket it as a self-same context, like a sealed container, and thereby treat it as an autonomous and revolutionary cultural site.

In what follows, I discuss some key aspects of a cultural studies approach to Internet study, starting with four basic issues in cultural studies and a loose definition of the field. Readers already familiar with cultural studies may wish to go directly to the following section, "Cultural Studies Does the Internet," which considers the current state of cultural studies work concerning the Internet. The final section of the chapter offers some suggestions for what cultural studies work can bring to future studies of the Internet.

If this chapter appears particularly polemical concerning the ideologies surrounding "on-lineness," it is because this work itself fits within the metadiscursive approach to Internet studies that I discuss later. In this case, I have endeavored to consider cultural studies of the Internet as a road into the critique of Internet discourse itself. The success of my readings will ultimately be measured by the degree to which this chapter helps others to move beyond the commonplaces and clichés of Internet scholarship and reconceptualize it in intellectually challenging and politically vital terms.

Politics, Context, Articulation, Theory: Issues in Cultural Studies

Perhaps because of the ambiguity in its name, cultural studies has become a notoriously difficult field to define.[1] Some people take the term at its most general, as a kind of cultural analogue of "social studies" that encompasses all of the humanities and qualitative social sciences. In this model, the reference to culture in the name is a reference to the object of the "studies" the scholar conducts: Any study of culture then becomes part of "cultural studies." Although such a definition may be useful for administrators seeking to downsize liberal arts programs, it is far too general and ill defined to be of much serious intellectual use. Imagine a single chapter in a book on Internet research covering "social studies approaches"; such a chapter would have to cover the work of economists and archaeologists, specialists in women's studies and area studies, political science and sociology. In other words, it would be too broad to be useful to its readers.

I have come to think of cultural studies more as a proper name for a genre of scholarship: Cultural studies is an orientation toward scholarship (which is different from a method—we will see how below), and this is how I use the terms *cultural studies* and *cultural study* in the remainder of this chapter. In this sense, *cultural* is an adverb modifying the studies; the *object* of cultural studies (e.g., the particular object that one subjects to "cultural study") remains unspecified in the name. Although the field takes its name from work done at the Centre for Contemporary Cultural Studies at the University of Birmingham, England, during the 1960s and 1970s, the Centre is now only one among many places where such work is conducted. Similarly, although one can trace a "tradition" of cultural studies back through work done at the center from the 1960s through the early 1980s (Hall, 1992), not all cultural studies work considers itself to be in dialogue with that particular body of work. Indeed, scholars in recent years have made claims for other "schools" of cultural studies originating in other places, such as the subaltern studies school in India or Latin American or Australian cultural studies (Barbero, 1993; Canclini, 1988; Frow & Morris, 1993; Guha & Spivak, 1988; O'Connor, 1991). As the term cultural studies gained currency among academics worldwide over the course of the 1980s and 1990s, definitions of the field proliferated—the confusing name giving birth to many attempts to define the field (Grossberg, 1997; Hall, 1992; Nelson, 1989; Nelson, Treichler, & Grossberg, 1992).[2] My definitions of the field below draw on Lawrence Grossberg's work (see Grossberg, 1997, for a range of his writings in this area), with a few modifications.

In general, cultural studies is a body of work concerned with, as Tony Bennett (1993) puts it, culture and power. This concern with culture and power is characterized by a set of shared intellectual strategies: These include attention to the political character of knowledge production, an orientation toward the analysis of context, a commitment to theory, and a theory of articulation. Although not every cultural study may exhibit all of these characteristics, they are useful starting points for getting a bearing in the field.

THE POLITICAL CHARACTER OF
KNOWLEDGE PRODUCTION

Although many fields have recently seen debates about the "politicization" of their subject matter (e.g., on politics and literature, see Berube, 1994; Graff, 1992), cultural studies sees all knowledge production as *inherently* political. In other words, cultural studies scholars simply acknowledge the political character of their own work, the work of other scholars, and their objects of study. Cultural studies scholarship is thus characterized by more frequent use of autobiographical and other self-reflexive strategies for putting the scholar *in* the analysis, frequent detours through theoretical concerns, and generally a preoccupation with the construction of its object of study and the construction of the scholar's writing style and speaking voice.[3] But cultural studies is even more political in its object choices: Ideally, it chooses objects for the purposes of political intervention. This may take the form of analyzing a present crisis (Grossberg, 1992; Hall, Critcher, Jefferson, Clarke, & Roberts, 1979), or it may take the form of an intervention in the conceptualization of politics (Hall & Jefferson, 1976; Morris, 1990). Of course, the term *political* is itself highly contested within the field; and one can easily slip into speaking of "politics" without being more specific. Styles of self-presentation on-line, gender relations on-line, the economics of computer use, and U.N. policy decisions are all political, but they are each political in a different way. Specificity is important lest one's claims about a particular kind of politics be interpreted as a claim about all politics. Finally, cultural studies is not so much a politics in itself as a response to politics both in and outside the academy. It is not a substitute for the work of activists or even for other kinds of politically motivated work in the academy. Ideally, it is antisexist, anticapitalist, antiracist, antiheteronormative, and anticolonial in its politics,[4] but it is also ideally strategic, meaning that any given cultural study is not bound to the requirements of critiquing all forms of domination at once (after all, even the most avant-garde scholarly writing is still a more or less linear form of expression).

For the Internet scholar, this commitment to politics takes at least two forms: the critique of object choice and the critique of the research practice. *Why* study the Internet? Is it interesting just because it's a trendy topic or because it points to something more significant than itself? Moreover, what is at stake in how the Internet is studied? What are the political dimensions of the intellectual choices the researcher makes and, more important, the connections between the research and larger political problems inside and outside academia?

THE PRODUCTION OF CONTEXT

If cultural studies' goal is to think politically, then its object choice shifts somewhat. Although cultural studies is often lumped with the humanities, it differs from many humanistic disciplines in that it is *not* primarily concerned with the interpretation of texts. On the contrary, cultural studies is primarily concerned with the production of context for a text, event, or practice under consideration. Thus, for instance, it is not the ultimate goal of a cultural study to determine what a given event on-line *means* for its participants (although this may be part of it) but, rather, *how the possibilities for meaning are themselves organized.* Interpretation of texts and artifacts is a necessary element of cultural studies research, but it is not the ultimate goal of cultural studies. Cultural studies seeks a richer understanding of the political character of cultural and social life, and this means examining the relationships among people, places, practices, and things. This move is, again, crucial for Internet researchers: Where does the Internet fit into the social universe?

What are the conditions of possibility for the particular practice or event being studied, both on-line and off-line?

ARTICULATION

One assumption underlying cultural studies' attention to context is that it is not possible, in advance, to know the effects of whatever is being studied. In other words, by looking at a text or event, the scholar cannot simply deduce its meaning or effect in the world. Similarly, cultural studies does not take its objects as given but as made. Thus, cultural studies requires a theory of how things in the world are connected with one another; this is called the theory of articulation. Articulation is the form of a connection between two or more previously unrelated elements (such as ideologies, practices, social groups, technologies, techniques, etc.) to make a temporary unity. Articulation also refers to the organization of said elements in their articulated relationship and the process through which that connection and organization is produced (Hall, 1984, 1986). Stuart Hall (1986) uses the metaphor of the articulated lorry: A truck that has been hitched to a trailer; any single cab can be hitched to many trailers.

A theory of articulation is based on the assertion that there are no necessary correspondences among different elements (people, ideologies, places, events) but, rather, these correspondences have to be made. All cultural phenomena are articulated: They are, internally, a set of connected elements, and these systems then in turn are connected with one another. Thus, any case of cultural change or reproduction must be understood as a process of disarticulation and rearticulation rather than as the combination of free-floating ideologies, practices, and constituencies waiting for their chance to get hitched.[5] Pointing out that something is articulated (and therefore, e.g., "socially constructed") does not in and of itself weaken the force holding together the articulation; it is the beginning of the researcher's work, not the end. For our purposes, articulation will be important in at least two different ways: in considering (a) *what counts* in a cultural study of the Internet and (b) *how to think about* and represent the Internet. Articulation is also a critical issue because it suggests that the language used to describe the Internet is itself the result of an articulation: There is no inherent connection between the Internet and the language used to describe it. For instance, the connection between millennial discourse and the Internet is itself an articulation that requires some analysis.

THE COMMITMENT TO THEORY

If cultural studies requires Internet researchers to critique the political dimensions of their research, attend seriously to context, and understand the Internet as articulated (i.e., *made* rather than given), it also requires the researcher to find new and more effective ways to describe the Internet—hence, the commitment to theory. Although cultural studies makes use of theoretical reflection in many different forms, cultural studies is not simply reducible to theory. In practice, this means that the cultural studies scholar is expected to, at some point in the research, take a "detour through theory" (although this need not appear in writing) to find an explanatory framework suitable to the object under study *and return from that detour through theory to a new analysis or description of a concrete problem.* The point is not to develop a pure theory but, rather, to use theory to help explain different dimensions of cultural phenomena. What theories the scholars use and how the theories get implemented can vary greatly, but all good cultural studies use theory in this fashion—as a means toward better understandings of the object at hand rather than as an end in itself.

Cultural Studies Does the Internet

Cultural studies, as opposed to an established discipline such as sociology or anthropology, has always been rather ad hoc in its approach to method: a little historiography here, a little ethnography there, a dose of hermeneutics, and a twist of some flavor of theory. Many scholars have leveled criticisms of the field from both inside and outside cultural studies for its lack of methodological rigor (Grossberg, 1992; Morris, 1990; Schudson, 1997; Sokal, 1996), and others have called for a new level of attention to and formalization of method in cultural studies scholarship (Bennett, 1993; Cunningham, 1991). Despite my flip description and this new attention to method (e.g., see the method-based critiques and reformulations of cultural studies in Ferguson & Golding, 1997), I believe its *experimental* approach to epistemology and method is actually one of cultural studies' strengths as a field. Rigid adherence to a particular theory or practice of method is good when seeking certain kinds of academic legitimacy but does nothing to guarantee the intellectual value or the political usefulness of research (Bourdieu & Wacquant, 1993, p. 30; Mills, 1959, pp. 50-76). This is another reason this chapter has less to say about method and more about the construction of the object: Rigidified and formalized method works against cultural studies' distinctively strong suits; methodologism limits the possible configurations of context and the range of possible theoretical and political moves a writer can make.

That said, the most important methodological principle for a cultural study of the Internet is simply to have one. To truly learn anything about the Internet, one has to ask carefully considered questions that can be answered only through some kind of organized research. Too much work on the Internet has hitherto thrived on other academics' ignorance of the medium. Despite the increasing availability of on-line services in colleges and universities, many academics are still relatively inexperienced with on-line communication. Explanations of e-mail, Netnews, flaming, Java, and so forth belong in introductions to the medium, although *analyses* of these phenomena are certainly appropriate objects of research. Similarly, some academic writing seems to have nothing to do with the actual character of the Internet. Very little is Internet specific to Sadie Plant's (1996) claim that "complex systems and virtual worlds are not only important because they open spaces for existing women within an already existing culture, but also because of the extent to which they undermine both the world-view and the material reality of two thousand years of patriarchal control" (p. 170). Plant can claim that the mere form or existence of cyberspace "overheats" the "patriarchal economy" (p. 182) only because her claims and language are so vague. Moreover, she uncritically repeats the millennial language of technological transformation that accompanies so much discourse about the Internet. Under what conditions would the mere presence or form of a technology ever "overheat" patriarchy? Has this ever happened before?

This is not to argue against theoretical and, more generally, speculative approaches to the Internet as such but, rather, to assert that theorizations of the Net require the same level of specificity as other objects one might theorize, such as literature, music, politics, globalization, or the relationship between time and space. Playing to other academics' ignorance and building a theory based on vague impressions are two major errors any scholar can avoid with minimal effort. The problem thus becomes the construction of the object: What should count as, and in, a cultural study of the Internet and why?

This central issue could be stated as a matter of borderlines: What is "the Internet"? Is it coterminous with concepts such as cyberspace, on-line culture, computer-mediated communication, or virtual reality? Thus far, cultural studies "of the Internet" have ranged widely. Rob Shields's (1996a) edited collection *Cultures of Internet* contains articles considering France's Minitel, the global information infrastructure, virtual reality, virtual polities, MUDs (multi-user domains), listservs, and the coming of the Internet to Jamaica. By calling the collection "Cultures of Internet" rather than "Cultures of *the* Internet," Shields appears to be taking a more processual approach—*Internet* referring to a wide range of processes. Steven Jones's *CyberSociety* (Jones, 1995a) is more oriented toward "computer-mediated communication" and ranges from analyses of computer and video games and virtual reality to Usenet and e-mail. The common link appears to be a person sitting at a screen controlled by a microprocessor. Yet both of these anthologies are quite scattered; they are far from systematic, comprehensive, or even coherent when read from cover to cover (they are, after all, anthologies). What would a full-length, fully developed cultural study of the Internet (say, called *The Internet*) look like? Would such a work even be possible or desirable?

At its best, cultural studies has produced seminal book-length works with a critical/political take on cultural phenomena. In their time, these works rethought their objects and the ways in which they were written about: They reworked the dominant metadiscourses of their objects and offered a viable alternative. Yet there has not yet been a similar cultural study of the Internet.

Seminal work in cultural studies has come in two varieties: collectively authored works and single-author works. Collectively authored works can either be a series of essays (Hall & Jefferson, 1976) or a book-length argument (Hall et al., 1979) but come out of collective and *actively collaborative* research endeavors. Although there have been a number of anthologies on the Internet and computer-mediated communication more generally, they are all collections of individual works rather than the results of collective research projects. Single-author works, such as Dick Hebdige's (1979) *Subculture* or Raymond Williams's (1973) *Television: Technology and Cultural Form,* offer a more conventional and synthetic scholarly argument but lack the richness of collaborative texts. Because it deals with a medium, I want to focus briefly on Williams's *Television* as an example.

Williams's (1973) *Television* is an exemplar of cultural studies work in its critique of existing discussions of its object of study, in its own construction of its object, in its theorization of the contexts and contours of its object, and in its approach to the stakes and politics of its object in broader cultural terms. Williams wrote that his book was an attempt to consider the relationships between television as a technology and television as a cultural form: "In the contemporary debates about the general relation between technology, social institutions and culture, television is obviously an outstanding case" (p. vii).

From the very beginning, his work is located in a broader intellectual and political context.

Williams engages contemporary debates about his object of study without submitting to their terminology or conceptualizations. So for instance, Williams's critique of technological determinism, especially the media effects approach (pp. 116-120) and the media theory of Marshall McLuhan (pp. 120-122), represented a significant challenge to the two dominant paradigms of academic television study at the time of the book's publication.

Television also examines the qualities of the object of study and retheorizes its approach based on distinctive conceptual problems Williams encountered. He coined the term "mobile privatization" (pp. 17-25) to describe the conjuncture that conditioned television's institutional and social development—the increased privatization and atomization of social life on the one hand and the increased dependence on transportation and communication technologies on the other. Similarly, he coined the term "flow" (pp. 72-112) to describe the texture and experience of television's textuality. Drawing from Williams's fertile suggestions, television researchers have made use of these two concepts for over two decades.

Finally, and most important, Williams understood his book as an intervention into the discourse about television—not only the critical, analytical, and descriptive concerns of academics but the *political* concerns of policymakers and users. His last chapter, rarely read today, deals with the future of television as a technology and an institution. Consider his prescient warning about future developments in cable television and videotape:

> We have always to remember that full development of the new video technology will take some twenty years: say between now [1973] and 1990. For this reason, some people, especially in the established authorities, manage to feel fairly relaxed about it: the problems will be sorted out as we go; it is no use trying to cross bridges before we come to them. But this is wrong on two main counts. First, some of the most serious problems will arise within the next few years: notably in relation to policies for cable television. Secondly, the history of broadcasting institutions shows very clearly that the institutions and social policies which get established in a formative, innovative stage—often *ad hoc* and piecemeal in a confused and seemingly marginal area—have extraordinary persistence into later periods. . . . (p. 141)

As Williams wrote, U.S. courts were clearing the way for Home Box Office (HBO) to begin broadcasting current movies, effectively breaking the network monopoly on entertainment television and thereby making viable a much larger consumer market for cable television in the United States. Williams's expressed concern with alternatives to the dominant media system and vision of an alternative future is sorely lacking in cultural studies today.

Through this example, we can see some of the key characteristics of a really good cultural study of a medium: It engages the dominant discourses about a medium without taking them at face value; it provides innovative descriptive material that allows other scholars to further reconceptualize the medium; it considers the past and present historical and institutional conjunctures shaping the medium; and finally, it considers the politics and the *future* of the medium without, again, taking available discourses on their own terms. Certainly, there are many issues missing from Williams's account; the point is not that Williams covered every aspect of television (of course he couldn't). Rather, the book's significance is as a platform for critique. In this sense, *Television* was very much a success.

But cultural studies itself is quite different from what it was in the 1970s, and this has presented another obstacle, perhaps the primary obstacle, to a Williams-like synthesis of the Internet. *Television* operates in a largely realist mode of social criticism; it derives its analytical categories from fairly commonsense conceptual categories and operates on the premise that analytical and descriptive language has some correspondence with the object it describes. Although seminal in many ways, the book operationalizes the premise that one can take a single medium as the object of a full-length study, a premise that has increasingly come under serious attack from cultural studies writers. Regardless of what medium is being considered, its users (or subjects or audiences etc.) never exist solely in relation to that medium, whether it is film, television, music, or the Internet. Thus, a number of cultural studies writers have turned toward analyses of "everyday life" or complexes of mediated experiences or media phenomena to better understand the relationship of communication and subjectivities (e.g., Morley, 1993; Morris, 1990; Silverstone, 1990; Silverstone, Hirsch, & Morley, 1992). Those who remain in a realist mode of analysis tend toward more localized studies, along, interestingly enough, Hebdige's "subculture" model even 20 years later. Other writers, such as David Morley and Roger Silverstone, also continue to have an impact in this area (even though they themselves have switched ethnographic orientations). In the context of Internet research, these localized cultural studies offer both on-line and off-line analyses, and often, their aim is to recover, describe, and analyze the distinctive features of subjective experience pertaining to the Internet or some cultural sphere related to the Internet.

SUBJECTIVITY, TEXTUALITY, AND EXPERIENCE

On-line analyses of Internet culture use a hybrid approach—often combining, in various degrees, ethnography, autobiography, and textual analysis. Often, their goal is to explain the workings of on-line culture in an ethnographic or discourse-analysis style. Many of these studies conclude by criticizing the on-line/off-line dichotomy that posits a split between the Internet and everything else. Although they offer this criticism, they do not develop it: Most subjectivity-oriented analyses of the Internet are founded on a dichotomy between on-line and off-line culture, in which on-line culture is mediated and off-line culture is not.

Michelle Tepper's (1997) analysis of the use of humor as a policing mechanism on the Usenet newsgroup alt.folklore.urban argues both by textual criticism and by analogy. By using humorous errors of fact or spelling, regular participants on the Usenet group create an insider/outsider status that is then reinforced through the use of invitation-only mailing lists and in-group jokes. In this way, on-line participants create "community" through verbal and physical exclusion. Gareth Branwyn's (1994) study of cybersex uses formal and informal interviews as well as his own experience with the practice. Branwyn's study is largely descriptive, but the combination of methods is certainly a useful approach to understanding a particular on-line phenomenon.

Two more autobiographical accounts deal with rape and death on-line. Julian Dibbell's (1994) widely reprinted "A Rape in Cyberspace: Or, How an Evil Clown, a Haitian Trickster Spirit, Two Wizards, and a Cast of Dozens Turned a Database Into a Society" deals with a rape scenario played out on LambdaMoo, a program designed to give its users a particularly vivid (text-based) impression of being somewhere. Although Dibbell was not present for the actual event, the article explores the stakes involved when people's on-line personas could be made (without their consent) to play out another user's sexual fantasies on-line. Similarly, Katie Argyle's (1996) "Life After Death" explores her own reactions to the death of a regular participant on a listserv to which she belonged, whom she'd never met, although she'd gotten to know him through his posts. Both articles problematize the distinctions between "virtual" and "real" life but in the context of specific problems related to the experience of Internet users. The autobiographical aspect of these descriptions helps to concretize the "virtual/real" split as more than just a conceptual problem but as a cultural and political issue as well.

Even the on-line accounts specifically written to problematize the virtual/ real split still seem to hold it up in terms of their own presentation of the topic. All of the aforementioned ethnographic studies spend most of their time analyzing events that happen on-line. Similarly, Aycock and Buchignani's (1995) "The E-Mail Murders: Reflections on 'Dead' Letters" is a fascinating tale of some of Valery Fabrikant's on-line activities prior to his murdering four people and wounding a fifth at Concordia University in 1992. Yet there is very little discussion of Fabrikant's activities off-line except as they are represented on-line. The logical next step for on-line analyses is to further their critiques of the virtual/real split by themselves moving beyond a primary focus on on-line experience in isolation from other experiences, both inside and outside other media. Theoretically, on-line analyses could also deal with the structure of the Internet, its content, and/or the organization of on-line practices, but as of this writing, no such more developed cultural studies exist.

Off-line analyses do successfully consider relationships between Internet activity and other parts of participants' everyday lives but retain this focus on recovering and describing experience. The large number of essays dealing with cyberpunk fiction would be an example of formal, off-line analyses related to on-line environments (the Dery, 1994b, collection is especially heavy on cyberpunk essays). In general, however, I've found that analyses of cyberpunk have more to tell us about cyberpunk than about the Internet. Similarly, writings about "hacker culture" (e.g., Hafner, 1991) are another possible angle for off-line analyses but tend to be more journalistic in orientation, focusing on telling a story and making the character of the hacker familiar. In other words, they are more concerned with narrativizing and representing experience than offering a cultural and political *analysis* of experience.

EPISODIC STUDIES

Based on the influence of French writers such as Michel Foucault, Gilles Deleuze, and Felix Guattari, the success of poststructuralist feminism, and strains of American pragmatism, writers ranging from Meaghan Morris (1988) to Andrew Ross (1991a) have taken to a more episodic, anecdotal, and momentary approach to constructing their objects of study. Here, the

Internet becomes one site among many in everyday life or a particular inflection of virtuality, cyberspace, or computer-mediated communication.

Writers taking this approach fall roughly into three camps. The first camp considers Internet communication as part of a larger problematic or cultural phenomenon. The second camp considers the metanarratives surrounding the Internet in other media—"discourses of the Internet." The third camp merges these two approaches in studying the Internet as part of a larger social and technical network.

Studies that consider the Internet as part of a larger problematic understand the Internet as one particular site among many to be studied as part of a cultural or political problem. Two examples of this approach will give a clearer sense of it. First, there are those scholars who approach the Internet as a subset of "technology" and who are particularly concerned with the role of "information technology" in the changing shape of work and leisure. For example, Aronowitz and DiFazio (Aronowitz, 1994, pp. 104-138; see also Aronowitz & DiFazio, 1994) argue that computer-aided design and manufacturing has aided in the integration of task at the General Electric engine plant in Cincinnati, shortening design time, eliminating jobs, and allowing closer interaction among management and employees. Aronowitz and DiFazio link the computerization of engineering and architecture to the de-skilling and loss of autonomy of the professional classes and shrinking of the job market: computer networking makes fewer workers necessary to serve the needs of the firm. Similarly, the contributors to the volume *Resisting the Virtual Life* (Brook & Boal, 1995; see also Bender & Druckery, 1994) critique information technology rather than the Internet per se, but the volume spans policy, agency, ideology, and alternatives to "virtual interactivity" through forays into policy, labor statistics, and even the aesthetics of screen savers. Here, the Internet is just part of a much larger complex of information technologies, industries, and ways of life.

Another approach to the Internet as part of a problematic is the rapidly growing area of body and technology studies among cultural studies scholars. Central to this area is Donna Haraway's landmark essay "A Manifesto for Cyborgs" (reprinted in Haraway, 1991; see also Haraway, 1997), an essay that offers an alternative to antitechnology positions in feminist and socialist theory through the figure of the cyborg, part organism and part machine.[6] The interplay among bodies and machines has since become a central concern among feminist scholars. Anne Balsamo's exploration of technologies of the gendered body, for instance, covers feminist bodybuilding, public pregnancies, cosmetic surgery, and virtual reality (Balsamo, 1996). Liz Grosz's

(1992) "Bodies–Cities" argues that telecommunications and information networks are part of the transformation of the bodily experience of cities, resulting in a kind of technical interchangeability of bodily and computerized functions.

The second "episodic" approach to the Internet is metadiscursive: It analyzes discourses of and about the Internet. Although this is a populous field, I will limit my discussion to four examples. Andrew Ross's (1991a) "Hacking Away at the Counterculture" was one of the earlier cultural studies analyses of computer culture. Ross's essay exemplifies the metadiscursive approach because it demystifies apparently given social relations, connects ideological positions to social relationships, and offers an alternative way to think about the problem being examined. His goal was to "describe a wider set of activity and social location than is normally associated with the practice of hacking" (p. 132). Ross begins his essay with an analysis of the media panic surrounding hackers, viruses, and computer security, moving quickly from antihacker hysteria to the cultural management of hacking through worker sabotage, a critique of techno-utopian discourses that includes an analysis of workplace safety in semiconductor production plants, a critique of the "technoculture" approach that sees a seamless interlocking of public and private media technologies to produce a society of surveillance, and a discussion of the possibilities for critiques of technoculture. Ross's concluding argument still reads with urgency: He attacks technophilic and technophobic positions alike: Cultural studies requires technological literacy to have a solid critique of existing technological formations and present an effective alternative vision.

Similarly, Laura Miller (1995) and Joe Lockard (1997) both offer critiques of the electronic frontier mythos through the very effective use of a fairly conventional ideology critique approach. Miller is concerned about how women's experiences on-line were represented in popular news media such as *Newsweek* and the *Village Voice*. For instance, a May 1994 *Newsweek* article argued that cyberspace was an environment largely hostile to women. Miller (1995) connects this ideology of female fragility with the frontier mythos and the movement for further regulation of the Internet (pp. 52-53). Miller is explicitly critical of Julian Dibbell's (1994) article cited earlier, worrying that the sense of female fragility based on men being bigger than women shouldn't operate in the same way in on-line environments. Although this remains an open (and difficult) question, Miller critiques the frontier mythos as gendered while also criticizing the usual gender-based critiques of cyberspace. Instead of working with the given alternatives, she offers the possibility of a different social vision for women's roles on-line. No doubt, the Internet was originally a men's club and is still male-dominated in many places. The question then is how to best approach the problem from a feminist position. As Miller suggests, feminists should be wary of "frontier" language precisely because of how it casts the possibility of women's participation in Internet culture.

Joseph Lockard (1996) also considers frontier myths in his critique of technophilic discourse that ranges from the conservative roots of the desire for a new frontier to the "invisible pricetags" behind computing. The final section of his essay connects the desire for universal communications expansion and the rhetoric of identity-less virtual community with first world-third world relations, American cultural imperialism, and the white ideology of racelessness. In fact, the absence of discussions of race in cyberspace re-instantiates a white ideology:[7]

> The [. . .] field of putatively null, anti-signified cyberspace is unmistakably signed with Euro-American whiteness. Race and ethnicity are simply not up for discussion in cyberspace social theory, and their very absence identifies unsubstantiated presumptions of community. The featurelessness of a presumptive non-raciality/ethnicity in cyberspace fails to correspond with the real and diverse communities around us. (p. 227)

The supposed racelessness of on-line culture thus is itself implicated in racial politics. Lockard, like Ross and Miller, takes a common issue in discourses surrounding the Internet and shows how different ideologies, practices, and technologies are articulated together to form what appears at first glance as a self-evident unity. All three critiques are expressly political, moving beyond a demonstration of the articulated ideologies and narratives to a political critique of social relationships.

Bolter and Grusin's (1996) "Remediation" uses the past to develop a metadiscursive critique. Rather than casting web pages and hypertext as wholly new forms of mediation, they contextualize these supposedly "new" visual conventions within the long flow of media history. Using examples from painting, photography, sculpture, and design, they argue that there is a vivid tradition among some new forms of expression simultaneously claiming their ability to supersede previous representational forms in terms of an aesthetic of immediacy (i.e., the new medium is supposed to be somehow "less" mediated than the old medium) and, at the same time, a hybridization of content that reworks and refigures the old media within the new, resulting in a multilayered textuality. The strength of Bolter and Grusin's argument is that they subject their own formal analysis of dimensions of new media to a genealogical approach (following Foucault, 1977), looking for the roots of current media forms in past activities. As a result, they are able to construct a social and cultural account of new forms of expression that attends to their specificity without relying on millennial rhetoric, technological determinism, or claims of absolute newness. The "new" dimensions of hypertext and the hybridized Web site are thus shown to have deep cultural roots of their own.

Perhaps the most developed cultural studies work to date on the Internet is J. Macgregor Wise's (1997) *Exploring Technology and Social Space,* despite its claims to be only partially about the Internet. It is also a good example of what is entailed in cultural studies' decentering of realist objects in favor of considering the Internet as part of a larger social and technical network, the third approach I mentioned above. Wise really advances two arguments that become simultaneous by the end of the book (and hence the qualification about the book "not entirely" being about the Internet and new communications technologies). The first has to do with how we think about technology. He contrasts three paradigms: the modern, actor-network theory (what he calls an "amodern" approach to technology), and Deleuzean theory, ultimately arguing for the third as the best theoretical framework for considering technology at present. Modern thought tends toward two poles in the consideration of technology: (a) technological determinism, in which technologies shape human activity independent of human actors, and (b) instrumentalism, which ignores the constructedness of technology and simply casts it as a means to an end. This vacillation in modern thought itself is based on a subject/object split, with agency frequently situated on only one side of the divide. Wise sees the amodern approach, after Latour, as overcoming the modern episteme's assumption of a subject/object dichotomy by theorizing both subjects and objects as possible agents in both "natural" and "social" elements of human life. But whereas actor-network theory is content to note the existence of agency, Deleuzean theory, he argues, reintroduces differential power relations into the analysis (pp. 58-59).

Wise shifts objects to mimic a progression he sees in the technology itself from the military-industrial complex, through large pedagogical institutions (he considers the communication technology exhibit in Chicago's Museum of Science and Industry), and into policy discourse and popular culture. Along the way, he considers the public relations apparatus of AT&T, the images of technoculture presented in *Wired,* the political forces behind the

National Information Infrastructure (NII), and the movement to expand the NII into a global information infrastructure.

Wise's book uses mostly documentary forms of analysis, developing critiques through interposing description and analysis. He seeks to move beyond an ideology critique (in which discourse either "represents" reality or fails in terms of that representation and functions as ideology) and make claims on social reality beyond the politics of representation. As a result, Wise focuses more on discourses about and around the Internet than on attempting a description of the Internet itself, although its ultimate goal is not simply a critique of the accuracy or inaccuracy of various representations. Wise's book represents a move in the right direction for cultural studies of the Internet but also highlights some of the difficulty in describing something in unfamiliar terms: That is, if one reads the book for its Internet content, one must first read 80 pages of theoretical argument before reaching a discussion of the object of study in any depth.

Doing Cultural Studies, Redoing the Internet

Given the existing work, the challenge facing cultural studies Internet scholarship is to retain its critique of realism while at the same time speaking to the real—refusing to concern itself exclusively with a politics of representation[8] and instead moving toward a more explicit and direct construction of its object. Insofar as cultural studies writing on the Internet retains its critique of realism, it also has the formal problem of representing itself. Writing is a linear form, and although some writers such as Meaghan Morris (e.g., Morris, 1988) have developed rather avant-garde solutions to the problem of writing outside realist constraints, an effective style such as hers takes years of work to develop. Such writing can contribute to the intellectual depth of the project, but it also reduces the possible audience. Conversely, more plain prose-style approaches such as Wise's take a great deal of time before the argument comes together for the reader.

Cultural studies' critique of realism, and my support of it herein, would suggest that it is neither epistemologically sound nor politically desirable to just study "the Internet" in isolation from other cultural phenomena. Our fictional study, *The Internet,* might at this point no longer be a study of a medium itself but its place in everyday life. To argue that the Internet is an autonomous sphere of social action is simply untrue based on the evidence offered by other areas of media studies; "subjects of cyberspace" are also subjects of television, telephony, radio, film, and music, as well as elevators, clothing, speech patterns, and food, not to mention the classic identity categories. That said, studies of subjectivity and cyberspace could possibly move toward a more Goffmanesque analysis that considers the "framing" of social activity and the performance of social roles independent of any subjective essence, but then this would no longer be a radical claim about how subjectivity is transformed through the Internet. Instead, it would simply be an acknowledgment of the role-playing that Goffman analyzed throughout his career (for two classic studies, see Goffman, 1963, 1974). Similar to Goffman's, Judith Butler's work on performativity in sexuality and gender practice may be of some use in conceptualizing the Internet and subjective processes (Butler, 1993, 1997) by highlighting that even constructed identities remain constructed only insofar as they are repeatedly performed. Such analyses, however, require an acute awareness of context: To do otherwise is to abstract the Internet from the complex media environment of which it is a part.

Internet research in general needs to be further integrated with research on other, related phenomena. Cultural studies should apply its collective wisdom to the construction of the Internet as an object of research rather than continuing to abstract the Internet from the media environment of which it is a part.

1. Cultural studies has the pedagogical task of disentangling the Internet from its given millennial metanarratives of universality, revolutionary character, radical otherness from social life, and the frontier mythos. This task can be fulfilled both through documentary research and fairly traditional ideology critique (the newest, most fashionable methods are not always the best). Most important for this type of research is its pedagogical function: It especially needs to reach beyond traditional scholarly audiences, although cultural studies scholars should be challenging other academics who are furthering an ideological formation that essentially amounts to advertising for the Internet. Also, an important qualification for this research is that it cannot resort to the simple antitechnology/alienation narratives so prevalent in philosophical and cultural critiques of technology. In my opinion, this is where cultural studies work (especially of the metanarrative type discussed above) has been most successful and perhaps where it can have the widest impact. Cultural studies scholars in this area have the challenge of finding a third voice outside the technophilic/technophobic dichotomy and of finding effective sites both in the academy and outside to intervene.

2. *Cultural studies scholars need to denaturalize and radically contextualize the Internet itself.* This can be accomplished through a variety of means. My own work in this area thus far has been of a comparative and media historical perspective. A simple exercise: Identify a claim about the Internet. Then choose another medium, see if the claim was made in the past and if so, how and where it surfaced. How does the claim figure in the discursive history of that medium? For example, the figurative language of AT&T's advertising campaign for universal telephone service (conducted from about 1910 through the 1920s) is very similar to more recent telecommunications advertising—mixing transportation and communication language to produce images such as "the information superhighway" that has been part of AT&T's public relations campaigns for the entire century. Similarly, one can find homologous millennial claims for all modern telecommunications media: radio (Khelbnikov, 1993), television (Denman, 1952; RCA, 1944), telegraphy (Czitrom, 1982), and some technologies we don't usually think of as modern telecommunications media—the electric light (Marvin, 1988) and the postal system (John, 1995). Bolter and Grusin's work (1996), discussed above, is also a fine example of this approach. In contrast to the mythology of electronic transformation, examples from media history suggest that as the Internet increases in importance and pervasiveness, it will simply become part of the mundane fabric of social and cultural life. Contrary to today's millennial predictions, the Internet's future and significance most likely lies in the domain of the banal.

Although there has been much analysis of representations of the Internet *through* other media, little has been written about other kinds of connections between the Internet and other media. Political economists and policy analysts have made much greater inroads in this area than cultural studies scholars (Herman & McChesney, 1997; Streeter, 1996). In addition to the important corporate connections between cable television, telephony, and the Internet, little has been written on the subject from a cultural point of view. For instance, as the World Wide Web expands, it becomes somatically more like cable television; although the visual and possibly cognitive content of the medium is different (and this would be an open question for psychological researchers), participation largely involves a user pointing and clicking a mouse to change screens. Services such as WebTV are in fact based on this presumed similarity; surfing the web and channel surfing share the same metaphor for a reason. Of course, this is just one example. The problems of presence/absence and real/virtual tend to get represented in a binary fashion: The Internet is virtual; the rest of the world is real. But notions of phantasm, absence, and unreality have plagued all "Western" forms of representation, both in technologically mediated and other expressive forms. Future cultural studies work should connect any discussion of virtuality to the larger problem of presence and absence that has surfaced in a wide range of contexts for hundreds of years; it is a central problem of media theory more generally (e.g., see classic writings by Anderson, 1983; Benjamin, 1968; Derrida, 1976; Warner, 1990).

Even in the spheres in which it is most significant, the Internet is only one of many technologies and media that its users encounter, and it may or may not be foremost among them in the subject's identity construction or the larger logics of subjectivity. Silverstone et al.'s (1992) turn toward the "moral economy of the household" is one such way of thinking about the subject effects (i.e., the effect of some practice that produces subjectivity) of multiple media.[9] As more and more cultural studies scholars shift their primary object of study from "culture" to "everyday life" (as suggested in Morris, 1990), they will have to develop more approaches for talking about multiple media encountered in multiple environments.

3. Cultural studies scholars should treat the Internet and computer-mediated communication more like other media and technologies. Like other media, the Internet represents the play of a whole range of cultural forces. Its form and content change over time, and its social significance varies from context to context: The Internet is more important to some people than to others.

Yet like scholars in other fields, Internet scholars have a tendency to universalize their own subjective impressions and dispositions, thereby grossly overestimating the impact, magnitude, accessibility, and universality of their object of study. Basic claims about the Internet presented with the air of fact often do not withstand even superficial scrutiny. Many writers have made wildly exaggerated claims about ease of access to the medium, its relative importance to the shape of modern politics, the Internet as a public sphere, and the Internet's rate of growth.[10] Mark Dery (1994c), for instance, claims that the "subcultural glimpses" of Internet discourse "offer a precognitive glimpse of the mainstream culture a few years from now, when ever-greater numbers of Americans will be part-time residents in virtual communities" (p. 6). Dery cites the astonishing figure that there is a 25% jump every 3 months in the number of computer networks hooked to the Internet (although the source he attributes does not cite a source for the statistic; it could well have been hearsay). Yet this simple claim is based on a wide range of faulty assumptions. It assumes that the Internet will continue to expand indefinitely at its present rate eventually achieving universal access (a feat not even accomplished by the present-day telephone). It assumes that as the Internet gets bigger, its content, form, and genres will remain the same. But no regular user of the Internet would support such a claim: Content changes drastically as size increases. Previously small newsgroups become huge and unmanageable; e-mail lists that used to put out 10 messages a day or in a week can suddenly spiral to more than 60 messages a day; advertising becomes more prevalent as companies scramble to find a way to make money on the Internet. The mechanics alone of dealing with a massive influx of new users can radically transform any on-line "community." As discussed above, as the World Wide Web grows, its cultural content—the *character* of its "interactivity"—changes.

Like other media, the Internet can also be considered a commodity. Silverstone et al. (1992) and writers such as Lynn Spigel (1992), John Hartley (1992), Liz Cohen (1990), and David Nasaw (1993), among others, all offer ways of examining the commodity status of communications technologies. All of these authors, however, stress that as commodities, media and technologies are bound up in differential power relationships and are endowed with different kinds of meanings depending on how they are situated. As exemplified by the stories of people getting e-mail addresses just for the prestige, Internet access is a sought-after service; it is very much a commodity. Similarly, making use of Internet access presumes access to and command of other commodities, such as computers, software, and phone lines.

In light of the Internet's commodity status, we should also ask other questions of Dery: His 25% jump doesn't account for who has and doesn't have Internet access. Although many corporate networks are hooked into the Internet at large, companies often limit the available Internet access for employees plugged into the corporate network. As Gilbert Rodman (1997) argues, statistics on how many people actually use the net need to be taken with a grain of salt:

> The decentralized nature of the net makes census taking difficult, the Net's rapid and continuing growth renders any data one collects on its overall size instantly outdated, and what actually counts as "using the net" varies fantastically from survey to survey. What numbers there are, however, suggest that barely 1% (if

that much) of the world and only 10-20% of the US are on-line in any capacity whatsoever.

In addition to considering those low numbers at least as seriously as the "25%" quoted by Dery and others, we have to consider what "being on-line" means. Claims about the "ease" of appearing on-line also should be carefully scrutinized. Rob Shields (1996b) asserts that "the required equipment is now available in North America at under $100 on the second hand market" and that "the very simplest PC equipped with the slowest of modems can perform adequately for the average typist" (p. 2). Although it is true that used computers are cheap, compatibility and applications are severely limited.[11] An old machine would work only for basic e-mail, gopher servers (which are widely being replaced by graphics and therefore memory-intensive web sites), and some Netnews and on-line database functions. Thus, as Joseph Lockard (1997) argues, "An ideology of computing cheapness . . . , along with its suggestion that a fully-accessible and democratic cyberculture is achievable in the not-too-distant future, is simply another social Ponzi scheme" (p. 221). Ironically, the more advanced a computer user, the more likely an old system will be of use. Inexperienced computer users are much more likely to require more advanced systems for access to on-line services (for one thing, hardware and software support for older systems is virtually nonexistent).

Similarly, Steven Jones claims in his introduction to *CyberSociety* that "unlike many other analyses and studies of contemporary society, one may enter the communities and discourse described in these chapters with relative ease" (Jones, 1995b, p. 3). "Relative ease" is a tricky term here, because in addition to the practical matter of access, we must remember that the proliferation of computer software has popularized the term *learning curve;* learning new software can take a lot of time, especially for the casual computer user. For the novice user, technical support for newer packages is relatively poor and expensive, and quickly goes out of existence for older packages. Of course, Jones was addressing his readers, largely a college- and university-based audience who would likely have more access to "free" facilities and more extensive technical support than other populations.[12] But the general ease and availability of Internet access is itself an issue open for discussion rather than being a closed case. As Lockard (1997) writes,

A pending FCC complaint by a civil rights coalition charges four Baby Bells with "electronic redlining" in their planning of advanced interactive video networks that will avoid (black, ethnic) inner cities and serve (mainly affluent white) suburbs. Access, community, and race are inextricably linked issues. (p. 227)

Proclamations of accessibility thus rest on erroneous assumptions about the economic and social foundations of Internet access. Computers, access to networks, and software literacy are themselves embedded in material and symbolic economies that require careful critical attention.

4. Finally, someone should write a cultural studies book titled The Internet *in the style of Raymond Williams's (1973)* Television, *or perhaps some other seminal cultural studies work.* Such a study would give a historical overview of the Internet from a more sociological, rather than an anecdotal, perspective. It could cover a range of domains both on-line (e-mail, Netnews, the World Wide Web, etc.), and off-line (home, office, library . . .). It could cover the industry, policy, content, and user practices. It could offer a theory of power dynamics on and around the Internet. In short, it would offer an effective critique of existing discourses around the medium, present some effective tools for thinking about it, and even provide a cogent discussion of its future.[13] Such a task could be undertaken by an individual whose research program has already provided a solid foundation for this kind of study, or it could be undertaken collectively by a group of scholars committed to working together and sharing a common understanding of the problem at hand. Given the current intellectual climate of cultural studies, there is no doubt that such a study would come under fire from many directions. But even as people leveled the criticisms, they would be reading the book, would look to it (or against it) for new research directions, reconsider and recontextualize its assertions and constructions, and retrace its steps to follow a different path. In short, it would wind up being a lot like any other seminal work in an academic field: effective, controversial, and of course flawed. Regardless of whether the goals of such a massive effort are truly attainable, the effort itself is often worth reading.

I have said very little about the mechanics of constructing an Internet study, and now this chapter is about to end. My reasoning is simple: Because cultural studies is committed to a willful and considered eclecticism of method, once you determine your method, you should learn it from experts in the area. *In principle,* hermeneutics, "pure theory," historiography, ethnography, and quantitative analysis[14] are all possible "methods," among others, for doing a cultural study. If you're doing ethnography, talk with ethnographers; if you're doing history, talk with historians; if you're doing textual analysis, talk with literary critics, art historians, musicologists; and so forth. More than likely, if your research goes beyond a single essay, you'll be using multiple methods. All the better. Talk with more people, and read more methodologies (if you find that helps). Cultural studies has even begun producing its own methodologies (DuGay, 1997), although as I have tried to show here, a methodological treatise is more or less antithetical to the work of cultural studies.[15]

Instead, I have offered some directions for the conceptualization of the Internet: It is both a productive cultural site and an artifact and element of social relationships. By attending to the construction of the object, researchers in cultural studies and other fields will be presented with a wider range of political and intellectual options throughout their research work. Clearly, the challenge is to move beyond the commonplaces of Internet discourse. Cultural studies' usefulness to Internet research should thus be measured by the degree to which it can get its readers to think beyond the technophilic-technophobic dichotomy, beyond the rhetoric of millennial transformation. Only by treating the Internet as one site among many in the flow of economics, ideology, everyday life, and experience can Internet research become a vital intellectual and political component of media and cultural studies. Only by recognizing the Internet's banality can Internet research move beyond the clichés of the millennial imagination.

Notes

1. That said, many other fields have struggles over the definition of central terms and prevailing notions of their objects; in this respect, cultural studies is not alone.

2. I should add that the definitions of the field are themselves heavily contested. As in most of the human sciences, there are widely divergent notions of what constitutes a "cultural study" and the purposes of the scholarship in general. For the purposes of this chapter, I will offer a heuristic definition of cultural studies as an orientation toward scholarship with four distinctive features but will not confine myself to discussing texts that rigidly fit my definition of cultural studies.

3. Of course, cultural studies has developed these moves in its own ways, but it did not invent them. On the contrary, the use of the autobiographical voice is a direct descendent of academic feminism and more recently the "reflexive turn" in anthropology; "the detour through theory" is a variation on Marx's approach to social research, and the critique of subject-object relations (i.e., the objective scholar removed from the object of study) is a product of a wide range of critiques of enlightenment-style empiricism and Kantianism.

4. The statement of its politics in the negative is useful here because the question of *what is to be done* remains an open issue for most cultural studies scholars. In fact, this is the point of doing the research: If you already know the political answers beforehand, why do the study?

5. This is not to argue for a voluntarist theory of articulation. That, for instance, discourses of "the frontier" are articulated to the Internet does *not* mean that it will necessarily be easy to disarticulate those metaphors from people's notions of the Internet. Articulations are held together by powerful social, economic, and ideological forces.

6. Carol Stabile's (1994) remains the most solid critique of Haraway to date and casts serious doubt on the political viability of technophilic feminism.

7. An interview with Samuel R. Delany, Greg Tate, and Tricia Rose appears in *Flame Wars* (Dery, 1994a), but deals with science fiction and the new form of music rather than with the Internet. Joseph Lockard's (1996) "Virtual Whiteness and Narrative Diversity" compares literary and on-line constructs of whiteness and racial difference.

8. This is not to suggest that representation is an unimportant political issue, only that the politics of representation is only one possible model of political action.

9. Although their excessive emphasis on the agency of consumption obscures other kinds of economic relations.

10. This is also a locational/biographical issue: Cultural producers tend to universalize their own experience, which is then confirmed by other cultural producers doing the same thing in the media they encounter. Thus, for instance, the "radio boom" of the 1920s was largely an artifact of media "snowballing" one another; coverage of radio bred more coverage of radio, and pretty soon, the phenomenon was "sweeping the nation," although radio had been widely available as a technology prior to the "boom" (see Douglas, 1987). One can find a similar "boom" in the 1990s as more and more journalists went on-line.

11. My own experience might be an instructive example here: Until 1993, I used a 1984 Leading Edge model "D" PC (bought new in 1984) for all of my computing and Internet needs. I finally had to stop using the computer when I discovered that newer versions of DOS and many DOS-based programs were no longer compatible with my machine. I then gave in to the prevailing market and bought the best computer I could afford so that I could postpone my next upgrade as long as possible. Since 1993, I have already found it necessary to upgrade the hard drive and the modem for basic everyday uses. I have also found that my RAM memory (8 megabytes was considered generous in 1993) is no longer sufficient for even my word-processing applications. Although the old Leading Edge is still usable as a stand-alone computer, the Leading Edge is no longer of any value for connecting with other computers.

12. Although computing facilities are often available for free to faculty, students' fees are usually required to support campus computing facilities—one reason that alumni have to pay to keep their university accounts.

13. Williams's predictions at the end of *Television* remain a rare example of cultural studies futurology. As Andrew Ross notes (1991b, pp. 169-171; echoed by Wise, 1997), the Left has largely ceded the practice of futurology to the Right. If the Left is to have any meaningful social vision, it must include images of the future.

14. Statistical analysis is more or less nonexistent in current cultural studies work, but as Justin Lewis (1997) has persuasively argued, it is no *less* valid a method when reflexively applied than any other qualitative approach to cultural studies.

15. As anyone who's done research knows, the difficult questions of method are most often encountered in the process of doing the research, as opposed to methodological expositions (such as this one).

References

Anderson, B. (1983). *Imagined communities: Reflections on the origin and spread of nationalism*. New York: Verso.

Argyle, K. (1996). Life after death. In R. Shields (Ed.), *Cultures of Internet: Virtual spaces, real histories, living bodies* (pp. 133-142). Thousand Oaks, CA: Sage.

Aronowitz, S. (1994). Technology and the future of work. In G. Bender & T. Druckery (Eds.), *Culture on the brink: Ideologies of technology* (pp. 15-30). Seattle, WA: Bay Press.

Aronowitz, S., & DiFazio, W. (1994). *The jobless future: Sci-tech and the dogma of work*. Minneapolis: University of Minnesota Press.

Aycock, A., & Buchignani, N. (1995). The e-mail murders: Reflections on "dead" letters. In S. G. Jones (Ed.), *CyberSociety: Computer-mediated communication and community* (pp. 184-231). Thousand Oaks, CA: Sage.

Balsamo, A. (1996). *Technologies of the gendered body: Reading cyborg women*. Durham, NC: Duke University Press.

Barbero, J.-M. (1993). Latin America: Cultures in the communication media. *Journal of Communication, 43*(2), 18-30.

Bender, G., & Druckery, T. (Eds.). (1994). *Culture on the brink: Ideologies of technology*. Seattle, WA: Bay Press.

Benjamin, W. (1968). The work of art in the age of mechanical reproduction. In H. Arendt (Ed.), *Illuminations: Essays and reflections* (pp. 217-252). New York: Shocken.

Bennett, T. (1993). Being "in the true" of cultural studies. *Southern Review, 26*(2), 217-238.

Berube, M. (1994). *Public access: Literary theory and American cultural politics*. New York: Verso.

Bolter, J. D., & Grusin, R. (1996). Remediation. *Configurations, 3*(3), 311-358.

Bourdieu, P., & Wacquant, L. J. D. (1993). *An invitation to reflexive sociology*. Chicago: University of Chicago Press.

Branwyn, G. (1994). Compu-sex: Erotica for cybernauts. In M. Dery (Ed.), *Flame wars: The discourse of cyberculture* (pp. 223-236). Durham, NC: Duke University Press.

Brook, J., & Boal, I. A. (Eds.). (1995). *Resisting the virtual life: The culture and politics of information*. San Francisco: City Lights.

Butler, J. (1993). *Bodies that matter: On the discursive limits of "Sex."* New York: Routledge.

Butler, J. (1997). *Excitable speech: A politics of the performative*. New York: Routledge.

Canclini, N. G. (1988). Culture and power: The state of research. *Media, Culture and Society, 10*(4), 467-478.

Carey, J. (1988). *Communication as culture*. Boston: Unwin Hyman.

Cohen, L. (1990). *Making a new deal: Industrial workers in Chicago 1919-1939*. New York: Cambridge.

Cunningham, S. (1991). Cultural studies from the viewpoint of cultural policy. *Meanjin, 50*(2-3), 423-434.

Czitrom, D. J. (1982). *Media and the American mind: From Morse to McLuhan*. Chapel Hill: University of North Carolina Press.

Denman, F. (1952). *Television: The magic window*. New York: Macmillan.

Derrida, J. (1976). *Of grammatology* (G. C. Spivak, Trans.). Baltimore, MD: Johns Hopkins University Press.

Dery, M. (1994a). Black to the future: Interviews with Samuel R. Delany, Greg Tate, and Tricia Rose. In M. Dery (Ed.), *Flame wars: The discourse of cyberculture* (pp. 179-222). Durham, NC: Duke University Press.

Dery, M. (Ed.). (1994b). *Flame wars: The discourse of cyberspace.* Durham, NC: Duke University Press.

Dery, M. (1994c). Flame wars. In M. Dery (Ed.), *Flame wars: The discourse of cyberspace* (pp. 1-10). Durham, NC: Duke University Press.

Dibbell, J. (1994). A rape in cyberspace: Or, how an evil clown, a Haitian trickster spirit, two wizards, and a cast of dozens turned a database into a society. In M. Dery (Ed.), *Flame wars: The discourse of cyberculture.* Durham, NC: Duke University Press.

Douglas, S. J. (1987). *Inventing American broadcasting 1899-1922.* Baltimore, MD: Johns Hopkins University Press.

DuGay, P. (1997). *Doing cultural studies: The story of the Sony Walkman.* Thousand Oaks, CA: Sage.

Ferguson, M., & Golding, P. (Eds.). (1997). *Cultural studies in question.* Thousand Oaks, CA: Sage.

Foucault, M. (1977). Nietzsche, genealogy, history. In D. F. Bouchard (Ed.), *Language, counter-memory, practice: Selected essays and interviews by Michel Foucault.* Ithaca, NY: Cornell University Press.

Frow, J., & Morris, M. (Eds.). (1993). *Australian cultural studies: A reader.* Urbana: University of Illinois Press.

Goffman, E. (1963). *Stigma: Notes on the management of spoiled identity.* Englewood Cliffs, NJ: Prentice Hall.

Goffman, E. (1974). *Frame analysis: An essay on the organization of experience.* Cambridge, MA: Harvard University Press.

Graff, G. (1992). *Beyond the culture wars: How teaching the conflicts can revitalize American education.* New York: Norton.

Grossberg, L. (1992). *We gotta get out of this place: Popular conservatism and postmodern culture.* New York: Routledge.

Grossberg, L. (1997). *Bringing it all back home: Essays on cultural studies.* Durham, NC: Duke University Press.

Grosz, E. (1992). Bodies-cities. In B. Columina (Ed.), *Sexuality and space* (pp. 241-254). New York: Princeton University Press.

Guha, R., & Spivak, G. C. (Eds.). (1988). *Selected subaltern studies.* New York: Oxford University Press.

Hafner, K. (1991). *Cyberpunk: Outlaws and hackers on the computer frontier.* New York: Simon & Schuster.

Hall, S. (1984). The narrative construction of reality: An interview with Stuart Hall. *Southern Review, 17*(3), 3-17.

Hall, S. (1986). On postmodernism and articulation. *Journal of Communication Inquiry, 10*(2), 45-60.

Hall, S. (1992). Cultural studies and its theoretical legacies. In L. Grossberg, C. Nelson, P. Treichler, L. Baughman, & J. M. Wise (Eds.), *Cultural studies* (pp. 277-294). New York: Routledge.

Hall, S., Critcher, C., Jefferson, T., Clarke, J., & Roberts, B. (1979). *Policing the crisis: Mugging, the state, and law and order.* London: Macmillan.

Hall, S., & Jefferson, T. (Eds.). (1976). *Resistance through rituals: Youth subcultures in postwar Britain.* London: HarperCollins Academic.

Haraway, D. (1991). *Simians, cyborgs and women.* New York: Routledge.

Haraway, D. J. (1997). *Modest-witness@second-millennium.femaleman-meets_oncomouse: Feminism and technoscience.* New York: Routledge.

Hartley, J. (1992). *Tele-ology: Studies in television.* New York: Routledge.

Hebdige, D. (1979). *Subculture: The meaning of style.* New York: Routledge.

Herman, E. S., & McChesney, R. W. (1997). *The global media: The new missionaries of global capitalism.* Washington, DC: Cassell.

John, R. R. (1995). *Spreading the news: The American postal system from Franklin to Morse.* Cambridge, MA: Harvard University Press.

Jones, S. G. (Ed.). (1995a). *CyberSociety: Computer-mediated communication and community.* Thousand Oaks, CA: Sage.

Jones, S. G. (1995b). Introduction: From where to who knows? In S. G. Jones (Ed.), *Cyber-Society: Computer-mediated communication and community* (pp. 1-9). Thousand Oaks, CA: Sage.

Khelbnikov, V. (1993). The radio of the future. In N. Strauss (Ed.), *Radiotext(e)* (pp. 32-35). New York: Semiotext(e).

Lewis, J. (1997). What counts in cultural studies. *Media, Culture and Society, 19*(1), 83-97.

Lockard, J. (1996). Virtual whiteness and narrative diversity. *Undercurrent*(4). Available: http://darkwing.uoregon.edu/~heroux/uc4/4-lockard.html

Lockard, J. (1997). Progressive politics, electronic individualism, and the myth of virtual community. In D. Porter (Ed.), *Internet culture* (pp. 219-233). New York: Routledge.

Marvin, C. (1988). *When old technologies were new: Thinking about electrical communication the late nineteenth century.* New York: Oxford University Press.

Miller, L. (1995). Women and children first: The settling of the electronic frontier. In J. Brook & I. A. Boal (Eds.), *Resisting the virtual life* (pp. 49-58). San Francisco: City Lights.

Miller, R. (1991). Selling Mrs. Consumer. *Antipode: A Journal of Radical Geography, 23*(3), 263-306.

Mills, C. W. (1959). *The sociological imagination.* New York: Oxford University Press.

Morley, D. (1993). *Television, audiences and cultural studies.* New York: Routledge.

Morris, M. (1988). *The pirate's fiancee: Feminism, reading, postmodernism.* New York: Verso.

Morris, M. (1990). Banality in cultural studies. In P. Mellencamp (Ed.), *Logic of television* (pp. 14-43). Bloomington: Indiana University Press.

Nasaw, D. (1993). *Going out: The rise and fall of public amusements.* New York: Basic Books.

Nelson, C. (1989). Always already cultural studies: Two conferences and a manifesto. *Journal of the Midwest Modern Language Association, 24*(1), 24-38.

Nelson, C., Treichler, P., & Grossberg, L. (1992). Cultural studies, an introduction. In L. Grossberg, C. Nelson, P. Treichler, L. Baughman, & J. M. Wise (Eds.), *Cultural studies* (pp. 1-16). New York: Routledge.

O'Connor, A. (1991). The emergence of cultural studies in Latin America. *Critical Studies in Mass Communication, 8*(1), 60-73.

Plant, S. (1996). On the matrix: Cyberfeminist solutions. In R. Shields (Ed.), *Cultures of Internet: Virtual spaces, real histories, living bodies* (pp. 170-183). Thousand Oaks, CA: Sage.

RCA. (1944). *Television.* New York: Radio Corporation of America Department of Information.

Rodman, G. (1997, May). *The net effect: The public's fear and the public sphere.* Paper presented at the Annual Meeting of the International Communication Association, Montreal, Quebec.

Ross, A. (1991a). Hacking away at the counterculture. In C. Penley & A. Ross (Eds.), *Techno-culture* (pp. 107-134). Minneapolis: University of Minnesota Press.

Ross, A. (1991b). *Strange weather: Culture, science and technology in the age of limits.* New York: Verso.

Schudson, M. (1997, August). Paper tigers: A sociologist follows cultural studies into the wilderness. *Lingua Franca, 7,* 49-56.

Shields, R. (Ed.). (1996a). *Cultures of Internet: Virtual spaces, real histories, living bodies.* Thousand Oaks, CA: Sage.

Shields, R. (1996b). Introduction: Virtual spaces, real histories, and living bodies. In R. Shields (Ed.), *Cultures of Internet* (pp. 1-10). Thousand Oaks, CA: Sage.

Silverstone, R. (1990). Television and everyday life: Toward an anthropology of the television audience. In M. Ferguson (Ed.), *Public communication: The new imperatives.* Newbury Park, CA: Sage.

Silverstone, R., Hirsch, E., & Morley, D. (1992). Information and communication technologies and the moral economy of the household. In R. Silverstone & E. Hirsch (Eds.), *Consuming technologies.* New York: Routledge.

Sokal, A. (1996). A physicist experiments with cultural studies. *Lingua Franca, 6*(4), 62-64.

Spigel, L. (1992). *Make room for T.V.: Television and the domestic ideal in postwar America.* Chicago: University of Chicago Press.

Stabile, C. (1994). *Feminism and the technological fix.* New York: Manchester University Press.

Streeter, T. (1996). *Selling the air: A critique of the policy of commercial broadcasting in the United States.* Chicago: University of Chicago Press.

Tepper, M. (1997). Usenet communities and the cultural politics of information. In D. Porter (Ed.), *Internet culture* (pp. 39-54). New York: Routledge.

Warner, M. (1990). *The letters of the republic: Publication and the public sphere in eighteenth-century America.* Cambridge, MA: Harvard University Press.

Williams, R. (1973). *Television: Technology and cultural form.* New York: Shocken.

Wise, J. M. (1997). *Exploring technology and social space.* Thousand Oaks, CA: Sage.

Index

About the Contributors

Elisia Cohen is a student in the master's program in communication at Wake Forest University. She also serves as one of the debate coaches for the University debate team.

Robert W. Colman (rwc@psu.edu) teaches at Penn State Harrisburg, where he serves as Coordinator of the Community Psychology Program, Associate Director of the Center for Community Action and Research, and Assistant Professor of Social Science and Psychology. A social psychologist, he joined the research project through his interest in its methodology.

James T. Costigan is pursuing a master's degree in communication at the University of Illinois at Chicago, where he works in Virtual Reality Research at the Electronic Visualization Laboratory (EVL). He has worked in the high-tech industry serving in the technical direction of conferences such as SIGGRAPH and the National Association of Broadcaster's Multi Media World. With several EVL alumni, he formed VRCO, a virtual reality software and consulting company.

Norman K. Denzin is College of Communications Scholar and Research Professor of Communications, Sociology, and Humanities at the University of Illinois, Urbana. He is coeditor of *The Handbook of Qualitative Research,* editor of the *Sociological Quarterly,* and coeditor of *Qualitative Inquiry.* His most recent book is *Interpretive Ethnography: Ethnographic Practices for* *the 21st Century.* In 1997, he received the George Herbert Mead Award from the Society for the Study of Symbolic Interaction.

Nicole Ellison (nellison@scf.usc.edu) is a doctoral candidate at the Annenberg School for Communication, University of Southern California, Los Angeles. She is currently writing a dissertation on information and communication technology and the changing culture and geography of the workplace.

Jan Fernback (fernback@colorado.edu) received her PhD from the Center for Mass Media Research at the University of Colorado and is Assistant Professor of Communication at Regis University in Denver. She has published works on the cultural and philosophical issues surrounding new communication technologies. She is currently writing on utopianism and new media technologies.

Laura Garton (garton@chass.utoronto.ca) is a doctoral candidate in the Department of Sociology at the University of Toronto. Her dissertation is based on a whole network study of computer-mediated communication within an organizational context. Employing a social network perspective, she examines how the introduction of a multimedia space technology creates new opportunities and new constraints on the relations and interaction patterns among distributed work groups.

Steven B. Goldberg (steve@tobor.usc.edu) is a Trustee's Scholar in the Department of Computer Science at the University of Southern California. He was the software engineer for the "Drinking Maiden" project.

Teresa M. Harrison (Harrison@Vm.its.rpi.edu) is Associate Professor in the Department of Language, Literature, and Communication at Rensselaer Polytechnic Institute, Troy, New York. She is coeditor of *Computer Networking and Scholarly Communication in the Twenty-First-Century University* (1996).

Caroline Haythornthwaite (haythorn@uiuc.edu) is Assistant Professor at the University of Illinois at Urbana-Champaign in the Graduate School of Library and Information Science. Her research examines who communicates with whom about what and via which media. Research includes a social network study of members of an academic research group, placing their information exchange and media use in the context of their work needs and interpersonal ties. Research in progress examines reciprocity and coorientation in computer-mediated communication, and information exchange and development of community among distance learners.

Steve Jones (sjones@uic.edu) is Professor and head of the Department of Communication at the University of Illinois at Chicago. His other books include *CyberSociety 2.0, Virtual Culture, CyberSociety,* and *Rock Formation.* He is editor of New Media Cultures, a series of books on culture and technology, and coeditor of *New Media & Society.* In addition to his scholarly work, Jones has provided Internet consulting services to many corporations and not-for-profit organizations. He has also been a featured speaker at numerous scholarly, government, and industry-sponsored seminars and conferences.

Sandra Lee Katzman (skatzman@nasw.org) teaches English in Tokyo and reports for Reuters Health. Her work has appeared in the *Journal of Computer-Mediated Communication.* Her opinion articles have appeared in the *Sacramento Bee* and the *Los Angeles Times.* She is an active member of the National Association of Science Writers of America.

Lori Kendall (lori@lucien.sims.berkeley.edu) received her Ph.D. from the Sociology Department at the University of California, Davis, and is currently a Lecturer in that department. Her research explores the performance of identities online. Her dissertation, an ethnography of BlueSky, focuses in particular on the intersections of masculinities and computer technology.

Jason Lucas (jlucas@scf.usc.edu) is a graduate student at the Annenberg School for Communication, University of Southern California, Los Angeles. He is currently finishing a master's degree and will pursue his PhD in communication at Ohio University next fall.

Margaret McLaughlin (mmclaugh@rcf.usc.edu) is Professor of Communication, Annenberg School for Communication, University of Southern California. She is coeditor of the *Journal of Computer-Mediated Communication* and coeditor of *Network and Netplay: The Virtual Group on the Internet.*

Ananda Mitra (ananda@wfu.edu) is Assistant Professor of Communication at Wake Forest University in Winston-Salem, North Carolina. He has published in the areas of critical studies, popular culture, and technology, particularly about the conditions in South East Asia and about South East Asian immigrants. He teaches courses in communication, technology, and culture.

Barbara F. Sharf (bsharf@tamu.edu) is Professor of Speech-Communication and Professor of Medical Humanities at Texas A&M University. She is the author of numerous journal articles and book chapters in health communication, medical humanities, and medical education. Recent and current research projects focus on the rhetoric of breast cancer discourse, narrative analysis of patient-doctor interactions, and a text in health communication.

Simeon J. Simoff (simeon@arch.usyd.edu.au) is Senior Research Fellow at the Key Centre of Design Computing, University of Sydney. Dr. Simoff attained his doctorate at Moscow Power Engineering Institute, Russia, where he was also an Assistant Professor. He has been a Visiting Professor in the Faculty of Arts and Sciences at the Middle East Technical University, Gaziantep Campus, Turkey, and at the Intercultural Open University, The Netherlands. His current research interests are in data mining and analysis, information systems, knowledge modeling and representation, multimedia communication, and distance learning. He has published more than 50 papers in journals, books, and proceedings and is coauthor of a forthcoming book on virtual design studios.

James J. Sosnoski is Professor of English at the University of Illinois at Chicago. He is the author of *Token Professionals and Master Critics: A Critique of Orthodoxy in Literary Studies,* and *Modern Skeletons in Postmodern Closets: A Cultural Studies Alternative,* as well as various essays on literary and pedagogical theory, computer-assisted pedagogy, and on-line collaboration. He has been a member of the Modern Language Association's Delegate Assembly, Ethics Committee, and Emerging Technologies Committee. He is collaborating with David Downing on *Living on Borrowed Terms,* a study of the use of terminology in literary and rhetorical studies, and with Patricia Harkin on *Arguing Cultures,* a textbook and Web site on contemporary persuasive practices.

Timothy Stephen (Stephen@cios.org) is Associate Professor in the Department of Language, Literature, and Communication at Rensselaer Polytechnic

Institute, Troy, New York. He is coeditor of *Computer Networking and Scholarly Communication in the Twenty-First-Century University* (1996)

Jonathan Sterne (j-stern1@uiuc.edu) is completing a PhD in communication at the University of Illinois at Urbana-Champaign. His dissertation, *The Audible Past,* is a history of sound reproduction.

Fay Sudweeks (fays@arch.usyd.edu.au) is Research Associate at the University of Sydney and a doctoral candidate in communication at the University of Wollongong. She also has degrees in Psychology and Cognitive Science. She has given lectures in Israel, Sweden, Germany, Bulgaria, and Russia and has coordinated a large international collaborative project on computer-mediated communication. Her research interests are the social, cultural, and economic aspects of computer-mediated communication. Her latest coedited book is *Network and Netplay: Virtual Groups on the Internet.* Recent activities include coediting a special issue of the *Journal of Computer-Mediated Communication (JCMC),* serving as editor of the *Design Computing Newsletter* and *JCMC Newsletter,* editorial board member of *JCMC,* and CMC editor of the interactive *International Journal of Design Computing.*

Barry Wellman (wellman@chass.utoronto.ca) learned to keypunch at Harvard in 1964. He is now Professor of Sociology at the University of Toronto, where he has been e-mailing since 1976. Wellman founded the International Network for Social Network Analysis in 1976 and is currently the Electronic Advisor to the American Sociological Association and the Chair-Elect of the ASA's Community and Urban Sociology section. He is also the leader of the Virtual Community focus area for SIGGROUP/ACM. In addition to his papers on community, computer-supported cooperative work, and social network analysis, Wellman coedited *Social Structures: A Network Approach* (1997) and edited *Networks in the Global Village* (1998).

Diane F. Witmer (dwitmer@fullerton.edu) is Associate Professor of Communication at California State University, Fullerton. Her research interests include computer-mediated communication and organizational communication, and her work has appeared in *Communication Monographs* and the *Journal of Computer-Mediated Communication.* She is an active member of the National Communication Association and the International Communication Association.